PROJECT 9

The American Military Experience Series
John C. McManus, Series Editor

The books in this series portray and analyze the experience of Americans in military service during war and peacetime from the onset of the twentieth century to the present. The series emphasizes the profound impact wars have had on nearly every aspect of recent American history and considers the significant effects of modern conflict on combatants and noncombatants alike. Titles in the series include accounts of battles, campaigns, and wars; unit histories; biographical and autobiographical narratives; investigations of technology and warfare; studies of the social and economic consequences of war; and in general, the best recent scholarship on Americans in the modern armed forces. The books in the series are written and designed for a diverse audience that encompasses nonspecialists as well as expert readers.

University of Missouri Press   Columbia

PROJECT 9

THE BIRTH OF THE AIR COMMANDOS IN WORLD WAR II

DENNIS R. OKERSTROM

Cataloging-in-Publication data available from the Library of Congress.

ISBN 978-0-8262-2027-1

☉™ This paper meets the requirements of the
American National Standard for Permanence of Paper
for Printed Library Materials, Z39.48, 1984.

Jacket design: Susan Ferber

Composition: Jennifer Cropp

Typefaces: Stencil, Helvetica, and Minion

CONTENTS

FOREWORD

R. V. Secord, Major General, USF (Ret)

This book, *Project 9: The Birth of the Air Commandos in World War II* is a very thoroughgoing and well-documented story of the famed 1st Air Commandos. It is important in that it not only fills in an interesting part of WWII, but also because this series of events explains the heritage and spirit of today's Air Commandos. USAF commandos of today are known officially as the Air Force Special Operations Command, which is aptly described by their unofficial appellation, "The Tip Of The Spear" or "Any Time Any Where." Our Air Commandos at the time of this writing have been involved in combat continuously in Afghanistan for over twelve years as well as current operations in a number of other hot spots in this era of unconventional warfare known today as Special Operations. The U.S. Special Operations Command (USSOCOM) is the unified command supervising this effort involving the Army Rangers and Green Berets and the USN Seal Teams along with a number of other small units. But the Air Commandos are the least known of these elite warriors, and I think of them as the "enablers."

Dennis Okerstrom's work clearly describes our commandos' roots, which were reinvented in the Vietnam War and were properly codified in 1986 when the Nunn/Cohen Amendment was enacted, thus ensuring the continuing existence of our Special Operations forces in spite of frequent "conventionalist" attempts to eliminate them. I knew Johnny Alison, described herein, for many years and had the privilege of meeting Phil Cochran at an Air Commando dining in during the 1960s after these Air Forces had been recreated largely for use in the war in Southeast Asia. These two heroes carried out unbelievable feats in WWII, and both evinced such humble personages that one would never have suspected they had done so. I see a similar situation in today's air commandos as they carry on the traditions so completely described in this very different book.

August 2013

(Gen. Secord spent many years in special operations at virtually every command level and is currently President of the Air Commando Association.)

PREFACE

I have had a lifelong fascination with World War II, and particularly the air war of that cataclysmic struggle. The origins of my interest are not hard to unearth: my father Carl was with the Mighty Eighth (he never referred to it as merely the 8th Army Air Force) stationed in England, where he met and married my mother, Mary Joan Sargeant. Dad's brother Tage was a B-17 navigator who held me a willing captive with his many stories (most spurious, I later learned) of the war, and many years later I was able to learn something of the Pacific air war from my father-in-law, Lynn Johnston, who flew sixty-eight missions in a B-29. Eventually I learned to pilot an aircraft, becoming a flight instructor and owning my own restored 1942 L-2B, an Army liaison plane.

Despite my background and interest in aviation, the genesis for this book (aside from the actual historical events) began in the sands of North Africa, not the jungles of Burma. My original interest was not in the American fliers of the 1st Air Commando, but in the British Tommies who became the Chindits, the Long Range Penetration Group that operated behind the Japanese lines in Burma. The seeds of that go back to the Raj of the 1930s, when my great uncle Leonard Raymond Nicholls was stationed in India with the King's Own Royal Regiment (KORR). Two photos of Uncle Leonard hang on a wall in my home: one of him as a young man in full uniform, his eyes staring straight into the camera, the lion badge of the KORR clearly visible on his cap and collar. The uniform looks uncomfortable—heavy wool, with a white sword belt and puttees, high, stiff collar—and he is awkwardly holding a sword. It's a formal photograph, one reminiscent of those made of the young warriors of the Civil War sitting in their brand-new blue or gray uniforms, trying to look fierce, wanting a likeness to send home to mothers and fathers.

The other photograph of Leonard is less formal, and more poignant, more human in many ways. It too is a posed shot, but at once informal and symmetrical. It is a group photo of the intercompany (novices) boxing champions of 1935. Sixteen young soldiers, Leonard among them, are grouped in three rows. In front of them sits a silver trophy flanked by pairs of leather boxing gloves. Behind the pugilists are several square columns and a couple of arched doorways. Later I learned that the architecture was part of Wellington Barracks in southern India, where Leonard served for most of his first tour in the army. In this photograph, the boxers are all in sleeveless jerseys and shorts; each has his arms folded, and most have tucked their fists under their biceps, exaggerating their muscles. As a youngster, it never once occurred to me that all of the soldiers in the old photo were instruments of colonialism, armed agents of a Western imperial force. Even now I find it hard to condemn them individually, young men seeking to serve king and country, defending the empire across the globe.

Leonard served eight years and received his discharge in late 1938. He was home for less than a year. On September 1, 1939, he was recalled; two days later he was on his way to Palestine as the war in Europe exploded. For the next two years, he moved around the Middle East and North Africa, until finally being sent to help the beleaguered garrison at Tobruk, Libya. There, a small British force was surrounded by Rommel's troops, unable to break out and with supplies diminishing rapidly. In November, a plan—Operation Crusader—was adopted for the British to break out. On November 21, 1941, the order was given for Leonard and his comrades to fix bayonets and move toward the east to link up with a British force advancing from Egypt. They had to walk through a minefield, climb through concertina wire, face German machine gun fire, and brave incoming German artillery rounds. Leonard and many other British Tommies, was killed. I have always thought that his dying before the U.S. entered the war, when Britain was alone fighting the forces of Hitler and Mussolini and the outlook was very dark indeed, was inexpressibly sad.

Mom began making an annual pilgrimage back to England in the late 1970s. I teased her that it was to renew her accent, which my friends always found so charming. Returning from one of those visits in the '90s, she brought me a book on the history of the King's Own, the Lions of England, the only British regiment ever entitled to wear the lion as its regimental badge. There I learned that Leonard's 2nd Battalion of the KORR, after the siege of Tobruk was broken, was sent to India. There it became part of Maj. Gen. Orde Wingate's Long Range Penetration Group, the Chindits, and was airlifted into Broadway as part of the invasion of Burma.

It was a few years later that I learned that the airlift was part of a joint Allied operation and that a colorful American group known as the 1st Air Commando had taken part. When my other teaching duties and writing projects allowed, I began research on this nascent special operations group. I learned early that General H. H. "Hap" Arnold, under whose tutelage the Air Commandos were formed, was clear in his initial command: "The hell with paperwork, get out there and fight!" This certainly made research challenging.

Still, after visits to the Veterans History Project of the Library of Congress and the National Air and Space Museum, both in Washington, D.C., the Silent Wings Museum in Lubbock, Texas, the Air Force Historical Research Agency at Maxwell Air Force Base, Montgomery, Alabama, and the Eisenhower Presidential Library in Abilene, Kansas, a picture began to emerge of a group of wildly individualistic, talented, and dedicated young airmen. The original group of 523 who made up the 1st Air Commando Group included Col. Phil Cochran, already immortalized in the comic strip "Terry and the Pirates"; Col. Johnny Alison, a much-decorated ace who previously had fought the Japanese in China and Burma; the former child star Jackie Coogan, who was one of the glider pilots; Buddy Lewis, a premier major league baseball player; and Dick Cole, the quiet, steady copilot of Jimmy Doolittle in the famous raid on Tokyo. They were all pilots. An astounding fact was that nearly 300 members of the group were pilots, a ratio of fliers to ground personnel that is truly mind-boggling.

This was possible because of the unique requirements imposed by Cochran and Alison. To become a member of the group, each airman had to possess not just a single valuable skill, nor even a secondary specialty; a tertiary talent had to be proven before any volunteer was considered. Pilots, for example, were quite often their own—and only—mechanics. A third specialty might be related directly to the mission, or it could be seen as enhancing morale. The ability to sing or play a musical instrument was often enough to qualify, provided the volunteer had two other skills essential to directly fulfilling the mission.

While the British troops under Wingate were training in India, the 1st Air Commandos began their initial training in the States before shipping to India for joint exercises with the Chindits. Conditions for waging combat in Burma were among the most severe in the world, with thick jungles, steep hills, wide and swift rivers, and a monsoon season that turned the ground to thick, muddy gumbo. The physical environment was not the only challenge faced by this highly unorthodox group, however. With a direct line to General Arnold and seemingly endless supplies, Cochran and Alison faced the envy and enmity of other theater commanders who sought to absorb the personnel and materiel into their own units. Fighting off these efforts seemed as difficult at times as fighting the Japanese.

The young men who formed the nucleus of one of America's first special operations groups are mostly gone now. I managed to wangle an invitation to the final reunion of the 1st Air Commando in October 2012, in Fort Walton Beach, Florida. Seven men attended, all of them gracious and welcoming, all in their late 80s and 90s. They seemed surprised that someone wanted to write about their exploits of seven decades earlier. For three days I interviewed these veteran warriors, listening to their self-effacing stories, shaking my head at their black humor, and telling myself how lucky I was to be there. Why was this their final reunion? I asked. They told me, "We don't want to hold a reunion and have no one show up!" At the conclusion of the reunion, they presented me with a souvenir cap. It hangs in a place of honor in my den.

This is the story of that first mission of the Air Commandos, Operation Thursday, and of the ordinary young Americans who performed so brilliantly. I hope you enjoy their story.

Dennis Okerstrom
Independence, Missouri
August 2013

ACKNOWLEDGMENTS

"We're born alone and we die alone" is a popular phrase in some circles, and that sentiment is echoed in many a pop song. Perhaps it is true in a literal sense, but one thing is for certain: no one writes a book alone. An author owes debts of gratitude to a long list of people and in naming them hopes against hope that no one will be forgotten in the accounting.

For me, the help rendered by so many people made a difficult job of research much less exhausting. Megan Harris of the Veterans History Project, Library of Congress, was extremely helpful in guiding me through the database of thousands of interviews. Donald Abbe and his staff at the Silent Wings Museum in Lubbock, Texas, were gracious and friendly, and they continually brought me new documents, photographs, and articles while I was there; Don continued to send me material long after I left Lubbock. John Q. Smith, director of the Air Force Historical Studies Office, was persistent in tracking down the office and telephone number of Gen. H. H. "Hap" Arnold in 1944, details that had eluded me, despite my best efforts. Mark Kahn and David Schwartz, archivists at the National Air and Space Museum in Chantilly, Virginia, were cheerful, helpful, and interested in my search for material on Col. (later Lt. Gen.) John R. Alison. Sylvester Jackson, Jr., and Leeander Morris, Jr., at the Air Force Historical Research Agency at Maxwell Air Force Base in Montgomery, Alabama, were extremely generous with their time, and I was most grateful for their perseverance in finding a misfiled interview of Johnny Alison, among other artifacts, and for their suggestions of additional files to study. Valoise Armstrong, Samantha Kenner, and Linda Smith, at the Eisenhower Presidential Museum and Library, Abilene, Kansas, were all very helpful in my research through the various documents related to the Quebec Conference of 1943. John Chapman, of Good Wear Leather, Seattle, and Dave Meyer, a longtime collection of World War II flight artifacts, of Overland Park, Kansas, were helpful in identifying various pieces of flight gear used by the Air Commandos; Dave also referred me to Mike Pope, who helped me locate an Air Commando glider pilot.

Family members of original 1st Air Commandos were beyond generous with their help as I sought letters, records, and photographs. Brad Smith, son of R. T. Smith; James Miller, son of Donald V. "Red" Miller; Randel Bailey, son of Tim Bailey; Jacob Sartz III, son of Jake Sartz; and John Forcey, son of Paul Forcey, were all enthusiastic in their support of this project and provided me with much primary research material unavailable anywhere else. Wes Fields, security director for Doolittle's Tokyo Raiders as well as for the 1st Air Commandos, opened many doors for me as I sought to interview anyone connected with the original group. Lt. Gen. Richard Secord, USAF, Ret., was equally generous in passing word of my interest along to a variety of special operations insiders, including Clay McCutcheon and Herbert Mason, both of whom offered their time and were very liberal in making photographs available from Operation Thursday. Gen. Secord was also gracious enough to read my manuscript, and I am humbled that he agreed to write the foreword to this account.

Of course, the seven original 1st Air Commandos who attended the final reunion of their unit in Fort Walton Beach, Florida, in October 2012, were not only fascinating men but were also open, friendly, and interested in my work. Richard Cole, Harry McLean, Bill Cartwright, Bill Ravey, Eugene Piester, Patt Meara, and Jim Eckert all were modest, self-effacing, and filled with good humor as they patiently endured my endless rounds of interviews and questions. To all of them, I will be eternally grateful and proud to have spent time with them. Air Commandos A. R. Van de Weghe, Chuck Baisden, Tim Bailey, and Charles Turner were also friendly and helpful by telephone and email, providing me with valuable firsthand accounts. Gretchen Hawk, executive director of the Waco museum, Troy, Ohio, provided me access to early training films for the Waco gliders.

This project might have died on the vine were it not for the exuberant embrace of it by Cindy Cole Chal, daughter of Dick Cole, whom I met at an airshow in Oshkosh, Wisconsin. She was delighted to learn that I was researching the 1st Air Commandos ("Nobody ever writes about

them! The entire China-Burma-India theater was the forgotten war!")
and invited me to the reunion in Florida. She went out of her way to
introduce me to each of the original Air Commandos who attended
and provided me with additional names of people to contact. Cindy has
an enviable collection of material, and her overall understanding of the
1st Air Commandos as well as the Doolittle Raiders is truly noteworthy.
She is fierce in her determination that the sacrifices of World War II
veterans will not be forgotten. I have incurred a debt to her I shall never
be able to repay.

My colleagues at Park University have been generous with their time
and encouragement of my writing projects; the administration has been
equally supportive in terms of release time from some of my teaching
duties to complete this book. Jane Wood, Emily Donnelli-Sallee, and
Jerry Jorgensen were especially helpful. I also am indebted to the university for its generosity with faculty endowment funds, a grant from
which enabled me to travel extensively to research this story of the 1st
Air Commandos.

Of course, the editors at the University of Missouri Press, particularly Clair Willcox, editor-in-chief, and John McManus, series editor
of the American Military Experience, were helpful with their whole-
hearted support of this book and patient with me as I added just one
more revision to the manuscript. Managing editor Sara Davis, as always,
was a delight to work with, gently but firmly herding me through the
long process of turning a manuscript into a book. Polly Kummel was an
eagle-eyed copy editor who never allowed to get lazy with my writing
or research.

Inevitably, errors will be found in this work despite my best efforts to
eliminate them. I am solely responsible for those.

PROJECT 9

PROLOGUE

5 MARCH 1944
LALAGHAT AIRFIELD, ASSAM, INDIA
TIME: 1800

A waxing, gibbous moon was just rising in the east, promising a measure of light in what otherwise would be near-total darkness. But a thickening haze was obscuring even that dim source, blurring the horizon and making the upcoming mission, already hazardous in the extreme, exponentially more dangerous. Added to the low visibility was the suffocating humidity, a dampness that made even normal breathing seem like sucking air through a wet sponge. The darkness and the dankness seemed to have merged into a single entity, an inky viscous element, dense and implacable, simultaneously both friend and foe. As an ally the night would cloak their movements; as an enemy it would similarly mask the small jungle clearings into which they must fly.

For the past two days tough-looking men—uniformed men with beards, in bush hats and other accouterments of war—had landed at Lalaghat, transforming the rough airfield into a raucous circus. Those men stood now in groups, smoking, chatting quietly, checking and rechecking their equipment. Punctuating their calm murmur was a cacophony of braying mules being coaxed or pushed into ugly squat cargo gliders, honking horns as jeeps raced up and down the grass strip, and shrill whistles blown by officers trying to organize their commands.

Lined up on one side of the wide grass runway were rows of Douglas C-47 Skytrains, the ubiquitous cargo plane called Gooney Bird by irreverent Americans and Dakota by the more staid British. All were painted a dull olive drab; some sported white stars in blue circles on their wings and fuselages; others were marked with red, white, and blue concentric circles, denoting the mixture of U.S. Army Air Force and Royal Air Force aircraft. About a dozen Gooneys displayed five white parallel stripes wrapped at an angle around the fuselage just forward of the tail. Painted on their nose sections was a variety of garish, brightly colored art featuring scantily clad young women; a few displayed comic-strip characters. They carried names like "Tail Wind" and "Peaches" and "Hairless Joe" and "Queen of the Ozone," artwork and names provided by cocky young American fliers a long way from home. The nose art granted a degree of pathos and humanity to the otherwise stark and utilitarian instruments of war.

Outnumbering the cargo planes were dozens of slab-sided Waco CG-4A cargo gliders arranged wingtip to wingtip on the opposite side of the grass strip. They were graceless flying machines, able to stay aloft only so long as they were towed behind a C-47. Once released from their tugs, they became carriages without horses and had only one flight profile: descent. They were somber machines, and many would make only a single flight. They were considered expendable, throwaway haulers of men and machines and weapons.

In the relative quiet of his cockpit, Col. Johnny Alison peered through the wide flat windscreen of the Waco at the tow rope snaking from the nose of his glider to the tow hook beneath the tail of the C-47 now parked fifty yards in front of him; the cargo plane's pilot was revving its engines and inching down the makeshift runway, the tow rope slowly straightening. A blast from the whirling props of the tug sent dirt and debris pinging against the Perspex windscreen, and Alison reflexively shut his eyes before once more staring intently at the C-47 and the tow rope. The tug's pilot was Capt. Jake Sartz Jr., a veteran Hump pilot who never got excited; he was a good match for the unflappable little fighter pilot-turned-gliderman. Competence bred confidence, and confidence augured well for success.

Alison surely felt the familiar tightening in his stomach, the old tenseness that he had experienced so often, in so many parts of the globe. It was not fear. It was a rush of adrenaline, the reaction of the human body to the anticipation of action or high stress levels. He was no stranger to perilous missions and no novice at night flying: a veteran fighter pilot, he had downed seven Japanese aircraft while flying with the U.S. 14th Air Force under Claire Chennault, destroyed more on the ground, and survived crash-landing his P-40 Warhawk in the Xiang River. Alison had served in England, Russia, the Middle East, and China; throughout it all he had not just survived, he had thrived.

Everyone agreed that Johnny Alison was a natural pilot, a "good stick" in pilot's parlance. Fighters, bombers, transports—it didn't seem to matter what the bird was, Alison could fly it if it had wings and an engine or two. But tonight he might be excused for having tiny doubts. The CG-4A was an aircraft, to be sure, but it was unlike anything he had flown before. It closely resembled a boxcar unnaturally mated to a pair of thick wings with a span of nearly eighty-four feet; its square fuselage squatted on a pair of wheels that seemed to hold the body far too close to the ground, and the nose wheel was not a wheel at all but a skid that looked like a fat overgrown ski. The cockpit was beyond Spartan: a single row of five instruments comprised the instrument panel; two large control wheels that might have seemed more at home in the cab of a truck were attached to the ends of an inverted V-shaped pedestal anchored above the windscreen. The two bucket seats for the pilots were bare metal painted olive green, and the depression that normally would have accommodated a parachute had been filled in with plywood; none of the troops being flown in would have chutes, so the cockpit crews would not be wearing them either. Across the windscreen were structural braces that suggested it was still under construction. Overhead several trim-control wheels were connected to exposed steel cables that ran the length of the cabin.

It would be a strange flight, to be sure. Alison was to drop his cargo of fifteen British and Commonwealth soldiers into a jungle clearing in Burma 150 miles behind Japanese lines, then oversee construction of a landing strip for conventional troop carriers, mainly C-47s. He did not have to worry about navigating or maintaining a constant altitude or monitoring the myriad instruments that displayed the health of a high-performance aircraft engine; he need not concern himself with forming up with other planes after taking off. It was a simple mission in some ways. All he had to do was stay in correct position behind and slightly below the tow plane, avoid slamming into the other glider being towed by the same Gooney Bird, fly for three-and-a-half hours at night with no lights on any of the aircraft nor any on the ground below, and then release from the C-47 and land in an unmarked, unlighted clearing in a vast jungle that might well be hiding Japanese troops waiting to ambush them.

Should be a piece of cake.

After all, he had made two takeoffs a couple of days earlier in the Waco, then released and landed safely. In the daylight with a large flat airfield below him. That flying time constituted his only piloting experience in the ponderous glider.

Still it was his job, as he saw it, to pilot one of the first gliders into the clearing code-named Broadway, in what the air force today calls the first-ever aerial invasion of any country. He was the deputy commander of the unit that would become the 1st Air Commando Group. The commander, Col. Philip Cochran, had wanted to go, but he had been instructed to stay at Lalaghat airfield to direct the air portion of the operation. It was an audacious plan conceived by the colorful British major-general Orde Wingate and authorized at the highest levels of both British and American war departments, reaching the offices of the president and the prime minister. The plan was to take thousands of British troops far behind enemy lines, along with mules, small artillery pieces, and other materiel, and then resupply the troops during a lengthy foray designed to harass the Japanese and disrupt their lines of supply and communication. The Air Commandos were also prepared to evacuate wounded troops and provide combat air support for the invasion force. The hope was that the operation would make it impossible for Japanese forces to invade India from Burma, which they had occupied since early 1942.

With few instruments to check before takeoff, Alison turned his attention to his personal gear: a .45-caliber pistol in a shoulder holster; .30-caliber M-1A1 carbine beside him in the cockpit; .22-caliber Colt pistol, his personal handgun, in a side cargo pocket of his paratrooper pants; musette bag full of grenades, spare underwear, and socks stowed behind his seat; a photo of his new bride in a chest pocket of his jacket.

The takeoff had been delayed more than an hour when last-minute aerial photographs revealed that one of the two original jungle clearings to be used as landing sites was now littered with large logs, thought to be trunks of teak trees. That left Broadway as the sole destination, and the question hung unanswered in the thick air: Were Japanese troops awaiting the gliders, ready to destroy them as they descended helplessly toward the black clearing? They would be large, slow, and vulnerable targets even on the darkest of nights. Alison's small arsenal was his guarantee that the Japanese would not take him prisoner.

Ten minutes earlier Capt. Bill Cherry's C-47, towing two Wacos, had been the first off. Jake Sartz's tow with Alison behind was second in the queue, to be followed by Capt. Dick Cole's tug pulling two more gliders. In all more than eighty gliders were to be towed to the clearing deep in northern Burma on this night, as the dozen specially equipped tugs shuttled back and forth, landing just long enough to hook up another pair of Wacos.

The towrope was taut now. Alison signaled to the soldier standing by the left wing tip that he was set. The man waved a green light to another standing near the C-47, who then signaled up to Sartz in the cockpit more than twelve feet above the runway. Sartz pushed the throttles full forward, and with a roar the tow plane began to roll forward on the runway, slowly—agonizingly slowly. A second glider hooked to the same tug was to his left, seventy-five feet ahead, and it added to his duties. The glider pilot on long tow, always on the right side, was charged with the additional task of keep his aircraft well to the right of the tug and to not creep forward on the towline. After months of intensive training, night and day, in heat and rain, in good visibility and bad, Alison trusted his pilots. It was not blind faith. It was founded in experience and training and close observation of the nearly impossible tasks that he had seen his handpicked fliers complete with an insouciance approaching cockiness. Although Alison had little glider time himself, he fully understood his job.

Something was wrong. The glider was not responding to his commands, and it seemed much heavier than in either of his previous flights. He sensed that the tail was rising, and the front skid seemed to be plowing into the grass runway. Alison glanced to his left and saw Lt. Donald Seese's Waco doing what must have seemed to onlookers like a choreographed synchronized dance with Alison's: the tail was slowly lifting, the nose skid digging a furrow in the earth. What was happening? Alison watched as several of the ground crew ran to Seese's glider and pulled down on the tail as it continued to move forward slowly. At the same time Alison felt the tail of his own glider start to drop. He watched the men run with Seese's CG-4A for as long as they could and knew the same thing was being done with his own. As the speed of the tug and the two gliders slowly increased, the tendency to claw nose-first into the earth subsided. He shouted for his copilot to trim the glider to counter the nose-heavy condition.

Then Alison realized that the banging of the main gear wheels had ceased; no longer did the oleo struts clunk jarringly against their stops. Even though it was heavily overloaded, the glider was airborne before the tow plane, a result of its huge wings. Alison pushed forward on the control wheel stay to just above the runway. If he climbed too quickly, the Waco would lift the tail of the C-47 and cause its pilot to lose control.

He was in the air now, but even so it was not quiet. The doped fabric covering the Waco thumped against the steel frame of the fuselage, creating a steady drumbeat, and he could still faintly hear the roar of the two engines of Sartz's tug.

He thought ahead. Alison knew there would be no lights along their route to broadcast a comforting sense of human habitation. The land itself was harsh, rugged, and deadly. If they were forced down, they could expect little quarter from their enemy even if they survived a crash landing. Some local tribes were reputed to be head hunters, and the jungle itself was known to be home to highly venomous snakes. None aboard the glider, including the pilots, was wearing a parachute. Nothing like this night assault had ever been done before, so they had no history to study, no checklist that might reduce mistakes. But there was no going back. Alison settled into his seat and grinned at his copilot, Capt. Donald C. Tulloch, a medical officer, who smiled grimly and nodded back. Ahead they could see their tug, and beyond that they could just make out the dark and ominous barrier that was the Chin Hills. Foothills to the mighty Himalayas, they would be called mountains anywhere else on Earth, towering thousands of feet higher than the pride of the eastern United States, the Blue Ridge Mountains. To clear the Chin Hills the pilots would have to climb to 8,000 feet before heading east to Burma and the jungle clearing called Broadway.

The combined force of British Chindits and American Air Commandos of the top-secret plan known as Project 9 was headed into combat.

CHAPTER 1

An axiom of World War II is that the campaign in Burma was largely "the forgotten war," the stepchild of the China-Burma-India front, a backwater battle in the Asia-Pacific theater. It was recognized as such even while events were unfolding. The end of the supply line. The war no one cared about. A writer for the prestigious journal *Foreign Affairs* said in April 1945 that the Burma campaign had been "overshadowed by the climax of the war against Germany and the great advances in the Pacific."[1]

What little most Americans knew about the war in Burma was focused largely on the exploits of Americans there: first, the dashing pilots who became known as the Flying Tigers, the American Volunteer Group under Claire Chennault; second, the exploits of Gen. "Vinegar Joe" Stilwell and his Chinese troops, which came to include the group known as Merrill's Marauders; third, the intrepid fliers hauling fuel and supplies over the Himalayas, the Hump pilots who battled ferocious winds, abysmal weather, and the world's highest mountains to keep the supply lines open and ensure that China remained an ally in the war effort.

A few movies featured the Burma front, but most were eminently forgettable: *Burma Convoy,* with wretched acting and amateurish settings; *Bombs over Burma,* a melodrama with a villainous Englishman serving as a double agent for the Japanese; and *A Yank on the Burma Road,* mostly set in Kunming, the China terminus. At the close of the war Errol Flynn enraged the British by starring in *Objective Burma,* a film that suggested that Americans had largely fought the Burma campaign themselves, with perhaps a bit of help from the British. The film was banned in Britain until 1952 and then shown with an apology.

In truth British and Commonwealth troops largely fought the war against the Japanese in Burma in one of the most physically demanding arenas of the entire global conflict, often in hand-to-hand combat with no quarter given or expected. Rugged mountains, swift-flowing rivers, tangled jungle, and horrific weather made Burma one of the least desirable places on the planet to wage war. In the north, head-hunting tribes were reputed to live in the Naga Hills, along the Hump route from Chabua to Kunming. Dense forests of hundred-foot teak trees made aerial reconnaissance difficult; marshy grasslands impeded land movement and in the rainy season turned vast areas into impassable swamps. These features, coupled with diseases such as malaria, dengue fever, and dysentery, and a plethora of poisonous snakes and other unpleasant creatures, meant that Burma wore out men and machines at an astonishing rate. Then, of course, there was the actual armed enemy, the Japanese, who often were fanatical in their attacks and cruel in their treatment of prisoners. When Rangoon fell to the Japanese in March 1942, British, Indian, and Chinese troops waged a quiet but deadly war against the occupying Japanese that would erupt into a full-scale battle by early 1944, when Japanese troops invaded India and British forces marched into Burma. The fighting was ghastly. Britain's 14th Army alone suffered more than 40,000 battle casualties.[3]

The reasons for the lack of American interest in Burma were complex and varied, but they centered on the view that Burma itself was not terribly important and certainly not worth the effort it would take to push out the Japanese. The British, having lost control of a valuable colony, naturally felt differently. However, American military planners believed that the northern part of Burma was important as a means of keeping China in the war by getting supplies to China from India. As early as mid-1943 top British and American military planners envisioned one key to defeating Japan would be a bombing campaign of the island nation by B-29 Superfortresses, and bases in China were vital to that strategic goal.[4] While the British believed that crushing Japanese forces and liberating all of Burma should be a key goal as well, American planners were unwilling to spend much capital—in men or materiel—to realize it. The Burma Road, and later the Ledo Road, which wound through northern Burma, were worth some considerable effort as pipelines for supplies to China, and Gen. Joseph Stilwell and his Chinese troops eventually prevailed, with coordinated help from British and American forces. But in the meantime advocates of American airpower showed what intrepid fliers and the mind-boggling capacity of U.S. industry could do. Roads were not necessary, it seemed.

The command structure in the China-Burma-India (CBI) theater was complex, a mixture of British and American leadership roles that did not reflect the numerical imbalance of their respective troops in the theater. The convoluted lines of command would present problems later. Lord Louis Mountbatten, operating from New Delhi, was selected as the overall leader—the supreme commander—of the South East Asia Command (SEAC), and he in turn asked U.S. Maj. Gen. George E. Stratemeyer to form a combined aerial force for the region. The Eastern Air Command had four air arms: the Tactical Air Force, Strategic Air Force, Photo-Reconnaissance Force, and Troop Carrier Command. The Troop Carrier Command (TCC) was under Brig. Gen. William D. Old, a capable and courageous U.S. flier himself, who often led from the cockpit. For ground troops the organizational chart was equally byzantine, with Gen. Joseph W. Stilwell a key and at times obstreperous player. Stilwell had no love for the British, and he held several simultaneous positions that made him virtually independent in the CBI: He was deputy supreme commander of SEAC, as well as chief of staff to Generalissimo Chiang Kai-shek; additionally Stilwell had operational control of Northern Combat Area Command. In the words of a popular song, he was his own grandpa. Relations among Allied ground commanders were frequently icy, but in the corridors of airpower the chill often thawed: as the Brits and Americans came to know each other well, and to depend on each other, the working relationships were often quite warm. Air lanes over the eastern end of the Himalayas and across northern Burma, while costly in terms of lives and goods, could in fact keep China supplied with fuel and the weapons of war.

A key to keeping the air routes safe for the transport of thousands of tons of war supplies was disrupting the lines of Japanese communications and transportation. That would be the mission of the eccentric British major general Orde Wingate, whose troops would operate behind enemy lines and would be inserted and then supplied by a colorful and unusual American air task force, originally called Project 9.

Comprised of a small select group of U.S. airmen, later to become known as the 1st Air Commandos, Project 9 was secretly tasked with providing aerial support to British troops operating hundreds of miles behind enemy lines. The original group of 523 men—of whom, astonishingly, 300 were pilots—would fly gliders, cargo planes, fighters, bombers, light aircraft, and the world's first operational helicopters as an extremely unorthodox and independent unit equipped so fully that it was autonomous. They would aid Wingate by inserting his troops into remote jungle clearings in Burma by glider. At night. They would then keep him supplied, evacuate his wounded, and serve as aerial artillery for the ground war. The Air Commando chief was an American fighter pilot, Col. Philip Cochran, a good-looking, glib, independent-thinking combat flier already immortalized as Flip Corkin in the comic strip *Terry and the Pirates*. His cocommander was Johnny Alison.

Cochran and Alison were given carte blanche to build an organization to support Wingate while simultaneously and unobtrusively displaying the capabilities of the U.S. Army Air Forces. Over six months, during which they also had to organize, train, and deploy their unit to India, they put together a group of men as colorful and individualistic as they and who included some of the best-known fighter pilots of the time, a member of the Doolittle Raid on Tokyo, a top major league baseball player, and the biggest child actor of the silent films of the 1920s and 1930s.

They answered only to Gen. H. H. "Hap" Arnold, commander of the U.S. Army Air Forces. The 1st Air Commandos were authorized by President Franklin Delano Roosevelt himself, as requested in person by Winston Churchill, the British prime minister, at the Quebec Conference in August 1943.

Before the war most Americans doubtless would have associated the name Burma with men's shaving cream, as the marketing strategy of Burma Shave used hundreds of jingles—white letters on small red signs—placed along the nation's highways.

"Our fortune / is your shaven face / it's our best / advertising space" was a blatant admission of the signs' mission. Some jingles were simply bad puns: "Ben met Anna / made a hit / neglected beard / Ben – Anna split." Others were fairly clever: "Said farmer Brown / who's bald on top / 'wish I could / rotate the crop.'" Virtually all the doggerel was written by Allan Odell, son of the founder of Burma Shave, Clinton Odell.

Between the wars it is doubtful, however, that the average American could have located Burma, if given a global map, or said much about the geography, history, climate, or potential strategic importance of the country. *Compton's Pictured Encyclopedia* of 1936, found in even the most remote farmhouses of the day, devoted barely a single page to the country; a lone black-and-white photograph depicted a tiny spired haven perched on a balancing rock. The caption read: "Thoughts of the next world should not be difficult to worshippers at the Kyaktiyo Pagoda, in the mountains of Burma. For not only does this boulder overhang a steep chasm, but it rocks gently back and forth when the wind blows."[5]

Mountains of Burma, indeed. In just a few years Americans would know about the mountains—the northern range would be given the not-so-affectionate nickname "the Hump" by pilots hauling cargo into China—as well as the rivers, jungle, hills and highlands, and coastal regions. Burma was a country of varied geography, with two major seasons—the wet and the dry—and a long history of conquest and war, some impossibly exotic-sounding rivers, fantastic crumbling pagodas and ancient ruins of long-ago cities, and a diverse population with ethnic tribal loyalties that were often united as much by their hatred of the British colonial regime as by their religion, Buddhism.

Geographically the country lies between India on the west and French Indo-China on the east, China to the north and northeast, and the Bay of Bengal to the south. It appears to have been constructed by a giant with a rake who left deep furrows and rows of hills, all going north to south. Four main rivers flow down from China to the Indian Ocean: the Chindwin in the west, then the great Irrawaddy, the Sittang, and the Salween in the east. If you squint your eyes as you look at a map, you might visualize the country as shaped rather like the head of a goat in profile, with a long beard that is the coastal region of Tenasserim. The country is a bit larger than the state of Texas, and about half of it is in the broad valley of the Irrawaddy. The upper valley is high, arid, intensely hot in the summer, and creased with steep gorges that quickly turn deadly as rain washes down from the higher places. To the south, including the coastal regions of Arakan and the Tenasserim, the land is lush, with teak trees, elephant grass, and thousands of other species of tropical plants fueled by the humidity and steady rains. Around the 1,000-mile valley of the Irrawaddy is a collar of highlands, forming a natural barrier that, while not preventing a series of invasions, at least made the efforts difficult for the invaders while also giving to the inhabitants an illusory sense of protection and isolation. On the west, separating Burma from India, rise the Chin Hills, rugged mountains that form a natural barrier between the two countries, and in the east a long frontier borders Thailand, or Siam. Teak and rice were Burma's major products for the Commonwealth, but Burma's strategic location gave it value beyond its commercial potential.

Historically Burma had been the scene for many centuries of a series of invasions and internal wars, not unlike other places where ideas, religions, and the promise of wealth clashed with competing views. Mongols, Chinese, Portuguese, British, and then Japanese invaded, and between invasions competing kings of city-states fought numerous wars.[6]

British interests in Burma had revolved around commerce and the need for raw materials for the empire's home industries, as well as its markets for finished goods. As European leaders from the time of the first voyage of Columbus began dividing up the globe through wars and treaties, the fear that old enemies might obtain some trade or strategic advantage in unclaimed corners of the world drove the actions of centuries of governments. For more than sixty years, beginning in 1820, the colonial armies of Great Britain, based in India, had clashed with a variety of leaders in Burma. In 1885 Lord Randolph Churchill, father of Winston, helped instigate events that would allow the British Empire to annex Burma without provoking too much outrage from the other European monarchies and republics.

Much as the American newspaper publisher William Randolph Hearst was able to stir up demand for war with Spain in 1898—helped by the accidental explosion of a boiler aboard the warship USS *Maine*—so too did the *Times* of London contribute to a shameless mercantile scheme to gain unfettered access to the rice, teak, and jade of Burma. A man of dubious morals but with extremely good connections, Giovanni Andreino (his brother was the Roman Catholic bishop in Burma, and Giovanni had been appointed representative of the three largest British trading firms in Burma), claimed to have a secret document sent by the French to the Burmese foreign minister. It proposed that the French would smuggle arms into Burma from French Indo-China, just across the Mekong, in exchange for monopolies on a variety of Burmese goods and raw materials.[7]

At the time Burma was under the watchful eye of the British. Lord Churchill, then a young and rising politician, saw political opportunity in the situation, although it would require skill and a certain amount of luck. Skill he possessed; luck was furnished him when the Burmese Council of State levied a huge fine against a British company with the exotic name of Bombay Burmah Trading Corporation. The Council of State determined that the BBTC had exported teak lumber without paying royalties, and the Burmese government, known as the Court of Ava, refused to reconsider the fine. This was a golden opportunity for the British to remove the king, Thibaw, and install a more compliant ruler. The British sent to Mandalay, the ancient city near the midpoint of the miles-wide Irrawaddy River, a list of demands for arbitration and other considerations, including Burma's surrender and the country's acceptance of a role subservient to India's. A deadline for compliance was set, and Gen. Sir Harry Prendergast was appointed to lead an expedition up the Irrawaddy to Mandalay.

The Burma Expeditionary Force made quick work of the ill-equipped and poorly trained legions of the Burmese king, all done in such a way that the French were unlikely to launch a counterattack. After all, what nation could allow a backwater country such as Burma to levy such a fine, thumbing its nose with impunity while also striking a most dangerous blow against free trade?

British colonialism thus arrived in Burma, and as happened too often in too many places, the colonial power made a mess of its relations with the indigenous people. The king was exiled to India, never to return, but the people around his teak palace later saw the carcass of his white elephant, virtually a deity itself, dragged unceremoniously from the grounds. Although it apparently had died of natural causes, this outrage was not to be endured. That, and other high-handed or thoughtless incidents, created an ongoing insurgency throughout Burma that left hundreds of British troops dead in countless ambushes and thousands of Burmese publicly executed by the occupying forces.[8]

The situation remained much the same throughout the first decades of the twentieth century. Although not exactly the blueprint for insurgency such as occurred in Iraq after the 2003 invasion by the United States and its coalition partners, the situation meant tension remained high between Burmese nationalists and British colonials.[9]

Meanwhile in Japan the effects of rising militarism and overcrowding were exacerbated by a lack of resources and a series of perceived insults by other powers. Determined to enter the twentieth century with prestige equal to that of industrialized Europe, Japan had gone to war with China in 1894 and with Russia in 1904, handily defeating both. In some ways Japan might have seen England as a role model, another small island nation that had expanded to control a global empire, often by the use of armed might. Japan entered World War I on the side of the Allies but was largely ignored in the ensuing peace treaties and suffered national humiliation when the League of Nations refused to include in the League Covenant a statement on racial equality. Japan was further humiliated by the naval treaty that allowed it only three warships to every five for the United States and Great Britain, and the decision of the U.S. Congress to restrict Japanese immigration in the 1920s must have felt like a kick to the groin. Japan received some consideration after World War I: mandates over islands thought to be largely worthless—the Carolines, Marshalls, and Marianas. Allied troops would reclaim them in bloody battles a quarter century later.[10]

If anyone doubted the ambitions of the Japanese for power in Asia, those doubts surely were put to rest by the Mukden Incident (also called the Manchurian Incident) of 1931. Using as an excuse the injuries of several Japanese troops on night maneuvers in Port Arthur and the Liaotung Peninsula (claimed by Japan following the Russo-Japanese War of 1904–5), the Japanese invaded Manchuria. Other incidents followed, and the influence of the militants in the Japanese government grew. In July 1937 the opening rounds of World War II began in China: the Japanese claimed that China had fired on Japanese soldiers on the Marco Polo Bridge north of Beijing. A full-scale invasion by imperial Japanese forces followed; they quickly entered Beijing, drove up the Yangtze, and by Christmas had captured Nanjing, a city that had served as a capital during centuries when China was divided. Anyone who thought that Japan was going to champion Asians against the racist policies of Western powers needed only view the slaughter of Chinese civilians in and around Nanjing. Japanese newspapers carried stories of contests among Japanese officers to see who could decapitate the most Chinese in a single day.[11]

Despite a Japanese attack on British and American naval vessels (including the sinking of the river gunboat USS *Panay*), neither power took any direct action against the Japanese, whose government had issued an apology when the shooting stopped. By early 1939 Japan had almost sealed off China. A naval blockade had closed the port cities, and only a few open routes allowed supplies to get through to the government of Chiang Kai-shek, who was now attempting to rally the Chinese from the city of Chungking. These routes went through Russia or up from French Indo-China. Or through Burma.

None of this is to suggest that Americans did nothing and watched the war building in China. Although they perhaps oversimplified the conflict, the Americans had already chosen sides, reducing the combatants to a Hollywood western, good guys versus bad guys. The long history of American missionary activity in China had established a paternalistic sense of obligation in many; besides, the beautiful wife of Chiang Kai-shek had gone to school in the United States, and she was extremely canny about publicizing the plight of the innocent Chinese. Magazines, including *Life,* ran articles about how to tell the difference between Chinese and Japanese using highly pejorative language toward the sons of Nippon; newsreels focused on the brutality of the Japanese in China.[12]

General Stilwell served three tours in China before Pearl Harbor (1920–23, 1926–29, and 1935–39) and was stationed in China during the Marco Polo Bridge incident of 1937 that led to the Japanese invasion. Stilwell spoke Chinese and would soon play a key role in the defense of Burma.

Before Pearl Harbor, Claire Chennault had retired from the U.S. Army Air Corps as a captain and had been recruited by the Chinese to train pilots. He wound up leading a group of mercenary U.S. pilots—the American Volunteer Group (AVG), which became much better known as the Flying Tigers. The small band proved to be an irritant to the Japanese in China—and in Burma. The group, secretly blessed by President Roosevelt, had been recruited from the ranks of Army Air Force and Navy fighter pilots. They got a late start and arrived at their intended base at Kunming, China, during the 1941 monsoon season. With the blessing of the British the Flying Tigers established their first base at Kyedaw Airfield outside Toungoo, in southern Burma. Their job was to keep the Burma Road open between Burma and southwestern China; barring that they were to prevent the Japanese from using the Burma Road to invade China across the Salween River bridge.[13]

When Japan, an island nation with global ambitions but few natural resources, launched the December 1941 attack on Western forces throughout the Pacific, the Burmese could be excused for not being overly outraged. The British were humiliated at Hong Kong, the French in Indo-China, and the Americans at Pearl Harbor. The imperial Japanese forces seemed invincible in the early days of the global war, marching—nearly effortlessly—from Singapore to the Philippines. When the Japanese turned their full attention on Burma, they quickly overran the British forces there, turning a strategic withdrawal from Rangoon into a full-fledged rout to India. For a time the British were all but inactive; much of the action was undertaken by Stilwell's Chinese troops in the north, and by the American pilots flying out of far northeastern India across the Himalayas with supplies for the Chinese.

Then the eccentric British officer Orde Wingate conceived the idea of a commando-style incursion of Burma by a mélange of Commonwealth troops. They called themselves Chindits and from February to April 1943 harassed the Japanese in northern Burma by wrecking railroads, blowing up bridges, cutting communications, and attacking Japanese positions far behind the lines. The operations were colorful, furnished good copy for newspapers and magazines starved for any positive news from the China-Burma-India theater, and ramped up morale in some quarters of the Allied military. But the first Chindit campaign was dogged by a lack of supplies, which had to be delivered by air, and, more important to the morale of the Chindits themselves, no means was available to evacuate the wounded or sick. Hundreds of British and Commonwealth soldiers had to be left behind in the jungles and hills of Burma, propped up against a tree, with a rifle and a few rounds of ammunition, to die or be captured by the Japanese.

In the summer of 1943 Wingate was preparing for a second Chindit invasion of Burma while searching for a way to avoid having to abandon disabled troops. What the Chindits needed, he concluded, was a small force of light planes that could land in jungle clearings and airlift the ill and wounded to hospitals in India. The British had few such aircraft, but American manufacturers were turning out thousands of versatile two-place, fabric-covered aircraft. These tiny aircraft would become the nucleus of the group that came to be known as the 1st Air Commandos. Wingate was a major influence on a new tactic of ground-air coordination that would revolutionize the conduct of future wars. A less likely figure would have been hard to imagine by those who knew him early in his career, although he had long exhibited a bent for imaginative, bold military enterprises.

CHAPTER 2

It is well to avoid a reputation for eccentricity.
                —H. H. "Hap" Arnold

Eliahu Epstein, who would one day become the Israeli ambassador to the United States and then to the Court of St. James, was an idealistic young Jewish activist in early 1937. He later would change his name to Elath, but in the prewar days in what was then called Palestine, Epstein was an ardent Zionist and a scholar of some local repute. His specialty was Persian literature, and he had been invited to a discussion of literature with a newly posted British Army captain named Orde Wingate, who spoke Arabic and was a graduate of the School of Oriental and African Studies in London.

Palestine was becoming a major headache for the British; the Arab Revolt, begun in 1936 as a general strike of Arab workers, had led to continuous violence between Jews and Arabs as each claimed sole ownership of ancient lands. It was not a posting to which many British career officers applied; most stationed there endured a three-year tour and then were greatly relieved to go elsewhere, anywhere.

Epstein had been told that Wingate's views were different from those of most professional British military men of the time, and he seemed to be genuinely on the side of the Jews, which was most unusual. He did have a few peculiar ways, however, it was said.

It was a hot day; Epstein knocked on the door of the Wingate residence and stood waiting on the doorstep as insects swarmed around a small date tree whose sweet aroma drifted over him. He heard stirring within the small house, and he self-consciously fingered the knot of his tie as the door bolt was released inside. The door swung open, and there stood a short, slight, dark-haired Englishman, with a welcoming smile and intense dark eyes.

It was Orde Wingate. He was stark naked.

He invited Epstein in, and for the next couple of hours the two men discussed Persian literature—Epstein was surprised at the range of the officer's knowledge of what was, after all, a rather esoteric subject—and then the concept of Zionism, which Wingate seemed to savor. Throughout the animated conversation the young Jew tried to appear nonchalant despite his extreme discomfort, and at the end of the visit Wingate saw him to the door, still wearing only a smile.[1] Nudity was just one of many quirks that marked Wingate as, well, eccentric.

Perhaps eccentricity, as well as self-assurance and perseverance, are required personal characteristics for those envisioning bold departures from the norm. Invading a country—any country, any time—is the end result of a series of events and the product of much planning, arguing, cajoling, persuading, and even threatening, and all that is just within the country planning the invasion. Endless rounds of meetings, countless reports and assessments, continuous intelligence briefings, and the inevitable foot dragging and push-backs from doubters all must be endured before such a monumental project ever is set in motion. The aggravations and complexity increase exponentially when two countries agree to partner in the invasion of a third.

In the case of Project 9 and the aerial invasion of Burma in March 1944, however, the plan came together rather quickly, primarily because of a few key individuals in the United States and Britain who were in a position to silence the naysayers and demand results. In this case British Army ground forces would join with American flying forces to effect a daring and unprecedented long-range insertion of troops more than 150 miles behind Japanese lines. The war in Burma was unlike the wars in Europe and North Africa: rugged terrain, pestilential jungles, monsoons, and a dedicated, highly motivated enemy, combined with a scarcity of cities, few roads, and poor communications, made the war in Burma both a challenge and an opportunity. Traditional strategies and tactics had to be modified, and eccentric leaders would become not only the norm but absolutely essential to success. Two young U.S. Navy officers conducted an official study at the end of the Air Commando campaign in Burma. They declared the results of the group spectacular and the personalities involved colorful. Indeed they were.[2]

British leaders were equally colorful. In the United Kingdom those both high and low often lionize military figures. They might be secretly loathed by their peers in uniform, but it wouldn't do to say so publicly. T. E. Lawrence (of Arabia), Gordon of Egypt, Clive of India—these were names the public recognized and adored. Wingate was such a leader. Eccentric, self-absorbed, disdainful of traditions and the opinions of others, the son of a strict puritan, the slight Wingate grew up always an outsider and, to put it charitably, not especially gifted in sports. He was blessed with a good mind while cursed with an obstinacy that would not allow him to use it conventionally; indeed he seemed determined at times to irritate those around him.[3]

Flamboyance might have seemed natural for a man who was a distant cousin of Lawrence of Arabia. Wingate himself was born in India. But Wingate's father, a career army officer, was a member of the Plymouth Brethren, a stern, puritanical sect that arose in opposition to the loose ways of the Anglican Church, and young Orde was reared in a strict, unsmiling, no-nonsense household. His father, stationed in India for most of his career, once refused to advance his men during a campaign in the Naga Hills. It was Sunday, after all. This zeal permeated the Wingate family. They had little time for amusement; God's stern visage, displaying anger at the laxity of those in the state church, was a constant presence in their lives.

When Orde was thirteen, his father, by then retired from military service, moved the family to a small town in England so that the boy could attend Charterhouse School, a private boarding school. Young Orde, however, went home each night; did not participate in the games, sports, and roughhousing that generally marked the non-scholarly activities of his peers; and simply failed to make much of an impression on anyone there, student or teacher. However, his lack of achievement did not prevent his entering the Royal Military Academy at Woolwich when he was eighteen, after which he was commissioned in the Royal Artillery.[4]

Discipline at Woolwich had to have been nightmarish for someone who had always been seen as an outsider, particularly someone as unprepossessing as Orde Wingate. At the military academy senior classmen handled infractions of the many onerous rules, and they could be merciless. However, military service was a family tradition, so completing the course was never a question. The young Wingate was not easily bent to discipline, and the jibes and jeers of classmates served only to push him further away from them and to emphasize his outlier status. He did discover one activity that seemed to spark his interest: he showed a remarkable—and hitherto unknown—natural talent for horsemanship. This newfound love of things equestrian led both to a hideous punishment from the senior class and a quite remarkable show of respect by younger students, respect that would continue through his tenure at Woolwich.

By tradition cadets marched to the stables, where they were assigned mounts, and then they rode together through a series of exercises. Wingate despised marching, and one day when the group arrived at the stables under the command of a senior cadet, they found Wingate already mounted on one of the best horses. It was a breach of discipline not to be tolerated, and he was ordered to report to the rugby pitch after evening meal to be run. This meant he would be stripped naked (does this account for his nudity at socially awkward times?) and run through a gauntlet of senior cadets, who would cane him with their swagger sticks, after which he would be thrown into the pond nearby. The punishment was humiliating, ghastly for most; cadets tried to run through the double line at top speed.

Wingate, however, showed his mettle that day. Uncowed, he walked slowly down the line, stopping to stare into the face of each senior cadet. His haughtiness brought him no sympathy there, but his own underclassmen were astonished and impressed by his grit. That night they trashed the rooms of the senior cadets involved in Wingate's run and thereafter accorded the outlier respect and friendship.[5]

Following his graduation from Woolwich in 1923 and his commissioning as a junior lieutenant in the Royal Artillery—and the award of numerous trophies for his fearless horsemanship—young Wingate was posted to the 5th Medium Brigade near Salisbury. Here he seemed resolved to sharpen his already laudable skills in horsemanship and hunting as well as to broaden his range of literary and musical interests. He gained admission to the Military School of Equitation, excelling both in riding and in irritating his instructors; he concluded the course by informing the commandant that he would thereafter specialize in motor transport. Money seems to have been a problem; few young British officers of the austere 1920s could live on their military pay, although many, if not most, had private means. Wingate did receive a small legacy from an aunt, but it seems he was generous to many people, including his sisters and brother, while not so quick to pay his bills.[6]

It helps to be well connected. Wingate went to see his father's cousin, Sir Reginald Wingate—Cousin Rex—who had been governor-general of the Sudan and high commissioner of Egypt. Shortly thereafter Wingate was admitted to the School for Oriental and African Studies, where he did quite well; following completion of the course in 1927, Rex had another recommendation: the young officer should do something in the Middle East to burnish his credentials. In the best tradition of an earlier generation of British Army officers, Wingate applied for a transfer from his regiment to the Sudan Defense Force, a posting that most officers would have viewed with alarm and disdain, the equivalent of being sent to Siberia. Undoubtedly helped behind the scenes by Cousin Rex, Wingate spent six years as a *bimbashi*, or local major, in command of a company of 300 native troops stationed at Gallabat near the border with Ethiopia. One of his company's main duties was preventing the poaching of elephants; a main diversion for Wingate was antagonizing other officers with long pedantic speeches on communism. In late 1932 he took a six-month leave and, together with an American archaeologist, mounted an expedition into the Libyan desert. The ostensible aim of the expedition was to find the lost oasis of Zerzura, a fabulous city in ancient myths that was protected by djinn who could call forth sandstorms when travelers approached. But it was to be as much a personal test as a journey of exploration; Wingate's idea of provisions included hard biscuits, dried dates, and cod liver oil. He drove himself, testing his body against the harsh environment, and in the end, despite not discovering a lost oasis or remnants of a lost army, the avowed aims of the expedition, Wingate felt victorious. He had proved something to himself about his ability to soldier on through deprivation and hardship.[7]

While he was returning to England in 1933 aboard a steamer, Wingate—although unofficially engaged to a young woman in London— met and fell in love with a stunning young woman, Lorna Patterson, who was sixteen and traveling with her mother. He awkwardly broke off his engagement, and three years later, in January 1936, Wingate and Lorna were married. Later that year Wingate, by then a captain, was posted as an intelligence officer to the 5th Division, which was preparing to depart for Palestine. His ability as an interpreter in Arabic and his previous experience in the Sudan were seen as valuable commodities in the tangled political and military milieu that was so vexing to Britain.

But Britain itself was to blame for the situation. To secure the financial and moral backing of worldwide Jewry during the Great War, Britain had issued the Balfour Declaration in November 1917, an artfully worded document that seemed to bless the Zionist movement's resolve to establish a Jewish homeland in Palestine. The diplomatic language, however, included a statement that the rights of indigenous Arabs—"non-Jewish communities"—should be respected. Therein was the rub.

A single-page letter, from the British foreign secretary Arthur James Balfour to Lord Rothschild, a leader in the World Zionist Movement, the Balfour Declaration was a monument to expectations and illusion:

I have much pleasure in conveying to you, on behalf of His Majesty's government, the following declaration of sympathy with Jewish Zionist aspirations which has been submitted to, and approved by, the Cabinet:

"His Majesty's Government view with favour the establishment in Palestine of a national home for the Jewish people, and will use their best endeavors to facilitate the achievement of this object, it being clearly understood that nothing shall be done which may prejudice the civil and religious rights of existing non-Jewish communities in Palestine, or the rights and political status enjoyed by Jews in any other country."

I should be grateful if you would bring this declaration to the knowledge of the Zionist Federation.
Yours,

James Arthur Balfour

Lord Rothschild, who owned an 11,000-square-foot apartment in New York and a fashionable home on Piccadilly in London, was the oldest son of the family of financiers who held such sway over institutions and governments. He was far more interested in zoology, however, and once had his photograph taken in Australia while riding a giant tortoise from the Galapagos; Rothschild is wearing a top hat. He was famous for driving a carriage around London drawn by four zebras. An eccentric, to be sure, but his influence in the Zionist movement was considerable.

The diplomatic language of the Balfour Declaration is striking in what it appears to say, but it never addresses how to attain the goal of a Jewish national homeland. The League of Nations adopted it, and in 1922 the declaration resulted in Palestine's becoming a mandate to be overseen administratively by Great Britain. A few thousand Jews emigrated to the area around Jerusalem in the next decade, with little fanfare and little resistance from the local Arabs living there. After 1933, however, tens of thousands of Jews fled Germany and eastern Europe following Hitler's rise to power. The Arabs, alarmed by the influx of Jewish immigrants, responded with deadly attacks, and Jews reacted in kind. Britain had created a Gordian knot from its too-clever linguistic coup; its army was sucked into the vortex of violence.

Captain Orde Wingate and his slim pretty wife arrived in Palestine predisposed to the cause of Zionism. Neither was Jewish, but Wingate apparently was impressed by the spirit and will of what he saw as the underdog, a small force with a long history of resistance. He saw energy and creativity and a ready supply of agricultural and commercial success stories from the collectives, which contrasted with what he saw as the filth and backwardness of the Arabs. His own early training in biblical history was also no doubt a factor in his less-than-neutral stance in the ongoing terrorism and warfare between Jews and Arabs.

Within four months of arriving in Palestine, Wingate had assessed the situation and concluded that the Jewish settlers were honorable, outgunned, and morally right. In a letter to his cousin Rex, who had been so helpful throughout Wingate's army career, Wingate pleaded that His Majesty's government do something "just and honorable" before the start of what he saw as the inevitable war with Germany. "Let us redeem our promises to Jewry and shame the devil of Nazism, Fascism and our own prejudices."[8]

The Arabs rejected out of hand a political settlement of partition, which the Peel Commission advocated. Appointed by the king and headed by Lord William Robert Wellesley Peel, the commission was charged with determining the cause of the Arab revolt and recommending a solution. The tiny area proposed for the Jewish state, about one-fifth the size of Wales, was too much land to give up; soon Arabs were rearming and attempting to assassinate British officials throughout Palestine. The Arab Revolt was in full swing. Wingate, the intelligence captain, soon was meeting regularly with Jewish paramilitary groups and now devised a campaign to halt the smuggling of arms to Arabs and to disrupt and destroy the armed gangs of Arabs that were attacking both British authorities and Jewish settlers. Wingate's plan was to seek out strongholds of Arab militancy by night, attack them, and rout the warriors by sustained effective firepower.[9]

Wingate, wearing two Webley revolvers at his waist and carrying a .303 Lee-Enfield rifle, led many raids himself. He was a distinctive figure in his trademark Wolseley sun helmet, full beard, and filthy field uniform. On one occasion he was wounded by his own men, who were firing submachine guns in pitch-black conditions. He told the sergeant who shot him that he must learn from his mistakes.[10]

In time the Special Night Squads, as they were known, were officially sanctioned, and the Jewish settlers were learning a lesson that Wingate was to preach over and over: the best defense is a vigorous offense.

By late 1938 Wingate had been leading night squads for nearly two years. He was tired, recovering from painful friendly-fire wounds, and ready for a rest; still a captain, he had had numerous run-ins with superior officers and had established a pattern that would remain with him: acrimonious relationships with many regular-army brass while a few high-ranking officers and officials sheltered, admired, and encouraged him. As he boarded the ship to return to England, he displayed a concrete emblem of official approbation above his left pocket: the scarlet-and-blue ribbon of the Distinguished Service Order, established by Queen Victoria in 1886. It was intended for award to senior officers and only for front-line service. That Wingate, a mere captain, was recognized for his unorthodox exploits in Palestine set him up for good assignments in the future while also placing him squarely in the sights of many in the regular-army establishment.[11]

When he returned to Palestine later that year, he was part of a much larger British military presence that, while not embracing local Arabs clearly rejected Wingate's championing of the Jews. A report issued by an intelligence conference objected to the Special Night Squads—which it called "dressing up Jews as British soldiers"—and called for more direct action by the British military and the elimination of the squads. Wingate was furious. But instead of giving way to hyperbolic vitriol, he wrote a reasoned fact-based response, pointing out that in the regions where the night squads had operated, sabotage of oil lines had ceased entirely and other violence was drastically reduced; moreover the cost to Britain was nil, since the local population fed and gave temporary housing to the squads. Still, the entire episode left Wingate with a particularly low regard for what he termed "military apes," those poor benighted souls who did not have his passion or vision for anything not included in published manuals. He made some lifelong enemies among the British officer corps, but the Jews considered him a hero. His name can still be found on buildings and streets across the present state of Israel.[12]

Not all Brits were antagonistic toward Wingate, however. The rogue, the outlier, the swashbuckler who gets things done and regulations be damned has always had a place in the hearts of many British citizens. When Wingate and his wife sailed back to England in May 1939 for reassignment to an antiaircraft unit in Kent, he met L. S. Amery, a close and powerful ally of Winston Churchill's—and Churchill was about to burst on the scene to counter the appeasement policies of the current political leaders.

The war with Germany began in September 1939, and for a full year Wingate fumed and fussed about his inactivity. Then Amery and Gen. Archibald Wavell, another staunch supporter and admirer, arranged for Wingate to be sent to Cairo, with a promotion to major, with largely unspecified duties beyond being generally helpful because of his background, familiarity with the Middle East, and knowledge of Arabic. He soon was involved in efforts to increase aid to Ethiopia, which had been invaded by Italy. Haile Selassie, who as emperor had claimed a direct line of kinship with the biblical King Solomon, had been run out of his kingdom and was now campaigning for more funds to fight a guerrilla war against the Italians. One can only imagine what Wingate began to ponder. Eventually the plan coalesced: attacks from the north, the south, and finally a force led by Wingate himself—he named it Gideon Force, after his favorite figure from the Bible—and accompanied by Haile Selassie would move into Gojjam Province. Gideon Force was conceived and organized along largely independent columns of men, camels, and supplies, a plan that presaged the later organization of Chindits in Burma.[13]

It would not be easy. Mussolini had placed 300,000 troops in Ethiopia, as well as 300 aircraft, and naval vessels at Massawa. The campaign, begun in February 1941, was complicated, with some British forces and assets already deployed but with several commanders unconvinced that Selassie and Ethiopia were worth the trouble and cost. Nor was Wingate's cocksureness appreciated, and his continuous wearing of his DSO ribbon served only to irk many British officers, who bridled at his forceful demeanor while he laid out his plan. After many months of campaigning, which included the judicious use of propaganda and misinformation, Wingate bluffed a superior Italian force into retreating from Burye, and in the months that followed he was able to claim other victories, although he was ill with malaria. This is not to suggest that Wingate was solely responsible for the liberation of Ethiopia and the return of Haile Selassie to the throne, because British, South African, and Indian troops in other regions of the country had also been routing the Italian army. But certainly Wingate was a factor.

The campaign ended in June 1941 with Haile Selassie reentering his capital, Addis Ababa, in triumph, riding a white horse and accompanied by Wingate in his pith helmet and columns of the crisply marching troops of Gideon Force. Backbiting, finger-pointing, and blame shifting followed, in what seemed to be the usual pattern for British military adventures involving Wingate. He made some bitter enemies, some friends, and some admirers, and he was recognized once more by His Majesty's government: a bar to his Distinguished Service Order. Two campaigns, two DSOs. His detractors fumed.

After Ethiopia Wingate was posted to Rangoon, an assignment he suspected was an attempt to get him out of the spotlight and off to the rear echelon of the war. But for Wingate the real war was about to start.

CHAPTER 3

To this point the experiences of Col. Orde Wingate—he was promoted as soon as he arrived in the Far East in late February or early March 1942—had been noteworthy, both for the detritus he left in his wake in the form of outraged or offended or perhaps jealous colleagues and for the honors his government bestowed upon him. That he was peculiar, eccentric, vain, opinionated, brash, dismissive, and headstrong was never a point for debate. Even his admirers allowed all the labels were true. That he was also brilliant, courageous, daring, passionate, loyal, sensitive, and scholarly were qualities that his enemies—and they were many and increasing—were loathe to acknowledge but were equally true.[1]

Wingate headed north out of Rangoon and scouted the countryside for several days, getting a basic and cursory sense of the land and the obstacles that an army operating there would face. The timing of his recce could not have been worse. Within days the seemingly invincible Japanese overran most of Burma, setting the stage for rolling westward into India and north into China. Rangoon itself fell on 8 March 1942. A long retreat by British troops and civilians through hellish terrain left the roads and trails littered with 14,000 of their dead, and the survivors who trekked into India looked like walking skeletons, hollow-eyed and gaunt, ill with dysentery and malaria. However much the Brits might like to call it a strategic withdrawal, it was an old-fashioned rout. The American general "Vinegar Joe" Stilwell, who had walked out himself, was blunt in his assessment: "I claim we got a hell of a beating. We got run out of Burma and it is humiliating as hell. I think we ought to find out what caused it, go back and retake it."[2] His acid comments did little to endear him to the British, but he had little good to say about them in any regard.

Wingate flew out of Rangoon and arrived in India soon thereafter, with an assignment to train guerrilla troops such as the Gideon Force in Ethiopia or the Special Night Squads in Palestine. The idea was to fight an irregular war in Burma, since conventional warfare was not going well for the Allies. Wingate, however, held that guerrillas were born, not made. Like the Jews comprising the night squads, the Gideon Force soldiers were experts in their own country. Moreover they had obvious incentives for fighting and winning: it was their country, and they could expect no mercy if they lost. Additionally, guerrillas ideally would have the support of the local population. In Burma this was hardly the case, as many Burmese looked upon the Japanese as friends who were throwing out and thoroughly humiliating the hated British colonial troops.[3]

No, there would be no Wingate-trained and Wingate-led irregular force of expatriate indigenous troops crossing into Burma. His fertile brain had been at work during the voyage to Rangoon from his last posting in Ethiopia: what was needed was a long-range penetration group made up of ordinary British troops (including Indian troops, West Africans, Gurkhas from Nepal, and a contingent of loyal Burma Rifles, in addition to several units of Brits) and led by extraordinary officers. He long had held the view that the keys to victory and good soldiering were good leaders.

The plan continued to evolve as the 77th Indian Brigade (so-called for reasons of secrecy) began training near Gwalior, south of Delhi. It was to cross into Burma from India's eastern province of Assam and divide into columns to attack rail lines, communications, and outposts, thus pulling Japanese troops away from the front. The brigade's actions would be coordinated with three major drives: Stilwell and his Chinese troops from the north, a spear into the south from the Burmese state of Arakan by British forces, and a push by an Indian army corps to the Chindwin River from Imphal in Assam.

Wingate was maniacal and unrelenting in his training; perhaps he needed to be. His goal was to train ordinary soldiers to accept the hardships, deprivations, and dangers of operating as far as 200 miles behind enemy lines and to create an esprit de corps that would make them relish being there. To Wingate's mind ennui had permeated much of the military in India. As during the Phoney War in France before May 1940, the enemy seemed to be faraway and not interested in further conquest, and to Wingate the Curry Colonels (he fairly spat the term) were worse than useless; in his eyes they shuffled papers all day and collected their pay. Even the enlisted ranks seemed less than eager to engage the Japanese in Burma. That would have to change. He drove everyone past what most thought was his limit of endurance; it was not, and they soon would learn that he pushed no one harder than himself. Walking was a waste of valuable time, and in short order he had all his officers following his own frenetic example and running to every meeting in the camp. No detail was too small for Wingate's scrutiny. With the nearly religious zeal of the ex-smoker that he was, he railed against the inclusion of cigarettes as part of a soldier's allotment. It had no effect; the cigarettes continued to be dispensed, and the men continued to smoke them. In other areas he was more successful. Sick call was reduced from, at one point, nearly 70 percent of one regiment sent from reserve duty in England to about 3 percent. Officers were simply ordered not to be sick, and commanding officers were to personally diagnose each reported case of illness. This directive made Wingate few friends, but he didn't care, and no one could argue with the success of the initiative.[4]

There was no let-up. Once, when a young officer told his Gurkhas to stand down while he sought out a missed rendezvous, Wingate happened upon the group of mostly teenaged Nepalese lying on their packs and smoking. He was furious, and when the unlucky lieutenant returned, Wingate demanded to know why the officer had not instructed his men to practice compass orienteering or concealment techniques or anything to keep them busy. Word soon got around: Stay busy. Another time, when a group of officers was called to a meeting with Wingate in an open-sided tent, they arrived to find him absent. They waited politely—who walks out on a meeting with a commanding officer?—when suddenly Wingate came storming out of concealment in bushes nearby, firing his Webley revolver in the air and screaming like a madman: "Hands up, the lot of you. You are all quite helpless, not one of you is armed." No one went about without a sidearm after that.[5]

The whole enterprise nearly came to an end in early 1943. Gen. Archibald Wavell flew into camp and explained that the plan for three main thrusts into Burma had been canceled or postponed, which would mean that the Japanese would be entirely focused on Wingate's irregular force. Wingate argued furiously against canceling the project, which might have been Wavell's hope; Wingate received permission to proceed with what was now code-named Operation Longcloth, a name with no special meaning and one that Wingate despised. He was rather more pleased with the name Chindit, which came about through his own misunderstanding of the Burmese word *Chinthe*, the mythological guardians of the temples.[6]

On 13 February 1943 the long-range penetration group under Wingate headed into Burma, more than 3,000 men divided into two groups. They walked, carrying all their gear; mules carried heavier equipment. The largest group, about 2,000 strong, comprised five columns and crossed the Chindwin River at Tonhe. The river, a south-flowing tributary to the Irrawaddy, was several miles east of the actual border with India but served as the true barrier. Heading the second smaller group was Lt. Col. Leigh Alexander; it split into two columns, which crossed at Auktaung and headed south. Wingate's hope was to deceive the Japanese into thinking it was the main force and was headed to Mandalay.[7]

The men, much leaner and tougher than before Wingate's severe regimen of training, each carried about 70 pounds of gear. They wore tropical uniforms and lugged a machete, rubber boots, light blanket and groundsheet, mess kit, first aid kit, bayonet, grenades, rifle or Bren gun, 50 rounds of rifle ammunition, and six days' rations. Daily rations were loosely based on Wingate's personal experiences in the Libyan desert many years earlier, as well as his more recent exploits in Ethiopia. Additionally he had continued to research the subject of nutrition, convinced that traditional rations did not provide enough energy and lacked the proper mix of vitamins, minerals, and fiber. A single day's rations thus looked like this: a dozen wholemeal biscuits, two ounces of nuts or raisins (nuts could be problematic for the large number of enlisted—Other Ranks in the parlance of the British military—who, because of poor dental health, wore full or partial dentures), cheese, dates, chocolate, twenty cigarettes (he hated this addition), tea, powdered milk and sugar, and salt and vitamin C tablets— about 3,000 calories per day. The force was accompanied by 1,000 mules carrying a few three-inch mortars, additional ammunition, and the key to communication and coordination, the indispensible RAF 1082/83 radios, each so large that three mules carried its parts when it was broken down. RAF Dakotas (C-47s to the U.S. Army Air Force) would drop additional supplies as needed. The success of the resupply airdrops would be a major factor in how long the campaign would continue.[8]

Columns became the basic organizational unit of the first Chindit operation, and Wingate eventually organized seven columns along lines that totally disregarded standard brigade structure. Each column consisted of about 400 men broken into platoon-sized units (about twenty-four men per infantry platoon); the infantry platoon was the nucleus, to which was attached a recon unit (made up of Burma Rifles, whose members carried civilian clothing with them to don when they entered villages), a support unit of heavy machine guns and mortars, and a demolition unit. The mules attached to the demolition unit were laden with high explosives; no one beyond the muleteers wanted to be close to them.

For a month the Chindits hacked and slogged through the Burmese jungles, wreaking a certain amount of havoc by blowing up bridges, tearing up railroad tracks, and attacking Japanese patrols. But they paid a heavy price in ill and wounded troops. It had been understood from their training days that those unable to walk would have to be left behind. It had seemed straightforward enough while they were in India, but the reality of leaving sick or wounded friends behind proved to be a terrible price indeed. Dysentery and malaria were endemic; as the columns snaked their way (the columns themselves were now called Snakes) through the hostile countryside, those with dysentery went naked so as not to foul their clothing when the urgent painful need to empty their bowels struck again and again. Wounded and seriously ill men were left propped up against trees, with a supply of food, water, and ammunition, and often with notes from officers appealing to the Japanese or Burmese who found them to treat them with the respect due gallant soldiers. But captivity by the Japanese was a nightmarish prospect; they could expect little mercy, and everyone knew it.[9]

Within two weeks the Japanese had ambushed two of the seven columns; casualties were high, and the mules stampeded, resulting in loss of weapons, supplies, and radios. Both columns were effectively eliminated while the survivors turned back to India. Column 1 lost radio contact for several weeks and was thought to have been lost to the enemy.

There were successes. "Mad Mike" Calvert's Column 3 moved into Nankan, Burma, and ambushed Japanese troops, blew up a bridge, and destroyed large sections of the Mandalay-Myitkyina railroad tracks with more than seventy mines. The column did not suffer a single casualty. Bernard Fergusson, an erudite soldier and poet who wore a monocle, led Column 5. His troops destroyed a bridge over the Bonchaung Gorge but in doing so suffered casualties, including six wounded who had to be left behind. After three weeks of silence Column 1 regained radio contact and announced it had pushed east and crossed the Irrawaddy. Wingate and his staff had been debating whether to cross the mighty river to test their theories about long-range penetration; the word from Column 1 affirmed their belief that all should continue to operate deeper within the Japanese-controlled interior of Burma.[10]

The crossings were perilous undertakings; in places the Irrawaddy is more than a mile wide, swift and dangerous, with hidden obstacles and strong undertows. Few soldiers were strong swimmers, and the mules were stubborn and vocal in their displeasure at having to swim behind the boats secured by the Chindits from local villages. They crossed at several locations, sometimes under fire from Japanese troops. These were desperate scenes of sheer bedlam, with explosions and gunfire punctuating the braying of mules and the shouts and screams of troops. Yet nearly all the Chindits managed to make it to the east bank of the Irrawaddy.[11]

It might have been a river too far. The area was far different from the jungle environment and generally friendly villages the Chindits had encountered. Here it was much more open, and very dry, the entire region crossed by roads that made it possible for Japanese to quickly send motorized troops in response to aircraft reconnaissance or radioed reports. The Chindits trekked on, now suffering horribly from thirst and malnourishment. The daily rations simply did not provide enough calories for men constantly on the move, and they all began the fantasy game of "what I'll eat when we get back." Airdrops now were absolutely essential to the survival of the columns but also marked their location for the Japanese or the pro-Japanese Burmese Independence Army of Aung San.[12] The drops were done with skill and valor—planes often had to circle a dozen times while supplies were pushed out of the Dakotas and Hudsons and included more than nourishment for tired and worn bodies. True to his penchant for detail, Wingate had recorded the lens prescriptions for those who wore eyeglasses, and impressions of dental plates for the many who required them as well; they were included in the drops for those who needed replacements. But by far the most valued item in the drops and the most longed-for was mail from home. Nothing assured continued high morale like the comforting words of loved ones.

But in the end the strain, constant fatigue, gnawing hunger and continuous thirst, debilitating illness from amoebic dysentery or malaria, injuries and wounds, combined with increasing Japanese pressure, forced Wingate and his commanders to pull back. They briefly considered several options, including heading northeast up the Burma Road or north to old Fort Hertz or recrossing the Irrawaddy and Chindwin. The decision was made for them when Lt. Gen. Geoffrey Scoones, commander of IV Corps and an old India veteran, ordered the Chindits back to India.

For Wingate it was a bitter pill. It was the right decision, to be sure, but it left him with a feeling of resigned failure. It had one positive side: the men would eat well, for the first time in many weeks, but at a high cost. All the mules and horses were to be slaughtered. Wingate himself demonstrated how they were to be killed silently, with a knife drawn through the carotid artery. The mule was tied and pushed to the ground, where a naked soldier sat on its head. Wingate—his old knowledge of horses gained in his early career helped here—felt for the artery and swiftly sliced it. A torrent of hot, slippery blood covered the naked soldier.[13]

When they staggered back into Imphal, the Chindits were a depleted force; men were emaciated, haggard, hollow-eyed. But they were the lucky ones: of the 3,000 who marched into Burma, only 2,120 returned. About 450 had been killed; 430 had been left behind or were known to be prisoners of war. Only 650 were considered fit for duty. Wingate expected to be court-martialed.[14]

But the British needed heroes, and they needed some assurance that ordinary Tommies and Commonwealth troops could defeat the super-men of Japan. The press went to work, and stories of derring-do filled the front pages of newspapers everywhere. Photographs showed the Chindits, dashing in Australian bush hats, in the wild jungle camps of Burma. Wingate was the darling of the hour; his cork-lined sun helmet, tangled beard, and bush jacket appeared in photos everywhere. The brass announced that Wingate had been awarded his third DSO; his scarlet-and-blue ribbon now carried two silver rosettes, an almost unprecedented distinction. He was forty years old.

Wingate wrote a detailed report of the Chindit operation and sent a copy to his friend and benefactor Amery, who shared it with Churchill. The prime minister was impressed; he ordered that Wingate return to London immediately. It was the end of July 1943. Wingate wasted no time, as he had not seen his wife, Lorna, in more than a year. He had just had new summer uniforms tailored, khaki cotton shorts and blouse, and did not have time to secure anything more formal. Being Wingate, he certainly didn't care, either. When he arrived in London, he reported immediately to General Sir Alan Brooke, chief of general staff, who informed the PM that Wingate was in the country. According to Churchill's memoirs, he was preparing to dine alone when he received the call and promptly invited Wingate to dinner at 10 Downing Street. Churchill was impressed: "We had not talked for half an hour before I felt myself in the presence of a man of the highest quality."[15] Previously, after reading Wingate's report on the incursion into Burma, Churchill had pronounced the daring leader "a man of genius and audacity" and intoned that questions of seniority should not block his further advancement. Wingate soon found himself a brigadier.

Now things took an unexpected turn. The prime minister was preparing to leave for Glasgow, to board the *Queen Mary* for the Atlantic crossing; he was to meet U.S. President Franklin Roosevelt in Quebec. The Quadrant Conference had been called to settle some matters regarding the further conduct of the war, as well as postwar strategy. The combined chiefs of staff would be present, and most of the senior military leadership of both nations. Churchill wanted Wingate to go with him.

Wingate expressed the proper eagerness to go but also voiced some disappointment at not being able to see his wife while home. Churchill promptly settled the matter: Lorna, aboard a train from Aberdeen to London, was removed at Waverley Station in Edinburgh and escorted to Glasgow; the *Queen Mary* was docked at Clydeside and would transport the prime minister and his party of 250 to Halifax. It was 4 August 1943.

Project 9 was now in gestation.

CHAPTER 4

The stately ship, 1,000 feet long and barely camouflaged by a coat of gray paint, steamed past McNab's Island, reducing speed at the north end as she entered the safety of the huge natural harbor at Halifax, Nova Scotia, in late summer 1943. The sheer grace of her main deck, the raked stem, and the three stacks slanting back from her superstructure made the *Queen Mary* unmistakeable in silhouette, and in daylight her lineage was undeniable. She was royalty in sackcloth, with clearly visible bloodlines. Her escorts, including a Royal Navy destroyer and the American aircraft carrier USS *Ranger,* had dropped astern, and the flagship of the Cunard–White Star Line—still regal despite bristling with retrofitted guns—sailed past the George's Island lighthouse and then the Sambro Island lighthouse, the oldest in North America. She cruised past Pier 21, the processing point for immigrants to Canada, a cousin of New York's Ellis Island.

Naval and merchant vessels anchored out of the main channel crowded the harbor; the docks were insanely busy. Cranes lifted huge nets filled with provisions and equipment onto ships' decks, some four deep at some berths, as the navies and merchant ships of nations at war prepared for the Atlantic crossing. Other ships were being repaired. The harbor was nearly overwhelmed by the vessels steaming in and out of the last stopping point before the long and dangerous journey to England. The *Queen Mary* slowed still more; outside the Narrows the crew began docking procedures at the Navy Yard, near the entrance to

Bedford Basin, the inner and most protected part of the harbor. Just visible in the northwest arm was Deadman's Island, final resting place of several American prisoners of the War of 1812.

Only twenty-six years earlier the area had been the scene of unimaginable horror. On 9 December, 1917 the *Mont Blanc,* a French ship loaded with munitions and explosive chemicals intended for the war raging across Europe, had collided with a Norwegian relief ship in the narrow channel to the basin. Sparks flew, the ship caught fire, and thousands turned out to watch as the *Mont Blanc* drifted into pier 6. Twenty minutes later the largest accidental explosion in history blew out windows fifty miles away, leveling much of Halifax, killing 1,600 to 2,000 people—reports vary—and injuring more than 9,000.

Five years before that the harbor had been the quiet somber landfall for survivors of the *Titanic's* collision with that iceberg in the North Atlantic; one hundred of the dead were buried in Fairview Lawn Cemetery in the center of old Halifax.

On this ninth day of August 1943 history was calling again. Lines were secured, the gangplank rolled out, and Prime Minister Winston Churchill, stout and bullish in a dark-gray pin-striped suit, his familiar blue polka-dotted bowtie, and a gray homburg, ambled onto the jetty. The five-day crossing from Glasgow had been shrouded in secrecy; to dispel suspicions about the identity of the large party boarding in Clydeside, the British had planted a story about a contingent of Holland's ministers, and to support the story posters had been plastered around the ship with messages in Dutch. Radio communications had been kept to a minimum; the VIP aboard was code-named Colonel Warden. Although the Battle of the North Atlantic was largely settled, German U-boats still prowled the shipping lanes, and the journey was perilous even with an escort of heavily armed warships.

Immediately after they disembarked, the prime minister and his family were driven to the nearby train station. Despite the tight cloak of secrecy, Churchill was mildly amused to see a large crowd gathered, waving British flags and flashing the PM's trademark V for victory. The Canadians cheered lustily when they recognized the famed stout figure, and, ever the showman, he listened and beamed as they sang stirring renditions of "Oh Canada" and "The Maple Leaf." For about twenty minutes he stood for photographs, shook hands with dozens of admirers, and signed autographs.[1]

A short time later, unrecognized and unheralded, a smallish dark-haired man in a naval uniform—the only uniform found aboard that would fit him—descended the gangway, accompanied by a young attractive woman who held his arm. An astute observer familiar with military decorations might have seen on his left chest a scarlet-and-blue ribbon adorned with two silver rosettes.

Brig. Orde Wingate and Lorna had been the toast of the younger set aboard the *Queen Mary*; the other wives aboard were thrilled to include in their dinner plans such a young, attractive, and rather exotic couple.

Wingate himself had spent the voyage preparing a presentation about the Chindits and the best tactical uses for long-range penetration groups. The prime minister had asked Wingate to address the Combined Chiefs of Staff, and Wingate threw himself into the assignment with vigor. The intellectual and solitary Wingate disliked social small talk, but among those aboard was the dashing Royal Air Force Group Captain Guy Gibson. The chatty and charismatic Gibson, awarded the Victoria Cross for leading his squadron in breaking German dams in the Ruhr valley, was more than up to the daunting social requirements of each evening, whereas Wingate toiled tirelessly in his cabin. Despite the new brigadier's solitude, Churchill appeared to consider Wingate's presence a personal success. In a telegram to the king Churchill said Wingate "made a deep impression on all during the voyage, and I look for a new turn being given to the campaign in Upper Burma."[2]

The British delegation rode the train to Quebec City, where Churchill was met by William Lyon Mackenzie King, prime minister of Canada and host of the conference. He was accompanied by a security detail of Northwest Canadian Mounted Police in their signature Stetson hats and scarlet tunics, who escorted the motorcade to La Citadelle.

La Citadelle was a massive brooding fortress overlooking both the old city of Quebec and the St. Lawrence River, evidence of the uncertainty of its nineteenth-century British architects as to the location of the greatest enemy: Americans sailing up the waterway or the French Canadians in the city of Quebec. The fortress, now a museum but still an active military garrison, stood as a symbol of the history of changing alliances and the ubiquitous presence of the dogs of war.[3] It was typical of defensive strongholds of its day, a large star-shaped fortress that dominated Cap Diamant and towered 300 feet over the St. Lawrence.[4]

In August 1943 the impregnable fortress built to repel American invaders and guard against Francophone rebellions played host to Churchill and Franklin Delano Roosevelt. The most powerful men on the planet, together with a phalanx of admirals and generals, planned the next phases of the war, including the liberation of France.

A truncated motorcade of three cars, carrying Churchill, his wife, Clementine, and their twenty-six-year-old daughter, Mary, the couple's youngest of five children (she was a lieutenant in an antiaircraft artillery unit of the women's Auxiliary Territorial Service), drove from the train station to the Dalhousie Gate of La Citadelle. To mark it as the preeminent entrance, the arched gate, which was actually a tunnel through the thick walls, was flanked by columns carved in relief out of the sandstone blocks. Here the vehicles turned into the fortress and were met by an RCMP honor guard; they stood stiff-backed in two ranks as the PM and his party emerged from the Packards in front of a block-long two-story neoclassical building in the inner courtyard. (A fourth motor car carrying Mackenzie King had taken a wrong turn and would arrive fifteen minutes late, much to King's annoyance.) The summer residence of the governor-general, originally officers' barracks, would be temporary home to both the Churchill party and the American president. In unspoken deference to FDR's polio-ravaged legs, wooden ramps had been constructed at key points in the building; the Canadians and British were far too polite to mention it. Code-named the Quadrant Conference, many of the working sessions would take place in the governor-general's residence as well as the Chateau Frontenac, a fairy-tale hotel with towers and dormers that rivaled anything built by King Ludwig II of Bavaria. The hotel served as guest quarters for the military and civilian members of the conference, both American and British. The steep verdigris copper roof and inverted ice-cream cones atop the many towers of the hotel were clearly visible from the ramparts of La Citadelle.

With a week to go before the official start of the conference, Churchill and Mary (Clementine stayed behind to rest) departed for the Hyde Park, New York, home of FDR, while the chiefs of staff and their aides worked out military details for the upcoming campaigns in both theaters of war.[5] Issues to be discussed included the cross-channel invasion of France, the anticipated surrender of Italy, strategy for the war in the Pacific, and questions of command in combined operations. Dozens of staff officers scurried around the Chateau Frontenac, and earnest intense meetings occurred at several levels days before FDR and Churchill's formal sit-down.

Although Wingate did not know it at the time, perhaps the most important man in Quebec regarding his military future, other than the president and prime minister, was the burly avuncular red-faced chief of the U.S. Army Air Forces, Henry H. "Hap" Arnold. Arnold was the antithesis of Wingate in many ways: nearly six feet tall, gregarious, profane, not often accused of being an intellectual but always decisive. Arnold was both intensely protective of his airmen and dedicated to the strategy of daylight bombing in Europe, which was costing thousands of young fliers their lives or their freedom. However, he, like Wingate, was disdainful of slackers and impatient with restrictive regulations.

Arnold was a 1907 graduate of West Point, where he had played some football, thrown the shot, and excelled in polo. While there he also had camouflaged a nighttime career as a bit of a hell-raiser. He compiled an impressive record of demerits for minor infractions of the strict rules at the military academy, and he once led a midnight raid on the cannon that sounded reveille at 5 a.m. Arnold and his gang of cadets rolled the small antique gun up the stairs of their dormitory and then hefted it out a window onto the roof, the wheels of the carriage straddling the ridgeline. It was an impressive bit of commando-style insubordination—much appreciated by his fellow cadets—for which Arnold apparently went undiscovered and unpunished.[6]

Arnold had been one of the army's first aviators—he had learned to fly from the Wright brothers in Dayton, Ohio, in 1911, and he was the first recipient of the MacKay Trophy, awarded annually since 1912 to the "most meritorious flight of the year" by someone in the air force. Below his medal ribbons he still wore his old-style solid gold Army Signal Corps aviator wings; fixed above his decorations were the new silver wings bearing a shield.[7]

Wingate's unorthodox views on warfare, and his obvious disdain for desk officers, might have appealed to Arnold. In any imaginable circumstances they probably would not have chosen to spend long hours in deep conversation or even to drink an occasional beer together. But the small dark intense Wingate, with his relish for the unusual use of men, weapons, and tactics, must have struck a positive chord in Arnold. The general was being criticized daily for his insistence upon the daylight bombing campaign—even the chief of staff, George Marshall, was beginning to question the wisdom of the strategy in view of the high casualties—so to hear of Wingate's success in Burma despite the naysayers must have had an I-will-prevail appeal for Arnold.[8]

On 10 August 1943, the day after he arrived in Canada, Wingate presented to the Joint Planning Staff and the British staff chiefs his carefully prepared plan for expanded long-range penetration groups. The first Chindit operation might have been seen as a training exercise of sorts, a lethal real-time way to test his theories. Now he was able to expand his vision, and in a crisp orderly no-nonsense presentation to the beribboned brass around a large mahogany table, the brand-new brigadier in the naval uniform displayed no eccentricities, no quirks, no unseemly passions. He had maps, photographs, reports, summaries, and recommendations, all carefully controlled and perfectly timed. He was complete but brief, not going beyond the limits of interest or exceeding the bounds of good sense regarding time. General Sir Alan Brooke, the British chief of staff, was impressed, calling Wingate's briefing first class.[9]

A week later the Combined Chiefs of Staff heard Wingate and were equally impressed. Meeting 17 August in room 2208 of the Chateau Frontenac at 2:30 in the afternoon, they listened intently as Wingate once more outlined his vision for long-range penetration groups in Burma. Among the Americans to hear his plan were Adm. William D. Leahy, joint chief of staff; George C. Marshall, general of the army; Adm. Ernest J. King, the navy chief; and General Arnold, head of the Army Air Forces. The British chiefs were Brooke; Sir Dudley Pound, admiral of the fleet; and Sir Charles Portal, air chief marshal.

Portal introduced Wingate and broadly outlined the theory of long-range penetration groups. Operating well ahead of main forces, the LRPGs would sever enemy supply lines through long flanking movements and would themselves be largely resupplied by air. Brigadier Wingate had experience in just such operations, Portal said, and would be pleased to report on his observations and conclusions.

After discussing the tactical use of long-range penetration groups, Wingate explained to the listening commanders how the units might be used in conjunction with other advances aimed at recapturing northern Burma. Wingate was wise enough to stress that the LRPGs must be used solely to disrupt enemy lines of communication and transportation while the main thrust worked to defeat the Japanese. He also stressed that any plans must be elastic enough to permit last-minute changes as Japanese forces reacted in perhaps unforeseen ways.

Following Wingate's presentation, Brooke told the assembled Combined Chiefs that the British chiefs had agreed to form six LRPGs, mostly from existing Indian Army units. One problem would be finding sufficient numbers of officers who had served with native troops and were proficient in their language, he said.[10]

"The operations outlined by Brigadier Wingate would enable us to seize sufficient of North Burma [sic] to open a road to China," Brooke confidently told the Combined Chiefs. "These operations must continue until the break of the monsoon [season] in order to avoid a Japanese reaction before the rains start." He also suggested that a second phase of LRPG use might be aimed at southern Burma, from the coast to the Mandalay-Rangoon line of communications. The Combined Chiefs, while apparently impressed with Wingate's ideas, agreed to defer action on the proposal until after they had considered the overall plan to defeat Japan. Regardless of how successful, how colorful, or how innovative a campaign might be, it still had to fit into the overall strategy to defeat the enemy. Although he may have been disappointed by the delay, Wingate listened intently, in the main pleased at the reception for his plan.[11]

His plan was audacious, but the record in Burma showed that audacity was a requirement for success against the Japanese. The first Chindit foray to cross the Chindwin had consisted of 3,000 men and about 1,000 pack animals, mainly mules. They had been supplied by a half-dozen Royal Air Force cargo planes that had to avoid Japanese fighters and ground defenses while searching the jungles below for signs of the Chindits. The Chindits ended their campaign when the RAF could no longer assure aerial supplies.

Wingate's new plan called for 26,500 troops in three groups, each organized into eight columns. He requested a dedicated aerial supply force of about sixteen C-47s, as well as a force of bombers that could provide close air support. The LRPG would be part of a three-pronged attack into Burma by British and Indian troops in the west, Chinese in the east, and a joint Sino-American force commanded by Joe Stilwell in the north. Wingate thus brilliantly explained the tactical use of the Chindits as part of an overall strategy to keep India and China in the war while inflicting a devastating defeat on the Japanese in Burma. With the approval of the Combined Chiefs, Wingate on 18 August at last presented his plan to Roosevelt and Churchill. The prime minister did not need to be convinced as he was already squarely in Wingate's corner. Roosevelt listened intently, nodding at times, asking occasional questions. He beamed his approval, directing Arnold to assist in any way possible.

Churchill was ecstatic. The little brigadier, who could be brash and dismissive, had, if not charmed, at least mightily impressed the Joint Planning Staff, the Combined Chiefs of Staff, and the president of the United States.

"You have expounded a large and very complex subject with exemplary lucidity," Churchill told Wingate after the meeting with FDR.

"Such is always my practice, sir," Wingate replied.[12]

At 5:30 the next afternoon, Thursday, 19 August, the president of the United States and the British prime minister met for the first time with the Combined Chiefs of Staff in La Citadelle. With Roosevelt on the American side of the table were Leahy, Marshall, King, Arnold, and Harry Hopkins, close adviser to Roosevelt. Churchill was flanked by Brooke; Pound; Portal; Anthony Eden, British foreign secretary; Field Marshal Sir John Dill, Vice Admiral Lord Louis Mountbatten, and Lt. Gen. Sir Hastings L. Ismay. They sat at a long wooden table that was shiny with wax; large oil paintings of celebrated British military leaders stared down at them from the paneled walls of the cavernous meeting room. A vivid painting of the Battle of the Plains of Abraham reminded them of where they were and of past British glories.

The meeting opened with a reading of the "Report of Progress" submitted by the Combined Chiefs, followed by a lengthy discussion of the war in Europe, in particular Operation Overlord, the planned cross-Channel invasion of occupied France. Roosevelt, chain-smoking through a slim cigarette holder, followed the conversations closely, occasionally rubbing a hand along a tire of his wheelchair. Churchill, sipping water from a crystal glass, presented no objections to the plan, suggesting only a 25 percent increase in the assault forces. Previously he had opposed Operations Sledgehammer and Roundup for a variety of reasons, but Overlord had his complete support.[13]

At last they came to the war against Japan. Under the cloak of geniality and bonhomie were some disagreements about how to proceed and when.

"Regarding the command situation in Southeast Asia," Churchill began. Roosevelt and the American brass looked closely at the prime minister, whose eyes swept around the table. "It seems to be that the setup to which we all agreed does not exactly coincide with the MacArthur model." There was no comment; no one could deny that Gen. Douglas MacArthur had assumed a transcendent command role in the Pacific. Churchill looked directly at Marshall and asked if it might be possible to have a British liaison officer appointed to MacArthur's staff.[14]

Marshall, a man of steel but with a keen sense of the diplomatic, smiled. "Arrangements to accomplish this are under way at the present time," he told the prime minister and the British chiefs. "In addition, I am taking the necessary steps to see that the situation in the Southwest Pacific is adequately reported to you, sir, at frequent intervals." Churchill nodded his approval.[15]

In general both leaders agreed to the plan to win the war against Japan. Much of it rested upon keeping China in the war, both to tie up Japanese troops and resources and to provide bases for the envisioned bombing campaign of the Japanese homelands by American B-29s. The importance of Burma in these strategic plans was emphasized; the shortest route for much-needed fuel and other supplies was through northern Burma, along the Ledo and Burma Roads, as well as its air corridors for overflights by C-46s and C-47s.

"The pressure being exerted by our operations against Japanese forces in outlying Pacific areas in Burma and perhaps Sumatra, will substantially contain those forces and prevent Japan from greatly reinforcing her air forces now deployed in China," declared a document from the Combined Chiefs of Staff. The Air Plan for the Defeat of Japan, in the form of a memorandum from the U.S. Joint Chiefs of Staff, declared as its mission: "To accomplish, by a combined aerial offensive, the destruction of the Japanese military, industrial and economic systems to such a degree that the nation's capacity for armed resistance is effectively eliminated, within 12 months after the defeat of Germany." An exponential increase in the number of airbases available, as well as the tonnage of fuel and supplies into China, would be critical to the success of the air plan.[16]

Where the British and the Americans differed was about whether the operations in northern Burma should be extended to the south of the country as well, to include the retaking of Rangoon and perhaps Singapore. The Americans favored this plan; the British did not, instead pressing for a strike at Sumatra, a move that in Churchill's view would replicate the previous year's Operation Torch in North Africa.[17]

"If a strong air force could be lodged in Sumatra, the Japanese could be brought to action, their shipping could be bombed, and they would be forced to gather resources to react against our initiative," Churchill intoned. He paused to light a foul-smelling cigar, exhaling a cloud of smoke that rose slowly to the high ceiling. Smiling, he looked around the table. "Options should be kept open for subsequent action in either direction. Whatever happens, we must not let an ultimate objective paralyze intervening action."

A short silence followed Churchill's assessment. Then, clearing his throat, the president spoke, with his patrician upbringing reflected in his voice to nearly the same degree as the titled Englishman's.

"I appreciate your view, Mr. Prime Minister." Roosevelt smiled disarmingly, in the way that had smoothed many a political contretemps. "However, I look at the problem from a rather different angle. The position occupied by the Japanese might be compared to a slice of pie, with Japan at the apex, and with the island barrier forming the outside crust." The metaphor brought a smile from Churchill. Roosevelt continued: "One side of the piece of pie passes through Burma, the other down to the Solomons. I quite see the advantage of an attack on Sumatra, but I doubt whether we have sufficient resources to allow both the opening of the Burma Road and to attack Sumatra. I would rather see all resources concentrated on the Burma Road, which I believe represents the shortest line through China to Japan.

"I greatly favor attacks which would aim at hitting the edge of the pie as near to the apex as possible, rather than attacks which nibble at the crust."[18]

Churchill, the embodiment of the British bulldog, smiled again. "I quite agree with your tasty simile. I am rather fond of pie myself." The admirals and generals chuckled. "But I wonder whether the conquest of Southern Burma is really necessary. The problem, as I see it, is not so much the finding of forces to deploy, but rather of overcoming the difficulties of an exiguous line of communication, and of a monsoon [season] which limits operations to six months in the year. Burma is the worst possible place in which to fight, and operations can only be carried on by a comparatively small number of high-class troops."[19]

He was referring, of course, to his protégé Wingate and the long-range penetration group.

Roosevelt nodded in recognition of the difficulties presented by the terrain and weather in Burma. He then revealed his concern: China must be kept in the war at all costs, and Generalissimo Chiang Kai-shek had specifically called for the retaking of Rangoon and Akyab, a town in western Burma, to disrupt Japanese communications. Somehow things would have to be smoothed over. "I am of the belief that the Japanese are not so dependent on their lines of communication as Allied troops," the president confided.

The following day, Friday, 20 August, the Combined Chiefs met again in room 2208 of the Chateau Frontenac. The Americans and Brits still disagreed about retaking all of Burma or only the northern half. Marshall voiced support for the former, while Portal, the British air marshal, emphasized the enormous numbers of aircraft and crew that would be available to fly supplies into China following the defeat of Germany, thereby virtually eliminating the need for ground transport and secure territory in Burma. Marshall agreed, and Portal went on: "I have been impressed by the small number of aircraft required to maintain three of Brigadier Wingate's groups. The air could be directed by these groups onto vital enemy points. Penetration by these methods with lightly armed forces assisted and supplied by the air, could, I feel, produce quicker results than the laborious advance of land forces, accompanied by the necessary building of road communications."[20]

Arnold, sensing that the moment was right, quickly chimed in. The end of the war with Germany would release not only cargo aircraft but fighters and bombers that could attack railroads and bridges, as well as troops and vehicles on the march, he said. A vision of a new kind of warfare, using irregular forces on the ground to coordinate air strikes, was slowly taking shape with no conscious impetus.

All that remained now was to placate the Chinese. Unhappy with the pace of progress in India—Churchill called it "lethargic and stagnant"—the Combined Chiefs agreed at Quebec to appoint Lord Mountbatten as supreme commander of a new South East Asia command. His deputy would be General Stilwell, who would continue to serve as Chiang Kai-shek's chief of staff as well. The Combined Chiefs further agreed that the president and prime minister would send a confidential letter to the generalissimo and that the Stilwell appointment would not be announced publicly until the Chinese commander had been notified.

On 23 August the president and the prime minister met again with the Combined Chiefs in La Citadelle and once again discussed the complexities of the war plan against Japan. Arnold raised the issue that competing goals might be at work.

"Mr. President, I would just like to point out that in giving priority to the operations in Northern Burma, the delivery of supplies into China might be reduced," Arnold said. "I don't disagree with the decision, but I have been charged with the responsibility for the delivery of supplies to China, and I would like to point out that giving first priority to the reconquest of Northern Burma might make it impossible for me to fulfill that responsibility." He looked directly at Roosevelt, but Churchill spoke first.

"I believe this would be largely a matter of judgment for the commander on the ground," he said. "For example, there is the necessity of sending some 2,000 men to Yunnan as part of Brigadier Wingate's force to cover the Chinese advance from Yunnan. This would be an instance in which the delivery of supplies to China would be temporarily interfered with."

Roosevelt nodded vigorously. "I should wish to establish some proviso which would prevent commanders on the supply lines in China [from] confiscating supplies intended for China to use in their own theaters."

Marshall addressed both issues, correctly identifying the competing requirements and the tendency of field commanders to see their campaigns as most urgent and most deserving of supplies and equipment. "I believe that situation (of confiscation) has been pretty well taken care of," he told the president and prime minister. He turned to Arnold. "It will be necessary for someone on the ground to have authority to make decisions regarding priorities." Arnold nodded, and Marshall continued: "If, for example, it is arbitrarily decided to use the entire capacity of the air transport route to supply General Chennault with gasoline, this very decision might jeopardize the success of the Burma operations which in themselves are essential to keeping China in the war."[21]

Churchill then broached once more the topic of southern Burma. At the Trident Conference in Washington, D.C., the previous May, the capture of Akyab had been seen as a necessary preliminary to the recapture of Rangoon, and both goals had been approved to please Chiang Kai-shek. But now the battle for Akyab would be a "dangerous, sterile and costly operation directed against a point where the Japanese would be expecting attack."

Roosevelt, responding, revealed the degree to which he had fallen under the spell of Wingate: "Brigadier Wingate has informed me that the capture of Rangoon would not cut the Japanese line of communications since they are now largely supplied overland from French Indo-China and Thailand." It was settled, then, except for placating the Chinese.[22]

The Brits and the Americans had some anxious moments when Dr. T. V. Soong and General Shih-Ming Chu attended the Combined Chiefs' meeting on Tuesday, 24 August. Soong, brother of Madam Chiang Kai-shek and therefore brother-in-law of the generalissimo as well as Sun Yat-sen, had been minister of finance for China and had bankrolled the American Volunteer Group, better known as the Flying Tigers. To say he was one of the most powerful men in China is to vastly understate the obvious. He asked some probing questions about the plans for the Allied war on Japan and wanted specific details about the expectations of the Chinese military machine. He expressed some fear that the Japanese would launch another attack on China. Brooke discussed the role of Wingate's long-range pentration group and invited response from Soong.

"I feel it would be of no value for me, as a civilian, to express my views on the situation," Soong said. The Combined Chiefs, now quite concerned, quickly began to reassure Soong that China was very much an important part of the overall strategy and that great efforts were being made to supply fuel and other needed supplies. Marshall called the effort to sustain China colossal and prodigious, and he said that security of the lines of communication was essential. Still, Soong seemed disquieted, and Marshall excused himself while he led the two Chinese delegates from the room.

When he returned some time later, he told the anxious Combined Chiefs the substance of his conversation. "I emphasized that he, Dr. Soong, must ensure unity of action from China on behalf of the united effort and that this unity of action must be accompanied by no holding back or reluctance. Only in this way could success be achieved and without it all our efforts would be futile." The generals and admirals of the CCS breathed a sigh of relief.[23] All in the room were aware that Chiang Kai-shek and Mao Tse-Tung were competing for the future of China after the war. At times, it seemed that politics prevailed over waging the war.

While Wingate's plan enjoyed acclaim in Quebec, it did not fare as well in New Delhi. Notified by telegram of the main points of the proposal, the British brass in India expressed profound reservations. Field Marshall Claude Auchinlech questioned Wingate's experience to command a large force, and Auchinlech insisted that transferring so many assets to the proposed irregular force would place serious demands on the British military in India. He labeled Wingate's plan "unsound and uneconomical."[24] Auchinlech obviously did not comprehend the esteem in which the PM held Wingate nor the degree to which the old warhorse was tired of the complaints and inaction from New Delhi. Churchill's response was explosive; at his request Wingate wrote an eight-page rebuttal of Auchinlech's memorandum and in the process also disparaged the lack of military success by nearly all the British brass in the Far East.

The governments involved presented the Quebec Conference to the public as an old-fashioned tent revival. In radio addresses both FDR and Churchill praised the harmony and progress of the conference. The truth was rather more complex, with some serious disagreements at times and hard bargaining, particularly when the discussions focused on a timetable for the cross-Channel invasion and when deciding whether southern Burma needed to be liberated. And FDR and Churchill signed a secret agreement on future use of atomic weapons, but the president fended off Churchill's suggestions that they jointly develop the secret superweapon.

A positive development, for the harmonious relationship of the two nations and for Wingate personally, was the U.S.-British agreement to the appointment of Admiral Louis Mountbatten as supreme allied commander of the new South East Asia Command (SEAC). Mountbatten, nicknamed Dickie, was a cousin of King George VI of Britain, as well as a strong supporter of Wingate and of the jointly approved plan for long-range penetration groups. Although Mountbatten was only forty-three, he had already headed several commands, including a flotilla of destroyers in the Mediterranean; German dive-bombers had sunk his ship, HMS *Kelly,* off the coast of Crete. Apparently no one ever questioned the decision to name a naval officer as supreme allied commander in a theater largely dominated by land battles.

Mountbatten, tall, handsome, and well connected, was also a bit eccentric; perhaps that is why he and Wingate got along so well. Churchill, in his monumental six-volume history of World War II, notes one instance in which Mountbatten's eccentricity was on full display during the Quebec Conference.

Things had gotten testy at one point during a session of the top leaders and their staffs. Serious disagreement had erupted over Britain's role in the major drive against Japan, and everyone agreed that the staff should leave the meeting and wait in a nearby room. The leaders settled their disagreement, but Mountbatten asked for a few more minutes without the staff present so he could discuss a secret project on which his naval engineers had been working. Of course, the time was granted. As long as you need, Dickie.

With a sense of the dramatic, Lord Mountbatten, resplendent in his admiral's uniform, nodded to an aide, who then wheeled into the room two wooden dollies on which rested a pair of large blocks of ice, perhaps three feet high and equally wide. Mountbatten explained to the Combined Chiefs, who doubtless wore quizzical expressions, that one block was ordinary ice. The other was Pykrete, a kind of super ice formed by mixing six parts water with one part sawdust or other wood products. He triumphantly held up a large splitting mallet and asked for a volunteer to crack the blocks of ice.

All eyes turned to Hap Arnold, quite visibly the strongest, stoutest man there. Arnold had suffered a series of heart attacks, which he and everyone else had quietly ignored, and his health seemed to be back in full bloom. Arnold smiled, removed his summer tunic, and rolled up his sleeves. Advancing to the block indicated by Mountbatten, the muscular Arnold hefted the mallet, flexed his shoulders, and took a titan's swing. The block shattered easily, ice chips exploding over the immaculate uniforms of the gathered generals and admirals. Arnold smiled, his normally pink face crimson with the effort and pride in his physical strength.

"Very good, General," gushed Mountbatten. "Now, if you will just repeat your performance with this block, please."

Arnold nodded and stepped up to the second chunk of ice. Once more he flexed his shoulders, gripped the mallet, and swung the heavy chopper as one would to split an oak log. This time the wedge bounced back without any visible damage to the ice, and Arnold screamed in agony as the shock tore into his elbows and shoulders. Mountbatten seemed quite pleased. Pykrete, he believed, might be used to build an unsinkable aircraft carrier; the mixture of water and wood pulp needed only minimal cooling to retain its frozen state and was nearly as strong as steel, he said.[25]

While Arnold grimaced and rubbed his shoulders, Mountbatten reached into a pocket of his uniform and pulled out a small Webley Bulldog revolver. Before anyone could react, he pointed it at a chunk of regular ice and pulled the trigger. The ice shattered, and he wheeled to fire at the block of Pykrete. The bullet ricocheted off the super ice, narrowly missing the British air commander, General Portal.[26]

One can only imagine the horrified thoughts of the staff officers waiting outside the room as they first heard Arnold's scream of agony, followed by two gunshots. In war sometimes judgment takes a vacation, even at the highest levels. But Mountbatten's lapse in judgment did not conceal his admiration for the unusual. This boded well for his support of the joint American-British campaign in Burma.

Wingate's vacation and time with Lorna were about to end, and hundreds of Americans would learn their plans were soon to change.

Project 9 was set to begin.

CHAPTER 5

While Roosevelt, Churchvill, and the Combined Chiefs met in Halifax to plan the war, Washington in late summer 1943 was a city focused on war. Nothing symbolized that focus more than the leviathan new addition to the skyline. In a city of monuments the Pentagon was both edifice to the country's military might and a practical no-nonsense office building—the largest in the world at the time—for the War Department and military brass.

As war had spread across Europe, it was obvious to everyone, including those who controlled the nation's purse strings, that housing the War Department in seventeen separate leased buildings along the National Mall and even across the Potomac in Arlington, Virginia, was inefficient and wasteful. A few months before Pearl Harbor, Congress had approved $83 million to construct what most thought would be temporary quarters—just for the duration of the war—for the planners and decision makers in the civilian and military hierarchy overseeing the conflict. (A common belief was that when hostilities ceased, the building would house a variety of government agencies and departments, since the War Department and the various armed services would shrink to a fraction of their wartime size.) But for now it was home to more than 30,000 workers, most in uniform but also many civilians, mainly young women.

The five-sided reinforced concrete building was a miracle of design, determination, and audacity. The first sketch of the building was done in the summer of 1941 by the chief architects of the War Department, George E. Bergstrom and David J. Witmer. The style was described as "stripped classical," a kind of spartan version of the Greco-Roman brand of monumental architecture called for in the 1902 McMillan Commission report, which blessed the style for lending dignity to democratic institutions. Construction began 11 September, 1941; 4,000 workers worked three shifts to complete it in sixteen months; the gleaming building was dedicated and fully operational on 15 January 1943. Five stories high, with an additional two stories underground, it covered thirty-four acres, including a five-acre central courtyard, contained 6.5-million square feet of space, and had parking for 8,000 cars. Each of its five sides was 921.6 feet long, and it rested on 41,492 concrete piles; more than six million cubic yards of earth had been hauled in to fill in the swampy lowland on which it was built.

Rising southeast of Arlington National Cemetery and in sight of the Lincoln Memorial and National Mall, the Pentagon sat just across Memorial Bridge on the Virginia side of the Potomac. The first site chosen was an area known as Arlington Farms, part of the large estate belonging to Robert E. Lee, but so many objected that it would block views of the national cemetery that President Roosevelt had ordered it moved three-quarters of a mile south to the present location, in an area commonly called Hell Bottoms.[1]

Lt. Col. Philip Cochran climbed out of the taxi and somewhat breezily returned the salute of the enlisted marine guard at the main entrance to the Pentagon. Inside he was directed to the office he requested—3E1009. Third floor, East wedge, tenth corridor, room 09. The new home of the War Department was a model of efficiency; it was constructed like five nesting boxes, concentric rings of concrete and limestone, with space between each ring so even offices deep within the monolith had access to light and air, although the building was also air-conditioned. Highest-ranking officers were ensconced in the outermost section, with offices facing the National Mall reserved for those with three or four stars on their shoulders, as well as the secretary of war and his staff. The sanctum sanctorum of this tabernacle to war had been inverted: the inner shrine to leadership was actually the outer ring, not the inner.

Cockran walked up several wide ramps to the third floor. To save material for the war effort, no stairs or elevators had been installed. He strode a short distance—despite seventeen miles of hallways, any place in the building could be reached in seven minutes or less—down corridor 10 to a suite of rooms numbered 9 and knocked on a door marked in gold lettering: Commander, Army Air Forces.

A secretary in an anteroom looked up pertly, first noting Cochran's rank, as she was trained to do. Light colonels were a dime a dozen in wartime Washington, and most were found in the Pentagon, so the silver oak leaves did not merit undue obeisance. She might then have noted the silver wings and rows of combat decorations, including the Silver Star and the Distinguished Flying Cross, and her interest level perhaps climbed a notch. Only then—the appraisal would have taken a fraction of a second—did she look at Cochran's face and his disarming smile. A handsome man by any standard, the stocky Irishman was also blessed with sparkling eyes and a grin that had melted many hearts. His face may have seemed vaguely familiar, and she might have wondered why, although she was certain she had never seen him before he walked in.

"Phil Cochran to see General Arnold." He was informal and friendly, although revealing just a trace of discomfort in the way he held his tan crusher cap in both hands. General Arnold would be available in a very few minutes. In the meantime please be seated, Colonel. He declined the offer of coffee. Where had she seen him before? She noted that he was casual for a middle-ranking officer summoned to the court of one of the highest-ranking generals in the Pentagon: his pants were tucked, nonregulation, into the tops of a pair of expensive-looking Natal boots, giving him a vaguely piratical mien.[2]

The irony, of course, was that Philip Cochran, the unorthodox, casual, perpetually smiling caricature of a fighter pilot, was known to millions of readers of daily newspapers as Flip Corkin, the unorthodox, casual, perpetually smiling fighter pilot with the square jaw, small nose, and eagle eyes who lived through a series of adventures fighting for justice and against evil in exotic locales. Milton Caniff, the series artist, had attended Ohio State University with Cochran; Caniff would create a bit of a stir within the intelligence community when some of the comic strip adventures came a bit too close to top-secret events in the combat zone.[3]

Cochran, born in 1910, was the second of five sons born to Bernard and Mary Cochran in Erie, Pennsylvania. Bernard Cochran was a lawyer and served a term as mayor of Erie, but the family was very much middle class. The family name was originally O'Corcoran and arrived with Philip's grandfather Bryan as he emigrated penniless to Boston from Ireland. The family Bible revealed two name changes in a single generation, as the O was dropped in favor of Corcran for Bernard's older brother, who died in infancy, and then to Cochran for his older sister, Stella. They were a family Irish and Catholic to the core. One of Phil's early memories was of attending mass at St. Andrew's during World War I and staring at a large American flag draped from the choir loft. The constellation of stars on the blue field was constantly changing, as a new star was added for each parish lad sent overseas. If one went missing or was killed in action, the star's color was changed to gold. It made a lasting impression on the young man.[4]

After graduating high school—where he played football, developed a fine baritone in St. Andrew's choir, and rebuilt several cars—Cochran worked in a papermill in Erie for two years to scrape together enough money to attend college. He chose Ohio State rather than a Pennsylvania school because it was less expensive, and he had two aunts and an uncle in Columbus whose presence might be handy. While studying business at OSU, Cochran met Caniff, the future cartoonist. Cochran's older brother, Paul, a talented musician, had attended OSU as well, after touring Europe with a band (Rudy Vallee was a band mate), and Paul introduced Philip to several band leaders on campus. He sang with a number of groups to finance his college degree, although he took a year off to work in the paper mill again, scraping together enough cash to complete his marketing degree.[5]

He applied to the Army Air Corps immediately upon graduation in 1935. He and another fellow were the only two of twelve candidates to pass the physical exam; Cochran was one of twenty-eight in a class of 110 to complete flight training. Because money was tight even for the military, the standard procedure was for those cadets who survived flight training to be assigned to a squadron as rated pilots but still ranked as cadets for as long as a year. The years before World War II were lean ones for young U.S. military officers. Despite what now seem like obvious indications that the world was drifting toward war, national leaders did almost nothing to increase the size of the armed forces. In 1939 the U.S. Army ranked seventeenth in the world in size, just behind Romania's, and the American air force had just 2,600 officers. Opportunities for advancement were few, but Cochran seemed not to mind either the paucity of promotions or the low pay. He reveled in the freedom that earning his wings had bestowed. He was, after all, a *fighter* pilot, not one of the lesser species, such as a bombardment or observation type.[6]

In the years leading up to the attack on Pearl Harbor, Cochran moved up the ladder in squadron positions. After the attack he was assigned as commander of the 65th Pursuit Squadron, stationed at Groton, Massachusetts, with the primary duty of teaching the pilots in his command the art of aerial warfare—tactics as well as dogfighting—and to do so, he declared war on the 64th Pursuit Squadron, which was stationed close by. For several months the two tried nearly daily to surprise each other with early morning or evening raids. Cochran, however, had devised an early warning system by charming a local young lady who lived near the field of the enemy squadron. Each time the fighters took off, she telephoned Cochran, who had his fighters up and waiting for them when they arrived over the field.[7]

His assignment at the Groton air base led to his fame in Caniff's comic strip. Although both had gone to Ohio State, Caniff was a senior when Cochran was a freshman. They knew each other but were not close friends. However, with the winds of war sweeping toward the United States, Caniff, by then a well-known cartoonist, had introduced a young character named Terry Lee into a series of adventures set in exotic locales somewhere in Asia. Caniff—like much of the rest of the country between the world wars—was fascinated by aircraft and the men who flew them. It was only a matter of time before he would bring them into the popular strip; mutual friends reintroduced Caniff, who was then drawing for the *New York Daily News,* and Cochran, and the cartoonist spent many days observing the cocky young pilots in their iconic gear as they worked hard and played hard. When Caniff had young Terry Lee join the Army Air Force to train as a pilot, he introduced the character of Flip Corkin. Cochran always insisted the obvious caricature was originally meant only as a joke, but it may well have been Caniff's way of thanking him for the opportunity to closely observe pursuit pilots at work. In any event mothers and fathers everywhere saw the character as the perfect, caring, fatherly commander of young Terry, and soon Caniff heard directly from the Army Air Force, which commended him for the strip and asked that the character of Flip Corkin continue. That made Cochran a permanent character in one of the most popular comic strips in the country.[8]

But while training the pilots of his squadron for war, Cochran had worked himself into the hospital. Fatigue had laid him low, and when the squadron received orders to ship out for the war in Europe, the commander was unable to go. Cochran was beside himself, but his opportunity for combat was not long delayed. Operation Torch, the invasion of French North Africa in November 1942, involved the use of army planes launched from navy ships, with the understanding that they would land at air bases in Morocco and not attempt the much trickier landing back on a carrier. Cochran was assigned to lead a group of thirty-five P-40 pilots as their aircraft were launched from the British carrier HMS *Archer.* Cochran's pilots were not an official unit as they were to be replacements for what some commanders believed would be high casualties among squadron fliers.[9]

As neither Cochran nor any of his pilots had ever taken off from a carrier before, he set out to learn as much as he could with just a few days' notice. He called a navy flier, who briefed him over the telephone: the carrier should always steam into the wind and had to make at least fifteen knots. When the *Archer* sailed in late October 1942, Cochran continued to ask questions about carrier operations. What he learned was not encouraging. The ship was capable of only eleven knots, and the British captain patiently explained that if a battle erupted, he could not be expected to maneuver in the midst of the flotilla to search for the prevailing wind. Additionally the P-40s were far heavier than the old carrier's catapult capacity. Cochran ordered the planes lightened: engine cowlings were removed, only four of the six .50-caliber Browning machine guns were loaded, and fuel was restricted to the lowest level that was safe.

At Casablanca, one of the three invasion sites, naval gunfire silenced most of the opposing fire of the French. A large majority of the French troops were undoubtedly opposed to the German occupation of their country, but they were still soldiers and sailors under the Vichy French government, so they obeyed orders, offering some resistance to the combined British and American forces. Much of it was token, however, and in just enough measure to satisfy honor.

Perhaps with the role of Jimmy Doolittle as his model, Cochran decided that his would be the first plane launched. The shooting had ended, but the takeoff still would be stomach churning for the army pilots, many of whom had suffered seasickness during their first ship voyage.[10]

Cochran sat in his cockpit, the canopy open, watching the British seaman with the colored flag; Cochran's engine was at full RPM, his feet on the brakes. When he got the signal for launch, the force of the mechanical assist shoved a stunned Cochran back in his seat, but he found himself alive and still flying just a few feet above the waves. "Piece of cake," he said to himself. He circled back over the carrier, waiting for the others to launch and form up. But no one else launched. He broke the strict rule for radio silence and learned the catapult was broken; it would take at least an hour to repair. Already low on fuel, a leader with no followers, he headed for the coast and landed at Port Lyautey in Casablanca. Eventually all but two planes launched safely—the pair ended up in the ocean—but when the young and jittery pilots arrived at the base, four crashed on landing. It was not a good beginning for Cochran's combat career.[11]

Since opposition to the invasion had been so light, Cochran's replacement pilots were not needed; in the confusion of the first days Cochran persuaded his superiors that he should move his planes and pilots to Rabat to institute a training program for his fledgling fliers similar to that which he had conducted at Groton. He was told to fly his P-40 to Rabat and check out the facilities there first. When he arrived, he taxied his fighter to the ramp. As he climbed out, he saw a formation of French troops standing at attention in front of a hangar. Intrigued, he walked toward them and soon realized that the group represented the official French delegation, which was awaiting the opportunity to surrender the airfield to the Allies. Cochran did his best imitation of a high-ranking officer expecting the formal surrender and requested a tour of the base. That concluded, he flew back to Casablanca and prepared to move his men and machines to Rabat.[12]

Because his group had no formal designation, Cochran christened his fliers the Joker Squadron; for the next several weeks he kept a rigorous training schedule that was paying off in increased flight proficiency and in confidence and morale as well. The men of Joker Squadron all wore red scarves. Eventually the Army Air Forces caught up with him, and he was ordered to take the six best pilots under his command and lead them to Thelepte, Tunisia, to bring a combat-depleted squadron back up to strength. Thelepte was the forward base of the Allies and therefore received few visits from the brass. Since he was now a major and the ranking officer, Cochran assumed command of the 58th Fighter Squadron, and for the next two months they were in combat daily, often improvising tactics.[13]

Like Wingate in the jungles of Burma, Cochran stressed that the mission was more important than personal hygiene. Men were unshaved, filthy, and red eyed, but they were harassing the Germans with self-taught low-level raids and close air support of Allied ground troops. Cochran lived in his grease-stained flight coveralls, and his haggard appearance was heightened by the loss of his two front dental caps, which snapped off on the gun sight of his P-40 during a bad landing. No dental work was available, so he continued on with the two stubs of his upper front teeth dimming his usual gleaming smile.

Jimmy Doolittle, the heroic leader of the raid on Tokyo, had been decorated with the Medal of Honor and promoted from lieutenant colonel to brigadier general. He was now the commander of Army Air Forces in Africa, and he arrived at Thelepte in his B-25 one day to inspect this isolated forward base. He was impressed, he said, with the way they had worked with the ground forces and with their hit-and-run low-level attacks on German truck convoys and railroads. What could Doolittle do for them? More planes was Cochran's answer. And so it was. The unit shortly thereafter received seventy-five brand-new P-40s. The 58th had steadily grown and, in addition to the new fighters, had already added A-20 Havocs (twin-engine light attack bombers), as well as some P-39s and more P-40s from the 33rd Group.[14]

For Cochran it was an exercise in unorthodox, guerrilla-like warfare, with his men continuously forced to adopt new tactics and forget what they had learned about formations and methods. With no one directly above him Cochran was free to be creative, and since he was not a graduate of a military academy and had no long family history of military service, he was not shackled to any traditions or an undue reverence for manuals, codes, or history. He was thus able to think in ways that might not have been possible for a career-oriented tradition-bound officer, who would first have considered the chain of command. For two months Cochran and his men flew daily missions, and eventually the strain of combat caught up with them. Cochran asked Doolittle for a flight surgeon to evaluate the condition of his men, many of whom he suspected were long past the point at which they should have received a rest. The doctor arrived, interviewed the men, and posted a list of pilots to be rotated to the rear for rest and recreation. Cochran's name was at the top of the list.[15]

He took some time to regroup and rest, and then the Army Air Force, recognizing that his intensive in-theater training had paid off, established the Northwest African Training Command, to which it posted Cochran, no doubt to his distress. Among the units he trained were the 99th Pursuit Squadron, which became known after the war as the Tuskegee Airmen, an all-black group. Cochran was impressed with the flying ability of the men and pushed for integrating them into existing combat units, but the service was not ready for that.[16]

By June 1943 Cochran was worn out with the strain of earlier combat and the almost daily training flights with the new inexperienced pilots being posted to the war zone. He was to be sent back to the States for an extended rest and then eventual reassignment to a fighter unit bound for the Big Show, the war out of England. He couldn't wait. But Gen. Carl "Tooey" Spaatz wanted Cochran to do one small thing before going on leave: Go to Washington, report directly to General Arnold, and impress upon him the absolute necessity of changing the policy of sending inexperienced pilots to the war zone to be trained there. Instead the air force needed to use combat-tested pilots who had completed their tours to train the neophyte aerial warriors at home.

Spaatz, who could be acerbic, left it hanging. Puzzled and perhaps a trifle intimidated, Cochran asked, "Now, what is it exactly that you want me to get across?"

Spaatz glared at Cochran for what seemed like minutes.

"Well, hell. I'm not going to tell you. You've lived it! I'm not going to tell you what to say. You get over there and say it!"[17]

As it turned out, Cochran did not meet directly with Arnold but did pass along his observations to the air staff before heading home to Erie, Pennsylvania, for a month. When he returned to duty, he was sent to

Mitchel Field on Long Island to begin the training advocated by Spaatz. The pilots preparing for war in Europe were being equipped with the newer, and more lethal, P-47 Thunderbolt. Cochran was soon able to persuade the 1st Army Air Force commander that sending Cochran to Europe for a tour in P-47s would be a good idea so that he could better instruct his charges.

Agreed, said the commander. Cochran was ecstatic; finally he was going to get into the real war, flying missions out of England.

Then he received a telegram telling him to report to General Arnold at the Pentagon.

CHAPTER 6

Philip Cochran was still sitting in the outer office of Gen. Hap Arnold. He tapped his fingers on his knees and idly flipped his cap. He cleared his throat, and the secretary looked up expectantly, but he did not say anything. He checked his watch for perhaps the tenth time in as many minutes.

Then they heard a sharp rap at the door, and in stepped a short unprepossessing man in the ubiquitous summer tans of an Army Air Force officer. On his epaulets were the silver leaves denoting his rank as lieutenant colonel, and on his left chest were silver wings and an impressive display of ribbons. One didn't see many Distinguished Service Crosses, even in the Pentagon. A Silver Star, Distinguished Flying Cross, Purple Heart, Legion of Merit, the usual campaign awards.

John Robinson Alison was small and muscular, with a cherubic face, protruding ears, and a high forehead accentuated by a prematurely receding hairline. But behind his tax-accountant appearance was a true warrior: He was considered a "good stick," a pilot's pilot who could instinctively fly anything with wings and fly it well. He apparently knew no fear—if he did, he had learned to control it and use it positively—and he had a talent for organization that was as legendary as his courage.

Cochran and Alison had been friends since their cadet days at Randolph Field near San Antonio. Cochran stood, extending his hand. They greeted each other warmly, both smiling in genuine pleasure.

It would have been difficult for anyone to imagine a more dissimilar pair. Broad-shouldered, suave, and charming, Cochran was the living embodiment of the archetypal devil-may-care fighter pilot, with a quick wit, a quicker smile, and a Yankee sense of practicality. Alison was small, with thinning sandy hair and a choirboy face, quiet, blessed with a fine, orderly mind and a southern martial spirit. At midwar he was already a legend in the fighter pilot community.

Alison, one of three sons of Grover and Edelweiss Alison, was born in Micanopy, Florida, in 1912. Despite his size he was a starting end on his high school football team and captain of the swim team. He also was elected president of his senior class.[1] He went to the University of Florida, where he majored in engineering with his eyes firmly skyward. Alison had wanted to fly since his high school days. He was so persistent that his father once paid for a few flying lessons, convinced that the exposure would quickly dissuade his son. It only made him more eager, however, and the lessons were discontinued. When college classmates John Taggart and Addison Pound applied to navy flight school, Alison thought he would join them. The following year, he drove to Pensacola to take the preliminary flight physical, even though the Army Air Corps had been his long-time goal.

He failed the physical. Too short by a quarter-inch to meet the navy's minimum requirement of 5'6",— he turned back to the Army Air Corps, where the minimum height requirement was 5'4". He was accepted for the cadet program and sent to Randolph Field in June 1936. The engineering program at Florida had prepared him well for the math and theory portions of the ground program, and he excelled in the cockpit as well.[2]

Alison learned to fly on PT-3s, BT-8s, and BT-9s. The BT-8 had a bad tendency to ground loop because it was so short-coupled, but the 9 had a worse fault: the wingtips tended to stall quickly, and several of Alison's cadet classmates were killed when their training aircraft stalled at low altitude as they were landing.[3]

Flying could be a dangerous enterprise, to be sure, but despite the rigor with which the military winnowed the aviation candidates, their instruction was often casual. Alison was assigned to an instructor for the second phase of training (called B-stage at the time; later called basic) who had developed a heart murmur and was grounded. However, he remained on instructing status; each day Alison reported to him, and the instructor explained the maneuvers that Alison was to practice. The cadet listened dutifully, then climbed into the training airplane alone, and flew what he thought the instructor wanted. Because of his size the parachute shop had to make Alison special cushions that allowed him to reach the rudder pedals and to see ahead.[4]

Philip Cochran was ahead of Alison at the flight school, but they became friends nonetheless. When Alison graduated from the demanding course in 1937, he was awarded his wings and was in the first class to be commissioned at the same time, without a waiting period in which he still would have ranked as a cadet. His first assignment was to Langley Field, Virginia, where he was roomed with Cochran. Langley was one of the oldest air bases in the country and had been the base of operations for Brig. Gen. Billy Mitchell during the summer of 1921 when he proved the utility of bombing ships from planes in experiments that used captured German warships off the Virginia coast.

At Langley Alison ran head-on into the realities of the prewar Air Corps: limited funds meant little flying. At one point he was so discouraged by the lack of flight time that he told his commanding officer he was considering resigning his commission. He received some good advice: hang tight, things are going to improve. Alison was shortly thereafter appointed deputy operations officer—Phil Cochran was the ops officer—and managed to schedule himself for every flight he could.[5]

At Langley Alison first exhibited a slight tendency to step around regulations and traditions if they seemed to work against good training for fighter pilots. He and his squadron mates spent as much time aloft as government funds would allow, but they were not merely boring holes in the sky. Instead they regularly held mock battles of one flight against another; these were followed by spirited discussion and analysis in the officers' club. The young fliers were perfecting their own formation and attack tactics while also polishing their flying skills.

There were accidents, and at one point the brass prohibited aerobatics until investigations assessing the causes were complete. Alison, already gaining a reputation as an outstanding pilot, believed the layoff would adversely affect his flying, so he began a series of night flights. Unseen by the brass in the dark skies over Hampton, Virginia, Alison practiced the aerobatics that he believed essential to aerial combat. He might have had the face of a choirboy, but he was also a southern boy and a bit of a rebel.[6]

Alison was sent to Mitchel Field in New York as operations officer for the 8th Pursuit Group. While there he had the opportunity to display some of his aerial gifts. He was asked to fly to Bolling Field in Washington, D.C., to demonstrate the abilities of the P-40 to Claire Chennault and a Chinese delegation that was looking to buy fighter planes for battling the Japanese. This was before Pearl Harbor, and Chennault had retired from the U.S. Army Air Corps as a captain before being recruited by the Chinese to train pilots. The Chinese were particularly interested in the rugged fighter plane, and Alison by now had considerable time and experience in the Warhawk.

Alison reported to the commander's office, where he chatted with Chennault and the Chinese. As Alison recounted it years later, two representatives from the Curtiss-Wright Corporation were also there and clearly were unimpressed with the diminutive pilot. They asked if their test pilot could fly the P-40 demonstration, but the commander said obtaining clearance would be time consuming. Alison asked Chennault what exactly he had in mind for the flight. After a brief discussion Alison climbed into the cockpit.

As the Chinese and Chennault watched, Alison took off, went to max boost, and pulled the nose straight up. Then he completed an Immelmann turn, a climbing maneuver with a half-roll at the top, turned back toward the delegation, and did a slow roll, five high-speed turns with the inside wing pointed directly at the crowd on the ground, then a split-S—a kind of reverse Immelmann, diving instead of climbing with a half-roll at the bottom. When Alison landed and taxied back to the Chinese, they were more than impressed.[7]

"We need 100 of those," they told Chennault. He turned to Alison, who was just walking up. "No, what you need is 100 of these," Chennault said, tapping the little flier on the chest. [8]

Back at Mitchel Field, Cochran and Alison were reunited, as Cochran took command of one of the three squadrons of the 8th Pursuit Group. Alison was soon promoted to command of a second squadron, after the original commander, John Aiken, died in a crash. But Alison's stateside assignments were coming to an end, and his overseas assignments would be marked by poor communications, obstinate Allies, lack of support, and sheer bad luck. Alison's training, perseverance, and diplomacy—topped by his burning desire to get into the fight—marked his peripatetic career for the next two years.

Because of his extensive experience in the P-40, Alison was sent to England in 1940 to advise and instruct British pilots in the fighter, 1,000 of which had been shipped by the United States to Britain under Lend-Lease. Alison and Hubert "Hub" Zemke, another rising star in the Air Corps, left the States for an assignment that Alison had been assured would last no more than a couple of months.[9]

As it turned out, Alison and Zemke spent a frustrating and relatively quiet four months doing their best to train pilots and ground crews alike in the quirks and peculiarities of the Curtiss-Wright fighter, which was already being outclassed by the best German fighters. The job was particularly difficult because no technical orders had accompanied the shipment of fighters, and despite repeated queries and best efforts, none were ever supplied. Because the United States was still a noncombatant, Alison and Zemke wore civilian clothing during their assignment in Britain.

At one point Wing Commander John H. Carey, a well-known British ace, had disparaged the performance of the American fighter, and Alison had quietly disagreed. The Brit challenged him to a dogfight, he in a Hurricane and Alison in a P-40. Despite Alison's lack of actual combat experience, he was able to get onto the tail of the Hurricane. The British pilot could not shake him, and when they landed he was complimentary in a reserved British way.

Then, in July 1941, Alison received a wire telling him to report to the American Embassy with all his gear. There he was told that he would accompany Harry Hopkins, President Roosevelt's adviser and special emissary, and Gen. Joseph McNarney to Russia to negotiate a Lend-Lease agreement similar to that with Great Britain. Despite Alison's demonstrations of the P-40's capabilities, British pilots did not care for the plane, and with Hitler laying seige to the Soviet Union, thereby diminishing the threat of a German invasion of England, it was suggested that some fighters still in crates might be more useful in Russia.[10]

After a series of meetings with Russian officials, Hopkins agreed to the Lend-Lease deal. Alison was told to stay in Moscow—he was promoted and assigned to the embassy—to await the arrival of the P-40s and Zemke.

When the crated fighters arrived, it was England all over again, with the added impediment that neither Alison nor Zemke spoke Russian. In time they learned enough to get by, but they still had no tech orders, and the Russians were at times less than cooperative. American freighters were taking fearful losses from German U-boats in the icy waters of the North Atlantic as they delivered supplies to the port of Murmansk. Someone on the American side suggested the aircraft be assembled in the States, then flown by American pilots to Russia by way of Alaska and Siberia. As air attachés in Russia Zemke and Alison were directed to secure Russian agreement; they sat down with their counterparts, held friendly meetings, and . . . waited. And waited. Zemke and Alison flew each of the P-40s assembled by the Russians; the Americans had little else to do. The delays continued, and each time they asked, smiling, nodding Russian officers assured them that the plan was being reviewed, and approval was only a formality. In November Lt. Col. Townsend Griffiss, an aide to Gen. George C. Marshall, arrived to personally conduct the negotiations; Alison and Zemke regarded his presence as a rebuke to them, a silent remonstration that they were not performing well at their assignment. In the meantime they heard that

Washington would be rotating one of them back to the States. Because Zemke was married, the bachelor Alison, who sorely wanted to leave Russia himself, told Zemke to pack up.

For a month Griffiss held regular meetings with more smiling, friendly, nodding Russian officials. But the plan for aerial delivery of the Lend-Lease aircraft was stuck on hold. In frustration Griffiss wired Marshall that he was going back to Washington. Frantic to leave Russia and get into the war as a fighter pilot, Alison fairly begged Griffiss to take him back with him. Griffiss, who was sympathetic, said he would authorize Alison's reassignment, and in January 1942 they left for the first stopover at Tehran, Persia.[11]

In Tehran Griffiss began to fret about his decision to bring Alison, in contravention of the junior officer's original orders. It would be best, he decided, for Alison to stay in Tehran; when Griffiss arrived in London, where he would have access to a trans-Atlantic telephone, he would quickly arrange for written orders to be sent to Alison recalling him to the States. In the meantime Alison had heard about a shipment of A-20 Havocs that were to land in Basra, Iraq, and asked if he might head to that port city and lend assistance. Griffiss quickly agreed, and Alison left for Basra.[12]

So now he was in Persia and Iraq without orders but with Griffiss's promise that Alison would be on his way out within a week. Since each of the A-20s had to be test-flown before delivery, Alison quickly checked out and test-hopped each of the light attack bombers. A week came and went, and then another, and Alison's unofficial presence in the Middle East began to weigh on him. After a month he finally learned that Griffiss's transport plane had been shot down as it approached England, and everyone aboard was killed.[13] Seriously concerned about his status now, Alison sent a cable to Arnold explaining his situation, with a plea to be transferred to a combat unit. He also stated, as diplomatically as possible—he was a captain writing to a four-star—that he did not wish to return to the Soviet Union and that he could be of far better use somewhere in combat in the Middle East.[14]

Months went by with Alison in his self-imposed limbo. Finally in June 1942 he received a wire from Arnold directing him to report to the 10th Army Air Force in Karachi, India (now Pakistan). This was closer to the war and had the additional grace of being official written orders. In Karachi came word that Alison was to report to Claire Chennault in Kunming, China.[15]

Combat at last. Alison was elated. He reported to Chennault in mid-June, and two weeks later the American Volunteer Group, the mercenary U.S. pilots who became better known as the Flying Tigers, were formally disbanded. Many of its pilots headed back to the States, while others were absorbed into the USAAF. Chennault himself was now a major general in command of the 14th Army Air Force. Alison was soon assigned to the 75th Fighter Squadron of the 23rd Fighter Group to serve as deputy to one of the most colorful and successful of the original Flying Tigers, Tex Hill, now a major in the USAAF. Within days of Alison's arrival in Kunming, the squadron was moved to Lingling. During the move he ran into an old squadron mate from Langley, Charlie Bond, who had been with the AVG since its formation. Like most of the original Tigers, Bond was sick, worn out, and eager to go home, but he was pleased to see Alison after more than two years.[16]

Living conditions were terrible in China, but the war was close. Japanese bombers hit the airfield almost nightly. Because airborne radars and other aids were nonexistent in China, no one was attempting nighttime interceptions. However, Chennault had established an early air warning system similar to that tried by Phil Cochran back at Langley: when Japanese planes took off, a series of telephone or radio calls alerted the American bases, and aircraft were pushed into revetments for protection.[17] As Alison looked up into the night sky during a Japanese raid, he was certain he could see exhaust flames from their engines. He went to Hill and said he would like to try a night interception the next time they were warned of an attack.

That came the next evening, and Alison and a wingman, Ajax Baumler, took off when the call came in that Japanese bombers were on their way. Hill stayed on the base with a radio to direct the two fighters. Alison came up behind one bomber; it was his first combat, and he was acutely aware that he was about to kill other humans. "Lord, forgive me for what I am about to do," he said aloud. But before he could press the trigger, the rear gunner saw him and opened fire first, badly damaging the P-40 and bloodying Alison's arm.[18] Although the engine was missing badly, the result of a huge hole in the crankcase, Alison shot down the bomber; it exploded, and the resulting flash revealed another that he had not previously seen. He stomped on the rudder to skid the fighter, sprayed the lead bomber with a nose-to-tail string of .50-caliber rounds, and it too went down.

But Alison was on his way down as well. The aerial fight had occurred directly over the air base, and he hoped for a landing on the runway. The P-40 was sputtering badly, and Hill ordered him to bail out, but Alison wanted to save the fighter if he could. He came in too high and fast, and now he was too low to bail out. He set the fighter down in the Xiang River nearby and was fished out by Chinese workers. For his night's work he received the Distinguished Service Cross, second only to the

Medal of Honor.[19] The fighter was later raised by ingenious Chinese workers using lengths of bamboo as flotation devices.

When Hill was rotated home, Alison became the new squadron CO. He spent a year in China and returned to the United States in July 1943 as an official ace with seven confirmed aerial victories and a deserved reputation as an outstanding leader, fearless combat pilot, and resourceful man when lines of communication and resources alike were lacking in far-off places.

After a short R and R, he was assigned to command the 367th Fighter Group in California, with a mission to train the fighter pilots who would deploy to Europe in time for the cross-Channel invasion, which Churchill, Roosevelt, and the Combined Chiefs were then planning in Halifax.

Alison had been in California barely a month when he received a cable from General Arnold: report to the Pentagon immediately.

CHAPTER 7

To hell with the paperwork. Get out there and fight!
    —H. H. "Hap" Arnold

Phil Cochran and Johnny Alison had just greeted each other when the door to General Arnold's office opened and the commander of the Army Air Forces himself walked out. He ushered them into his office, a large room well lighted by several windows. They found two more general officers seated at a table. A globe, three feet in diameter, nested in a floor stand to one side.[1]

Alison noted that Arnold, who had received many decorations during his thirty-year career, wore only three ribbons on his summer uniform: the Distinguished Service Medal, the Distinguished Flying Cross, and the Air Medal.[2] Arnold introduced Cochran and Alison to Maj. Gen. Hoyt Vandenberg, deputy chief of staff, and Lt. Gen. Barney M. Giles, deputy commander of the USAAF. It was a time of rapid promotions—Giles had been a lieutenant colonel in 1941—and of fighting generals.[3] Vandenberg had just returned from a tour as chief of staff under Jimmy Doolittle in the Northwest African Strategic Air Force, where Vandenberg had flown numerous combat missions. There was no saluting; the senior officers nodded and offered their hands. Arnold got right to the point: "Boys, I got a big job for you."

Cochran and Alison already knew the details. Each had arrived a couple of days earlier and had had private initial conversations with

Arnold, but both had kept that information to themselves and did not discuss it with each other. Cochran also had had a long conversation with Vandenberg, whom he had met during the North African campaign, and to whom he had delivered Spaatz's plea for more stateside training before sending pilots into combat. In fact Vandenberg had recommended Cochran for the position after Arnold requested the names of five men who could best command an unorthodox secret organization of fly-guys. Cochran had been adamant during his conversation with Vandenberg: no way did he want to go to a backwater theater when the real fighting was raging in Europe.

According to Cochran, he vented his frustration for several minutes, but Vandenberg had been clear: Cochran would still meet with Arnold, and the final decision would be Arnold's. Cochran said in an interview several years later that it did not go as he had hoped. As Arnold began to soft-sell the Burma plan, Cochran, brash as always, interrupted his commander and said he wanted "no part of it."[4]

Cochran, desperate, pushed ahead, knowing it would be his last chance to avoid the assignment and go instead to Europe with his P-47 group. Arnold asked him why he did not want to go to Burma.

"General, I have been in Africa, as you know." Arnold nodded nearly imperceptibly, and Cochran pressed on. "I worked hard and I studied hard. I believe that right now I have more combat experience than any fighter pilot in your Air Force. I am going to be brash enough to tell you that I think I know more about the practical side of fighter aviation than anybody in the Air Force. I've done it the hard way, and it's an attribute to the Air Force, and here you are sending me over to an alley fight, some doggone offshoot, side-alley fight in some jungle in Burma that doesn't mean a damn thing.

"The big show is in England, and I've got this job ready to go over there, and I think I can contribute a hell of a lot more with what I know and have been studying for seven years."

The fighter pilot paused, partially for effect, partly to gauge the reception of his intemperate remarks. If anything, Cochran thought Arnold looked kindly, perhaps a bit amused. Cochran gambled on another minute of forbearance from the general.

"By the way, there's one guy that I have learned about. That's the guy you ought to take, he's a grand person and that's Johnny Alison. He's from that area. He was in China. He is that area-oriented, he is a fine guy, and he will do the job." Cochran grinned at Arnold, his best Irish charming-as-hell full-bore grin that had gotten him out of trouble so many times.

"You get out of here," Arnold said, turning to pick up a report from a stack on his desk.[5]

Gnashing his teeth at what he saw as a waste of his talents and the dashing of his dreams to get to the fight in Europe, Cochran went back to Vandenberg. Vandenberg stopped him midstream.

"You guys, you smart-asses, do you really think Arnold is going to pick you? He probably doesn't want any part of you," Vandenberg declared. Cochran began to believe he had dodged the four-star bullet and convinced himself that Alison or Charlie Bond, one of the original Flying Tigers, would be selected. Bond's name had slipped out in conversation with Vandenberg.[6]

The next day Cochran was ordered back to Arnold's third-floor office in the Pentagon.

Arnold was sitting behind his desk this time, and he did not rise when Cochran entered. His face was carved in stone. Cochran knew that whatever happened, he had used up all his goodwill. Finally Arnold stood up and said, "Well, I made my decision, and you are going."

So that was that. Cochran knew it was pointless, and undoubtedly detrimental to his career, to argue further.

"Okay, when and where?"

Arnold laughed and stepped from around his desk. "Now, that's better." The air had been cleared, and the general had gotten his way, as generals do. "When and where will come later. I want to get that other monkey in here."

"Who's that, General?"

"That Alison is going with you."[7]

The next day was 30 August, and Cochran and Alison were listening intently to Arnold. For the next fifteen minutes Arnold related the story of Wingate and his Chindits in Burma, of how he operated far behind Japanese lines, of the strategy of long-range penetration groups, of the colorful and unorthodox commander himself, of the esteem in which Wingate was held by Churchill and others. Arnold talked about the Quebec Conference. He told them of the plans for an expanded guerrilla action to be coordinated with other strikes against the Japanese in Burma. He discussed the desperate need for light planes to support the Chindits' upcoming strike, and FDR's approval for a joint British-American operation.

Cochran and Alison concentrated on Arnold's discourse, as lieutenant-colonels do when a four-star is talking to them. Arnold concluded his prologue by saying, "Churchill and Mr. Roosevelt have talked, and the president told General Marshall to get Wingate the help he needs. That's where you men come in."

Alison, who still was unclear about his status in regard to the assignment, asked exactly what was expected.

"General, what are you going to give us to do this with?"

"I am going to give you L-5s." The L-5 was a liaison plane, little different than many prewar private aircraft, covered in doped (treated) cotton, with a high wing and a 185 horsepower engine. Alison turned red. At the time liaison pilots wore wings with the letter *L* in the center of the shield. "Real" pilots frequently asked if it stood for *little* or *low*.

"General, I'm a fighter pilot," he began. "I have a fighter group at [Fort] Hamilton, and in a few months I'm going to be taking it to England, and I expect to see some pretty exciting warfare." He took a deep breath and continued. "I've spent my career in the service learning to be a fighter pilot. I've had a year of combat experience. I like the business, and I believe that I can be of value to the Air Force. If all you're going to give us is some L-5s, you don't need me, and I don't want the job."

It was a rerun of Cochran's initial response. The Irishman from Pennsylvania correctly read Arnold's face, which had turned to stone once more, and quickly intervened.

"General, he doesn't really mean that."[8]

Who were these damned lieutenant colonels who thought they could tell the general of the entire Army Air Forces that they would not accept an assignment? But Arnold was also fair, and he had some sympathy for their position. What fighter pilot, already battle tested and with the chance for more, would opt for a posting to tiny puddle jumpers? They needed to know his plan in full; it would involve more, much more, than puddle jumping.

The general outlined his thoughts. L-5s would be perfect for picking up wounded from Wingate's columns, but why limit their role to flying ambulances? Arnold envisioned taking the Chindits in by air, perhaps by using gliders and cargo planes, and resupplying the campaign through pinpoint aerial drops for the duration of their mission. Arnold would fulfill the directives that came out of the Quebec Conference, but nothing specifically prevented expanding the role of the Air Force in the operation.

Arnold appointed them cocommanders of the project and offered them authority to obtain anything they needed. But their preparations needed to be carried out in total secrecy, and very quickly, since the Chindit campaign had to start at the beginning of the dry season in Burma. They had six months at the most to assemble the right men and equipment, train them, and get the entire outfit to India to launch the first-ever aerial invasion of a nation. Arnold wanted them to devise a plan and report back to him.

Project 9 had officially begun. Secret projects of the Army Air Forces during World War II were designated by a number, resulting in an innocuous-sounding name. Project 1 was the Doolittle raid on To-kyo. The paper trail for Project 9 would be scant, and Arnold himself would run interference if necessary. The first step would be to design an organization that would support Wingate's long-range penetration groups but would also showcase the capabilities of the burgeoning Army Air Forces. Arnold sweetened the deal by eliminating irksome record keeping, the lifeblood of historians and the bane of military pilots everywhere.

"The hell with paperwork. Get out there and fight," he told Cochran and Alison.[9]

That might have been the wrong thing to say to military officers, particularly fighter pilots. Modern warriors depend on a rigid command structure and well-documented accounting, procurement, training, and logistics procedures, but modern warfare was in its infancy in 1943. World War I had used modern weapons with nineteenth-century tactics. Strategy and tactics had begun to adapt to the new technology by the start of the second round of global war, but they were evolving as conditions warranted and technology blossomed. Arnold was launching a new untested idea, and he did not want to impede his commanders with burdensome paper pushing.

Shortly thereafter the two flying officers set up a command head-quarters in the Hay-Adams, the elegant hotel on Lafayette Square near the White House, where they rented a suite from which to begin building an entirely new kind of air war unit. Project 9 at that point underwent its first name evolution—they called it simply CA-281, for Cochran-Alison and the room number in the Hay-Adams. The hotel was a swanky place, an Italian Renaissance edifice with wood-paneled walls, views of the Washington Monument and the White House, and an A-list of previous guests, including Amelia Earhart, Sinclair Lewis, Ethyl Barrymore, and Charles Lindbergh. Alison and Cochran began making phone calls to former squadron mates and old friends, men they thought would fit into the new unit. Within a month they had decided that a cocommand simply would not work, so Alison insisted that he be the deputy commander since Cochran was a couple of months senior on the list of lieutenant colonels. In practice they were effectively cocommanders, but that arrangement was too unorthodox for those with whom they worked.

Arnold had advised them to learn all they could about Wingate and his plans for a long-range penetration group and to determine exactly how he anticipated using an aerial force. As Cochran later phrased it, in a way that might hint at how both men initially viewed Wingate: "Well, somebody's got to go talk to that nut."[10] To that end Cochran and

Alison, without clearing it with anyone, agreed that one of them would have to go to London to meet with the British commander. Alison had plans to get married soon, so Cochran went, hitching a ride on a transport to England. In London he checked in with Lord Mountbatten's staff; the lord had him to lunch, then sent him to the War Office to meet with Wingate.[11]

Neither was impressed with the other; it was not a good start. Later Cochran confided that he found Wingate intense, opinionated, and difficult to understand "because he was so British and talked so fast."[12]

"If there is anyone I hate, it's another opinionated person," he told an interviewer years later, with a laugh.[13]

The encounter of Cochran and Wingate might reasonably be seen as a clash of similar, highly individualistic, talented men who were accustomed to respect for their views, conclusions, and experience and who prided themselves on unorthodox thinking. It usually takes a large room to accommodate two such individuals, and Wingate's office on the top floor of the Combined Operation headquarters was small, dark, and cramped. The tiny space had been temporarily allocated to the hero of Burma until he returned to India for the next campaign.

Cochran introduced himself, explained his assignment from General Arnold, and then asked what Wingate had in mind for aerial support. Wingate kept no record of the meeting, but the breezy informal American fighter pilot was probably a new type to him. The brigadier began a long monologue with a description of the Chindits' first campaign, the theory of long-range penetration, and the critical need to evacuate wounded and resupply the ground force. The meeting was forced and awkward. Almost grudgingly they agreed to meet again the next day.

The second meeting went much more smoothly. A couple of Chindit officers joined Wingate and Cochran, and the American flier quickly noted their enthusiasm for the first campaign as well as the upcoming operation. As Wingate and his lieutenants explained the overall strategy of the long-range penetration groups, Cochran began to see it in terms of aerial combat, with squadrons being vectored to locations for rendezvous and interception, and he was drawn into their enthusiasm. These were men just like him: caught up in a war that no one had asked for, they were exercising daring and audacity outside traditional paradigms. They were not desk-bound brass. They were taking the fight to the enemy.

The talk turned to aerial support, and Cochran said that supplying small planes for evacuation of the wounded was no problem. He then proposed that the entire ground force, including the mules, be taken in by gliders and cargo planes, supported throughout the operation by fighters and bombers. Wingate and his officers were ecstatic at the possibility.

Cochran stayed in London another day or two, a guest of Lord Mountbatten and his wife, Edwina. On 7 September 1943, on his flight back to the States, thick fog grounded his and all other planes in Iceland. While waiting idly in the officers' club, he was invited to attend a briefing for Hap Arnold given by Bernt Balchen, the famous Norwegian pilot who had flown in the Roald Amundsen polar expedition. Balchen, who had been an Olympic boxer, was also an expert marksman and skier, and renowned for his skill in wilderness survival. Arnold had recruited Balchen early in the war to direct operations in Greenland, establishing secret air bases that would allow U.S. planes to be ferried instead of freighted across the Atlantic. Now Balchen was going to bring Arnold up to date on events in Greenland, including the rescue of several airmen by Balchen's crews.

At the briefing Cochran saw Arnold and several of his staff across the room. And the general had obviously seen him. Finally a staff officer approached Cochran, saying that the general wished to see him.

"Cochran, what are you doing here?" Arnold appeared neither pleased nor displeased to see him but clearly puzzled.

"Well, General, I'm in the same boat you're in; I'm stuck." He went on to explain that he had been to England to visit Wingate in order to best build and equip the unit that would support him.

"You've been to England? It's too bad you didn't get to see Mountbatten. I would have wanted you to see him, but he's in the hospital."

Cochran nodded. "Yes, General, I know. I took him."

Now Arnold did look surprised. "What do you mean, you took him?"

Cochran told him about staying with Mountbatten and his wife and described how, on Cochran's last day in London, an old polo injury had flared up in Mountbatten's arm. As the American understood it, tendons in the admiral's right hand had been injured and were beginning to shorten, making it difficult for Mountbatten to fully open his hand. He needed surgery, and, while it was not a serious medical emergency, it required a short stay in the hospital.

Arnold listened, taking stock of a man he had tapped for a top-secret project where independence, initiative, and the ability to work with the Allies were qualities crucial to success.

"You'll do," Arnold told him.

Cochran grinned.[14]

CHAPTER 8

There wasn't any animal like this in the Air Force zoo. We were inventing a new one.

—Col. Philip Cochran

It was late September 1943, and the sweltering, enervating heat that had gripped Washington and much of the Northeast for weeks was beginning to ease. The steaming summer was slowly simmering into fall, but the passage of time was not the ally of the men planning the invasion of Burma, half a world and half a year away. After Cochran's visit with Wingate, Cochran and Alison set to work feverishly on a plan.

General Hap Arnold, in a khaki shirt and tie, wore glasses as he carefully read the typed report of Cochran and Alison that outlined a plan far surpassing that originally conceived in Quebec. He occasionally made noises that could be construed as approval—or not. He glanced up once as he flipped pages, but his face was implacable. Arnold was widely known for abhorring long reports; usually anything more than two paragraphs had an immediate response: sent back to the writer, with an acerbic demand that it be condensed. "Get to the point" was the phrase that seemed always about to burst from the general's mouth.[1]

Alison and Cochran sat silently, half-wanting the AAF commander to explode and reject their report as unrealistic and far too ambitious. Both still harbored some faint hope they would be sent back to their respective fighter groups and ordered to leave for Europe immediately.

Alison ventured a look at Cochran, slightly raising his eyebrows in a silent question. Cochran replied with a barely discernible lift of his shoulders.

At last, after about ten minutes during which the only sounds were the crackle of pages being turned, Arnold laid the report on his desk and removed his reading glasses. He rubbed his eyes, then looked at both young officers. He turned to Gen. Hoyt Vandenberg.

"Van, does this thing make sense?"

The AAF deputy chief of staff nodded. "Yes. It's a very, very ingenious plan."

Arnold took out his pen and scribbled his initials on the report. He turned to Cochran and Alison. "All right, do it."[2]

With a squiggle of Arnold's pen the promise that had been made in Quebec to extend American assistance in evacuating wounded British troops had grown exponentially. It was now an audacious plan to provide not only evacuation of sick and wounded Chindits from Burma but also insertion behind Japanese lines using gliders, resupply using heavy and light cargo aircraft, and close air support of the Wingate columns using fighters and—eventually—medium-range bombers. And for good measure the plan would press into service the world's first military helicopters, despite screams from the evaluators at Wright Field that they had not even completed preliminary testing.

Alison and Cochran had no time to waste and precious little time to perform even the most basic necessities of organizing the new unit, assembling personnel, acquiring assets, instituting training, and deploying a force sufficient to ensure the success of the joint British-American venture. The monsoon season in Burma runs from June through October, and during that time the rain is nearly constant. More than 200 inches drench the countryside, causing freshets to become streams, streams to engorge to rivers, and rivers to become raging torrential floods. Paths become slippery quagmires, marshes turn into swamps, and the entire countryside, never an ideal battleground in the best of weather conditions, becomes a nightmare of physical misery, a sodden muddy horror in which moving on foot, let alone sustaining offensive action, is nearly impossible.

Cochran and Alison had felt a definite sense of urgency as they worked up plans for Project 9.

After Cochran's return to Washington from London, he and Alison had sat in the suite in the Hay-Adams and let their imaginations go. "What If" became their favorite game. Gradually the outline for a self-sustained, autonomous aerial fighting force took shape. In less than a month they put together a table of organization and a "dream sheet" of equipment and personnel that would be necessary to effect their pie-in-the-sky vision.

The idea of a couple of battle-tested fighter pilots' acting as couriers or ambulance drivers was just too galling for Cochran and Alison, and they soon saw the possibility of making the operation a full-blown combat opportunity. To some degree the meeting with Wingate had at least partly persuaded Cochran that the Chindit operation was worth supporting. While Wingate himself might indeed be a nut, he was at least a fighting nut. He and his men were taking the battle to the Japanese, in a theater that was seriously short of Allied victories or even offensive operations.

Cochran was impressed with the Chindit concept as it had worked so far. But now, with a directive from the AAF commander to support it, he and Alison set out to design their own version of guerrilla warfare.

"As we studied it more and more, our natures came to the fore; we began to want to support him [Wingate] with combat action," Cochran said years later. "We said that he not only needed to get his wounded out but that when he got in place, they could point out targets on the ground. He could use ground-air support; he could use bombardment; he could use fighters; he could have a lot of direct military action brought to bear after he got into an area."[3]

The two lieutenant colonels—both soon would be promoted to full colonel—had been handed a rare opportunity: authorization to plan an entirely new concept of warfare, with few, if any, limits on what they could do or what assets they could use.

"The more we thought of it, the more we built and built," Cochran recalled after the war. "Then we figured that we could turn this thing around and make it partially a doggone good air combat effort and really be of great assistance to these ground troops. We could be their artillery, we could be their supply, and we could be their air combat forces. So, really unconsciously, what we were doing was building a whole small region of warfare where we had ground troops, artillery, infantry, air-ground support, fighter support, and bombardment support, plus finding a way to fly them into their area and get them in rather than have them spend months on the ground walking.

"The bare bones of those ideas started to form in our minds as we were building this thing. Every time we thought of a new thing, we'd kick it around and say, 'Why don't we learn about that technique and see what it's about.'"[4]

The plans expanded, the requirements for men and equipment ballooned, and the excitement of Alison and Cochran grew, although this was at least partly because of the heady exercise of unlimited authority.

At times it seemed unreal to both men, and at other times they realized that they were only partly serious about the Burma mission.

"We just searched out all these things and read them into our plan. And as we built and built, our plans became more and more complicated and grandiose. So we, in a laughing kind of way or in a half-serious kind of way, said, 'What we will do is design this thing. It will be so big and so ambitious that General Arnold will get mad and kick us out. Then we won't have to go.' We kept building and building, and although we were kind of half-kidding, we were serious about what we were doing," Cochran recalled.[5]

They were designing something that had not been done before, they had no precedent, and they had to consider every detail. Both knew that the China-Burma-India theater was last on the list for supplies, the last stop on the line. The Allies had determined from the start of U.S. involvement that, despite the attack by Imperial Japanese Navy's torpedo bombers at Pearl Harbor, the main target of the Allies would be Nazi Germany. When the Third Reich was defeated, they would turn their full attention to Japan. In the meantime U.S. efforts in the Pacific were at best a holding action, with enough might and enough encouragement to keep India and China from falling to the Japanese.

The Project 9 combat team would not be able to call upon existing forces in the region for support. Everything, from cigarettes to combat aircraft, would have to be planned for before they headed out. "We had to figure what aircraft we wanted, what we wanted them for, how many pilots we needed, how many mechanics we needed, and how much ammunition you needed, because there wasn't any animal like this in the Air Force zoo. We were inventing a new one. There was no precedent," Cochran said of the planning stages.[6]

"We had to plan on supplying ourselves. We were to be superimposed as a task force on an already beleaguered region, being China, Burma, India. They didn't have any supplies; they were destitute out there. The big effort was going on in Africa and Europe, and they were not getting all the things they needed. . . . So we had to plan to take much of our own supplies. We even took, for instance, our own cigarettes and our own powdered milk."[7]

What had begun as a grudging acquiescence to orders from Arnold gradually became a serious effort at inventing the first guerrilla war supported largely by aerial forces.

After Arnold approved the overall plan, they were able to draw on logistics experts and other specialists on the general's staff in the Pentagon. One problem to consider was the transportation of the small air force to India. They determined that most of the aircraft would have to be disassembled and crated, then off-loaded at an Indian port and shipped by rail or truck to the proposed base in Assam. There they would be reassembled, using pilots to assist the ground crews.

Cochran and Alison outlined the organization and personnel requirements for a self-sustained, autonomous aerial fighting force. Before October was out, they had put together a table of organization and list of assets and forwarded it to General Arnold. The AAF commander forwarded it with his approval to Marshall, who quickly signed off as well.

Cochran and Alison's next job was finding the right men to head each of the sections: light plane, cargo, glider, and fighter. At the Quebec Conference the Royal Air Force had agreed to supply bombers as needed, so Cochran and Alison did not consider bombers at first. Both men had been in the Army Air Corps—the name changed to Army Air Forces in June 1941—for six or seven years, had combat experience, and knew enough pilots to call on, men they trusted and could be counted on to lead in a new and untested organization. They tapped their key men, and soon the word was out that volunteers were needed for a secret assignment, one that would last no more than six months and would include combat, a description guaranteed to attract the adventurous.

The first men assigned to Project 9—CA-281 on typed orders—were Maj. Samson Smith as executive officer; Maj. Arvid Olson, a former AVG pilot, as operations officer; and Capt. Charles Englehardt, administration. Even the smallest unit needs a formal system of organization, so additional officers were assigned to the various sections: Capt. Robert Moist, adjutant; Maj. Edwin White, supply; Capt. John Jennette, engineering; Maj. Richard Boebel and Capt. Temple Moore, intelligence; and Maj. Ernest Bonham, communications. Men with more than a single specialty got preference, and piloting was valorized above other skills. When Maj. Robert Page, a flight surgeon working in the Pentagon, received a memo asking him to choose medical specialists for a secret combat assignment—primarily doctors who could also fly—he immediately put himself at the top of the list.

And so it went. Despite the need for secrecy, the response was immediate and enthusiastic. Alison and Cochran called close friends, and the friends called top men they knew. As fighter pilots, Alison and Cochran focused first on the section they knew most about, and selected Maj. Gratton "Grant" Mahony, another ace from the Pacific who had flown with Alison, to head up the fighter section. Other fighter pilots well known to either leader also eagerly signed on, including R. T. "Tadpole" Smith, a giant of a man who often had trouble squeezing into the cramped cockpits of fighters, and A. J. "Ajax" Baumler, who had first flown combat in the Spanish Civil War. Smith was a former AVG pilot who had known Alison in China; Baumler was flying with Alison the night he shot down two Japanese bombers.

Cochran and Alison decided to divide the transportation section into three units: transport, glider, and light cargo for small unit resupply. They chose Maj. William T. Cherry to head transportation, and he too already had a colorful history. A year earlier Cherry had been the pilot of a B-17 carrying World War I's top ace, Eddie Rickenbacker, on an official tour of the Pacific theater. A faulty navigation instrument had sent them hundreds of miles off course, and they were forced to ditch; Rickenbacker and the flight crew had drifted in a life raft for twenty-four days before a U.S. Navy aircraft spotted them. Named as engineering officer for the transport section was Capt. Richard "Dick" Cole, who had been Jimmy Doolittle's copilot on the first B-25 to launch from the USS *Hornet* for the famed raid on Tokyo. Doolittle, Cole, and the rest of the crew had bailed out over Japanese-occupied China and spent a harrowing several weeks dodging Japanese patrols while being guided to safety by friendly Chinese. Following that, Cole had remained in India for a year, flying the Hump in C-47s to Kunming, China, carrying gasoline and other much-needed supplies for Chennault and the Chinese. In June 1943 he was rotated home and was in Tulsa, Oklahoma, a ferry command control officer and acceptance test-pilot flying a variety of aircraft that were being modified at Air Force Plant No. 3 there. Cole had flown the Hump with Capt. Jacob Sartz, who knew Johnny Alison from their China days. Sartz recommended Cole, and in October, 1943, Alison called him with an offer of a secret and dangerous assignment. He didn't hesitate. "Sign me up."[8]

Sartz had been pilot for Gen. Claire Chennault for a time in China. When Burma fell, Sartz had evacuated British residents to India; on one flight he took off from Rangoon with seventy-one passengers crammed into a C-47. When he landed, he had seventy-two. A woman had given birth in flight. For his valor in flying despite the imminent threat of Japanese fighters, Sartz was awarded the Silver Star.[9]

Cherry, Cole, and Sartz were joined for Project 9 by additional pilots from the Transport Command, including Buddy Lewis. John K. Lewis Jr. was best known as the third baseman for the Washington Senators. When the war started, he had gone through basic training as an infantryman, then was accepted for flight training. When posted overseas to the CBI to fly the Hump, he had buzzed Griffiths Field during a game to say good-bye to his teammates. Luckily no one thought to get the tail number of the plane that zoomed low over center field before disappearing to the south. In India he had named his transport "The Old

Fox," for Clark Griffin, the Senators' owner. Lewis flew more than 350 missions over the Himalayas into China.[10]

Neither Cochran nor Alison knew much about gliders beyond what they had read in the newspapers, but they knew the army had to have an expert. They asked around the Pentagon and got the name of Bill Taylor. A captain and qualified glider pilot who had had a tour in Panama, Taylor had become interested in glider landings in jungle terrain and had done some experimenting there. Might Taylor and his assistant, First Lt. Vincent Rose, be interested in a combat assignment in an area similar to Panama? They asked no questions. Sign us up, they said.

Cochran and Alison selected Taylor to head up the glider section and named Rose his deputy. They immediately began selection of glider pilots and glider mechanics from Bowman Field, near Louisville, Kentucky. Among those chosen was the former child movie star Flight Officer John L. "Jackie" Coogan.

Chief of the light cargo section would be Lt. Col. Clinton Gaty, who was also an engineer out of Wright Field, and Cochran and Alison counted on him to also oversee maintenance for the entire operation in addition to his duties with the light cargo aircraft.

Once they had selected the key men for the nascent organization, they turned their attention to the hardware and materiel they would need for the coming campaign. The assigned mission initially dictated the aircraft needed. The expanded role of Project 9 radically altered that first assessment. Aircraft were about to be used in ways that were new to American forces, and the tactics devised would have profound effects on future battles and subsequent wars.

Wingate's original plea had been for light planes, a force of small rugged aircraft that could land in jungle clearings and evacuate a wounded Chindit. The L-1 Vigilant seemed ideal for the job, able to take off and land in spaces scarcely larger than a football field. But far too few Vigilants were available, so Cochran and Alison began to look for alternative aircraft that could operate out of rough strips and carry enough weight to be useful for a variety of missions.

The L-5 seemed perfect: It cruised at 115 mph, stalled at 43 mph; with its flaps it could take off from and land on short fields; its range was more than 400 miles. It had two doors on the right side (all the L-2 class liaison planes had a single door on the right) for easy access to the rear seat, and many had been converted to flying ambulances by modifying the fuselage to accept a litter.

But that was only a part of what they now envisioned as a complete miniature air force, a unit different from any other organization then in existence. Light planes were the foundation, but the Waco CG-4A glider would take in Wingate's troops, supplies, and mules. Douglas C-47 Skytrains would tow the gliders to the landing sites far inside Burma. Fighters would protect the cargo planes and gliders, and light bombers would support and protect the ground troops during the campaign.

Cochran and Alison had been given free rein to build their new command, and they did it with a vengeance.

CHAPTER 9

As Phil Cochran and Johnny Alison put together their fleet of small planes to support a British Army operation in Burma, they did so during a time of tight budgets—both the United States and Britain were still suffering the effects of the worldwide depression—and no small amount of controversy about how best to use aerial assets, and what they should be, in modern warfare.[1]

The controversy was rooted in linguistics and definitions, especially of the word *observation,* on both sides of the Atlantic. Because of evolving technology and tactical realities, its definition began to change and became the center of an ongoing dispute between factions within the military establishments of both countries.

Observation balloons had been used extensively in battle since before the U.S. Civil War. A tethered balloon lifted an observer several hundred feet into the blue, where he could see and report on the movements of a proximate enemy. Obviously the observer could not see whether another force was advancing just over the distant hills or what strategists were thinking in the enemy capital hundreds of miles away. Even so, observation by balloon was better than what had existed before—confused communiqués from a small cadre of scouts on horses—but it soon became obsolete, an easy target for winged aircraft. Those aircraft quickly assumed the observation-reconnaissance role, and military strategists soon learned that the mission dictated the type of aircraft needed, not the reverse.

In army flying schools of the 1930s young aviators received at least basic instruction in the four kinds of military airplanes of the day: pursuit, bombardment, attack, and observation.[2] Military theorists of most nations followed the precepts of Gen. Giulio Duohet, the Italian air minister who held that future wars would be fought and won by bombardment aircraft, heavily armed, that would bomb enemy cities into terrified submission.[3] Fighters, then called pursuit ships, were considered of minimal value (although most pilots still aspired to fly the fast and nimble machines), and attack aircraft were generally lightly armed pursuit planes with little real chance of changing the course of a closely fought ground battle. One of the Wright brothers' early models was the 1912 Model D, built to meet the U.S. Army's request for a "speed scout."[4] Between the world wars observation aircraft grew into large awkward-looking airplanes, with crews of two or three, driven by powerful radial engines. They were armed with several machine guns and often had retractable gear. They were sophisticated, complex, heavy, and slow, requiring hard runways and highly trained ground crews, as well as large supplies of fuel, equipment, and parts. Planes such as the North American O-47 and the Curtiss O-52 Owl were capable of extended flights and what today is called loiter time, time spent over a target or area of interest, but would have been helpless against the fast heavily armed fighters that Germany and other countries were developing.

By the time shooting started in earnest in Europe in September 1939, the day of the elephantine observation plane was past. It was not only easy prey for fighters, but its appetite for parts and fuel, and dependence upon hard runways, rendered it clearly impractical for use by ground forces such as artillery units. So the brass debated: Should they develop a single, multipurpose aircraft for general observation and reconnaissance, or multiple aircraft, each designed for a specialized purpose? In military parlance *observation* came to mean visual sighting in the area of front lines. *Reconnaissance* came to mean flights far behind the lines, requiring high-speed aircraft capable of flying long distances.

The Air Corps—which did not become an independent service until after World War II—did not have the same requirements as the field artillery. The Air Corps preferred a fast high-performance airplane capable of flying deep into enemy territory and returning quickly. However, that was the last thing needed by ground units, who saw an airplane as a means of directing fire, as well as coordinating and communicating among units. The Air Corps needed a small, simple, and rugged plane. The Stinson O-49 Vigilant had proved to be a good general purpose observation plane. It could handle short fields, thanks to its 295 horsepower Lycoming radial engine, Hamilton-Standard constant-speed prop, and slotted flaps and automatically deploying leading-edge slats (manufactured by the British firm Handley Page). It was capable of extremely slow flight, stalling at a mere 31 mph, and was rumored to be capable of flying backward in a strong wind. It was large, with a wingspan of more than fifty feet, which made it an ideal flying ambulance. But its very sophistication was also its biggest drawback: it took 6,000 man-hours to produce, and not nearly enough were available to meet the demands of the military.[5]

During field maneuvers in Tennessee, Texas, and Louisiana in 1940, army commanders had listened to the pitches of manufacturers of light civilian planes and used Taylorcraft, Piper, and Aeronca planes as liaison aircraft. The term *liaison* was not new, but the concept as applied to military aviation was. Liaison aircraft were small, light, inexpensive, and simple planes, easy to maintain and capable of flying in and out of grass fields. Their other major virtue: they were immediately available, and production of each aircraft required only 300 man-hours, ensuring a ready supply if approved by the materiel command. The seeds for a new type, the liaison airplane, had been planted.[6]

Not everyone was smitten with the tiny airplanes. They certainly had their flaws: fragile, with no blind-flying instruments, and too small for a pilot sheathed in sheepskin and strapped into a parachute. But at a conference in Washington in January 1942, an overall need for 4,000 light aircraft was determined by the Army; this was soon upped to 5,000, and six months later increased by another 1,960.[7]

From the late 1930s until the outbreak of war, the debate in Britain between advocates of high-speed reconnaissance planes and low-speed puddle jumpers had proceeded much as it had in the States. The Air Ministry preached that unarmed slow-flying observation and liaison aircraft would simply be sitting ducks for enemy fighters. But artillery and other ground unit officers saw little value in aircraft that were not easy to maintain or could not be flown from grass fields near the front. The chasm between them was wide and deep. A Royal Air Force officer, quoted in a postwar U.S. study of liaison aircraft, said, "Our view is this, 'Let the soldiers play with their toys, it amuses them and doesn't do us any harm.'"[8]

Despite the demonstrated abilities of the German Fieseler Fi-156 Storch (Stork), and the use by the French of commercial light airplanes for the role of liaison, the British decided not to build a light airplane, a determination reinforced by the immediate need to build large numbers of fighters and bombers. Besides, the British did not have a large base of independent small aircraft manufacturers, such as could be found in the United States, that they could press into war production.

However, a British company heeded the call of the Royal Artillery and other combat units for an air observation post (AOP)—a small airplane to direct artillery fire—and began building the Auster AOP under contract with the Taylorcraft company. It was a variant of the L-2, used by the U.S. Army, with a larger de Havilland Gypsy Major engine. The British used the Austers in combat theaters around the globe, including Wingate and the Chindits' first foray into Burma, where the 656th RAF Squadron, an observation unit, flew them in support of operations there. The problem for Wingate was not proximity but numbers: too few RAF light aircraft were in-theater.

By late 1942 the U.S. Army Air Forces had concluded that the thousands of L-2 class (L-2, L-3, and L-4) light aircraft built by Taylorcraft, Aeronca, and Piper were not adequate and began using the Stinson L-5 Sentinel, which was larger, had a bigger engine, and included flaps, radios, a variable-pitch propeller, and more instruments. Although heavier than the L-2 class, it could carry more useful load and still could operate from short undeveloped grass strips. The army ground forces, meanwhile, continued to rely on the smaller L-2 class Grasshoppers.

More than 3,690 L-5s were built during the war and were in plentiful supply when Wingate asked for aerial help in evacuating his wounded and in resupply; the L-5s were far more plentiful than the more powerful, and more useful L-1, which was the new designation for the former O-49 Stinson Vigilant.[9]

The Piper L-4, Taylorcraft L-2, and Aeronca L-3 were all quite similar, little more than the iconic prewar light plane, the Piper Cub, with a single door that could be removed or latched open for flight and a 65 horsepower Continental engine that could be replaced in a couple of hours with common tools and two mechanics working out of the back of a truck. All had a fixed-pitch wooden propeller, a half-dozen instruments, and no flaps. None had an electrical system; they were started by the occasionally exciting method of grasping the propeller and forcefully swinging it through its arc, a method known as prop starting. In a curious divergence of policy army ground forces who completed liaison flying school at Fort Sill, Oklahoma—artillery, for the most part—were qualified to fly a machine only a tiny step removed from the Wright Flyer. But they were rated as pilots and commissioned as officers. The AAF, on the other hand, with liaison flying schools around the country, declined to offer commissions to graduates and made them sergeants instead. They would fly aircraft much more sophisticated and complex than the Piper Cub but had a lower rank and received far less pay.

L-pilots, as they came to be called, came from a variety of training backgrounds. Some had washed out of regular pilot training courses, others came from the Civilian Pilot Training Program, still others had volunteered expressly for the Grasshoppers, as the L-planes were called.[10] Bill Cartwright, who became a pilot in the 1st Air Commandos, was typical of many. He had volunteered as an aviation cadet and passed primary flight school in Texas flying the bi-wing Stearman PT-17, but then he washed out of basic flight training on BT-13s. He was sent to a service unit to become an aircraft mechanic, then told to report to Liaison Pilot Training. Flying a Grasshopper was a piece of cake after the Stearman, and after just a few hours he was given a check ride, rated as an L-pilot, and awarded silver wings—while still a buck private. Next he was sent to Fort Sill to be trained as an artillery-spotter pilot. He completed the course but did not want to fly for the artillery.

"I was an Air Corps guy, that's what I wanted. Probably could had been commissioned had I followed that route, but I wanted back with the Air Corps section. I was made a staff sergeant, and sent to Illinois, where my job was to fly L-2s with a student radio operator in the back seat, a minimum of an hour and forty-five minutes in the morning, and another in the afternoon."[11]

Cochran, Alison, and their handpicked section leaders for Project 9 began their search for aircraft by looking for a hundred or so Stinson L-1s, which they determined to be the most desirable for the upcoming Burma campaign. But so few were available that they had to turn to the smaller L-5, which they were able to procure in the numbers they needed.

Next they turned their attentions to gliders, the aircraft that Hap Arnold had envisioned using to take the first contingents of Chindits to Burma; Alison and Cochran now saw this aircraft as the heart of their aerial task force.

Gliders were perhaps the most unusual aircraft used in World War II, the only conflict in which they have been used. In the aftermath of World War I the victorious Allies had placed restrictions on Germans' use of powered aircraft. To get around those limits thousands of young Germans learned to fly gliders and thus formed the nucleus of pilots for the powerful Luftwaffe by the mid-1930s. The United States and most European nations, including Britain, did not see a military function for the small open-cockpit sailplanes.[12] Nor did American and European civilian fliers have much interest in gliders, since they did not come under the Treaty of Versailles and were free to develop powered aircraft. A small group of enthusiasts in the United States finally established the Soaring Society of America more than a decade after the first German gliding clubs had been formed. Among the early flying sportsmen was Richard C. DuPont, descendant of the founder of the DuPont Chemical Company, who perhaps more than any other individual managed to maintain some minimal American interest in nonpowered aircraft.[13]

Gliders as military assets grew out of the early German interest in soaring that followed World War I. Applying what they knew to military possibilities, German glider pilots shocked the world in May 1940 by quickly and easily attacking and overrunning Fort Eban Emael, Belgium's new and seemingly impregnable fortress across the Meuse. The bastion stood directly in the path the Panzers planned to follow days later as they blitzed into Belgium and then northward to outflank French defenses at the Maginot Line. A ground attack against the fort was certain to be bloody and prolonged; aerial bombardment was seen as futile because of the deep underground spaces within the fortress.

But the Belgians had built a large parade ground atop the mighty walls of Eban Emael, and the German intelligence staff took note. After sitting idle for many months in the so-called Phoney War, the German war machine overran the mighty Belgian fort with glider-borne troops and burst into Belgium and then France. Forty-one JU-52 cargo aircraft had taken off in predawn darkness, each towing a DFS 230 glider carrying nine fully battle-equipped German troops. They had landed silently on the grassy area atop the walls, and before the stunned Belgian defense troops could respond, had captured the fort within twenty minutes. Other glider troops seized bridges over the Meuse, demonstrating to the world the military effectiveness of silent flight.[14]

Britain and the United States scrambled to catch up to this new instrument of war. The British won the heat in November 1940, rolling out the Hotspur Mark I, a cargo glider capable of carrying eight troops and their equipment, or 2,200 pounds of cargo. The Hotspur never saw battle but was used extensively in training. On the U.S. side of the pond, glider development went a bit slower since the nation was not yet in the war. In March 1941 General Arnold directed the experimental and testing site at Wright Field to develop a combat glider capable of carrying twelve to fifteen men plus four machine guns, to be towed singly or in pairs behind a transport aircraft. Such a machine would be used to land combat units behind enemy lines. Arnold was thinking, of course, of a cross-Channel invasion, which even at that early stage was the obvious end-game strategy for liberating Europe.

A second memorandum from Arnold directed Wright officials to seek glider designs only from companies not already building powered aircraft for the military. Eleven small companies received invitations to submit plans for a military cargo glider, but only four responded. The design submitted by the Waco Aircraft Company of Troy, Ohio, won the construction contract. Its glider featured a box-like fuselage with an upturned nose that would accommodate fifteen troops or a jeep, a small artillery piece, or even a miniature bulldozer. Eventually sixteen companies, including Ford Motor Company, subcontracted with Waco to build the big gliders. Ford's plant in Kingsford, Michigan, which had been building wood-sided motor cars before the war, built 4,190 CG-4As. Ford was by far the largest producer of the gliders and offered them to the government for $15,400, nearly $10,000 less than the next lowest unit price.[15]

A horrific accident in St. Louis on 1 August 1943, just before the Quebec Conference opened, might have quashed plans to use gliders for aerial assaults, but perhaps the public and military alike had simply grown used to aircraft accidents. Hurried training and occasional short-cuts in manufacturing exacted a fearsome toll on student and veteran aviators alike. Nearly 15,000 died in stateside training accidents alone.[16]

The crash in St. Louis was especially public, however, and involved high-profile city officials. On a hot late summer Sunday, the mayor of St. Louis, William Dee Decker, boarded a CG-4A glider built by Robertson Aircraft, one of four aircraft builders in the city turning out combat gliders. Accompanying him were the presiding judge of the St. Louis County Court, the president of the area chamber of commerce, the city's director of public utilities, the municipal deputy comptroller, the president and vice president of Robertson Aircraft, and an officer of the AAF's Materiel Command. Capt. Milton Klugh piloted the glider; in the right seat sat his glider mechanic, Pfc. J. M. Davis. A C-47 towed the Waco aloft, pulling the glider directly over Lambert Field so the crowd of several thousand could get a good look at this silent bird of war. Klugh then released from the transport. The glider climbed. Then the onlookers heard a loud sharp crack and watched in open-mouthed horror as the right wing flipped up and separated from the glider, which then dived vertically straight into the earth. There were no survivors.[17]

The cause was found to be a wing-strut bracket that had been improperly machined by a subcontractor for Robertson. The accident seemed to magnify the distrust of an unpowered cargo glider held by many at the time. The crash was Page One news across the country, accompanied by a stark photograph of the doomed glider in its fatal one-wing dive.

However, the St. Louis tragedy probably did not affect the efforts of Uncle Sam to recruit young men for glider pilot training. They already had plenty of reasons to stay away. Arnold, who wanted to produce a glider force quickly, initially had called for 1,000 volunteers from the ranks of already commissioned power plane pilots. Few were interested. Arnold nonetheless raised the number of glider pilots needed to 4,000, and a month later to 6,000, and the slots still went largely unfilled. Platoon sergeants regularly extolled the virtues of powerless flight to the enlisted ranks in a concerted effort to attract candidates. Still there were few takers.

Convincing many potential candidates that being towed behind a transport plane, then landing troops under fire in a flying crate, was a desirable thing to do was proving difficult. Easing test scores and other requirements while dangling promotions also failed to interest young men in becoming glider pilots.

Then the military tried a psychological ploy, distributing pamphlets at flying clubs and universities across the country that appealed to machismo: "It's a he-man's job for men who want to serve their country in the air." Gradually the inducements began to have an effect, and by October 1942, ten months before the Quebec Conference, more than 10,000 men were in some phase of glider pilot training. Six thousand eventually completed the rigorous training.[18] They pointed to their silver wing badges with the G on the shield. "The G stands for guts," they said, with more than a touch of pride.

Glider pilots suffered morale problems, with long waiting periods, poor living conditions at some bases, and broken promises. In November 1942 a new directive raised the spirits of the fledgling glider pilots: all glider pilot school graduates would be promoted to the rank of flight officer, a wartime flying version of warrant officer. The pay would be much better, the uniforms snappier, and their duties restricted to flying, with few collateral duties.

Flight officers wore a warrant officer badge on their caps, and on their shirt collars or jacket epaulets they wore a blue oval bar with a single gold band bisecting it horizontally; the badge was often called the blue pickle. Flight officer was a hybrid rank, denoting neither officer nor enlisted man, that had been created only for flight personnel in World War II, a kind of third lieutenant. Flight officers had access to officers' clubs and were generally accepted as officers, but they also were not expected to have the same "officer and gentleman" demeanor of lieutenants. The pay, however, was identical to that of a second lieutenant.[19]

One problem was that no one knew exactly what a flight officer was. Ed Cook, who completed glider training in August 1942, was promoted to staff sergeant and assigned to initial instruction in gliders. When the order came down that as of 5 November 1942 all glider pilots were to be promoted to flight officer, the base commander acknowledged he had no idea what that rank was but thought it was similar to a pilot officer in the Royal Canadian Air Force. The newly promoted glider pilots were advised to wear a second lieutenant's bar with a vertical blue stripe, which was later changed to a horizontal one. "We bought out the Woolworth's supply of blue nail polish," Cook wrote years later.[20]

Glider pilots trained at a number of airfields in the South and Southwest, primarily Texas and New Mexico, and the regimen usually started with flying small single-engine L-class airplanes before moving on to gliders. The experience of Flight Officer Tim Bailey in learning to fly gliders was both typical and unusual. Already a graduate of the Civilian Pilot Training Program, he was sent to Tucumcari, New Mexico, for primary training in small powered airplanes; he did well in the same aircraft he had first learned to fly. After several weeks he was sent to Clovis, New Mexico, where fledgling pilots practiced dead-stick landings until they could shut their engines off and land within fifty feet of a chalk line drawn on the runway. On to Fort Sumner, New Mexico, where for the first time Bailey and his fellow cadets flew gliders, small two- or three-place Taylorcrafts or Aeroncas. When he graduated from light glider school, he was promoted to staff sergeant and designated an instructor for the incoming class.

While flying with a student one afternoon, they released from their tow plane, and Bailey ordered the student—on track to become an instructor himself—to do a spin to the right, then one to the left. The first spin recovery went well. On the second Bailey thought they were holding the spin too long and motioned for the student to pull out. Nothing happened, so Bailey looked back and saw the cadet struggling with the control stick. Bailey immediately tried to pull his own stick back, but it was jammed forward; he pulled back so hard that he bent the hollow metal tube. Finally the small glider pulled up, too steeply, and stalled, once more going into a dive. Bailey ordered the student to bail out, and he quickly followed.

However, when Bailey tried to jump, his flight suit snagged on the handle of the door and he was caught, held fast to the diving glider. He managed to kick free and pulled the D-ring to his parachute. It snapped open, and he was suspended below the white canopy. Then he stared in horror at how close the glider was to him. The pilotless aircraft seemed bent on killing him; it dived and climbed in a series of oscillations perilously close to him and his parachute.

In the end, of course, he survived, but he was closely interrogated by a lieutenant who was convinced the pilots had bailed out needlessly. Later it was determined that one control stick had become stuck under the canvas cover of the seat ahead of it.[21]

Cochran and Alison asked for a hundred of the big CG-4A gliders, as well as twenty-five TG-5 training gliders. The latter were small two-place machines similar to that flown by Bailey; they were built from the fuselage and wings of the L-3 and were used to keep the glider pilots sharp. The TG-5 could be towed behind an L-5, so Cochran and Alison envisioned much more glider flight time. They also thought that the miniature glider would be useful for inserting a small group behind enemy lines, but that never happened.

Clearly the Waco gliders would need something large to tow them, and the obvious candidate for tug was the Douglas DC-3, now in olive-drab uniform and renamed C-47 by the AAF. It was a rugged versatile craft, much loved by its pilots and capable of flying even with major battle damage. The Douglas airliner had been developed in the mid-1930s as a sleeping car, with berths for passengers on long night flights. That idea was scrapped, and starting in 1942 the U.S. military purchased more than 10,000 C-47s, which operated from rough fields in every theater of the war. Plants in Santa Monica and Long Beach, California, and Oklahoma City turned out the cargo aircraft day and night, and military pilots, including Capt. Dick Cole, Doolittle's copilot, test-flew every fourth or fifth one off the line before delivery to a military facility.[22]

For lighter cargoes and rough short-field operations, the Project 9 commanders selected a rugged Canadian bush plane, the Noorduyn Norseman. The Norseman, never a beauty queen, had aerodynamic fairings over the upper half of its undercarriage that looked like stunted wings; the airplane's single Pratt & Whitney R-1340 radial engine produced 600 horsepower while giving it a blunt-nosed, no-nonsense look; it could be fitted for skis or floats, neither of which were likely to be used in Burma but which had made it a favorite of bush operators in Canada. The Norseman could carry 2,000 pounds and would prove to be an important asset in the Chindit campaign. Cochran had seen one in Canada on his return trip from England; when he inquired about it at the Pentagon, he learned that the AAF had just purchased fourteen. He asked for and got twelve, a dozen planes intended for another command but now diverted to Project 9.

Each time Alison or Cochran put in an order for aircraft, they were met with incredulous stares or hoots of derision. "Sure, Lieutenant Colonel, I'll just get you those hundred L-5s right away. Right away after the five-dozen orders ahead of you."

Alison or Cochran would patiently explain that they had top priority. "Everyone has top priority, there's a war on." They would return to the Pentagon, General Arnold would type a letter directing that one hundred L-5s be placed at Alison and Cochran's disposal, and sign it. The planes immediately became available.[23]

Fighters gained the special attention of Cochran and Alison. Both had extensive experience in the Curtiss P-40, but by 1943 machines in the Axis arsenals had outclassed the venerable fighter. They debated the merits of several fighters, including the twin-engine P-38 and the rugged P-47. This time they were unsuccessful in commandeering their first choice. The P-38 was a long-range fighter, one that in their professional judgment would be perfect for forays into Burma from India. But they were highly prized assets in both the Pacific and European theaters, and even Arnold could not justify their use in the area that Cochran himself had called "an alley fight."

They eventually ended up with thirty P-51As, the razorback version of what would become the premier Allied fighter of the war. The A-version of the Mustang was armed with four .50-caliber wing-mounted machine guns (later models carried six) and could carry as much as 2,000 pounds of bombs affixed to hard points under the wings. Originally built by North American to meet the requirements of the Royal Air Force, the '51 was transformed into a first-class fighter by replacing its Allison engine with the Rolls-Royce Merlin engine, built under contract in the United States by Packard.

Even then, Alison and Cochran were not totally satisfied, and they let their fighter-pilot imaginations roam freely. Fifty-caliber machine guns were fine against other aircraft and lethally effective against troops on the ground. But if railroads and river barges were the targets—and Cochran and Alison now envisioned that they would be—then perhaps they could try something else.

Rockets were the newest weapon in the aerial arsenal and were still being tested. When Alison and Cochran tried to requisition some for the fighter section of their miniature air force, they ran into another stone wall; no rocket-launching tubes were available anywhere to fit the Mustang. They asked the North American plant in Dayton to make the equipment, but officials there refused: they were building P-51s as fast as they could and did not want to waste time tooling up for a minor project. So Cochran and Alison asked Arnold for the money to have the launching equipment built by a small machine shop overseen by Ajax Baumler. For $27,000 they equipped their thirty P-51s with rocket launchers and would be the first combat unit to use them.[24]

The aerial task force was nearly complete. But the pair had heard rumors about a new rotary-wing craft called a helicopter, designated the YR-4 and then being tested at Wright Field.[25] It was rumored to land and take off vertically, making it ideal for small spaces. They determined to get as many as possible for the campaign but once more ran into a solid chorus of disapproval. Fewer than a dozen had been made, and everyone, it seemed, had claimed the choppers when testing was complete. The army wanted them, the navy wanted them, even the Royal Navy claimed priority.

The men in the helicopter-testing unit at Wright Field were adamant. No way in hell were the helicopters leaving Wright Field. They were being run through a demanding regimen to determine whether they were even viable candidates for inclusion in the nation's arsenal; no, they would not be released to anyone, not even General Arnold.

A terrific argument continued. Cochran's main point was that the 'copters were vitally important, life-saving equipment. "We don't want to do just proving, we can use them."[26] When Cochran left for India, he told Alison to keep working on obtaining the 'copters. Alison appealed to Frank Gregory at Wright Field but was also rebuffed. Gregory was the Army's rotorcraft expert, working with Igor Sikorsky, the designer of the craft.

According to Cochran, Alison ran into Harry Hopkins, the man he had accompanied to Russia on the Lend-Lease deal two years earlier and a close adviser to President Roosevelt. Hopkins invited Alison to dinner, and during the evening's conversation the subject of the helicopters came up, along with their importance to a top-secret project involving the little fighter pilot and others.

Six helicopters were suddenly mysteriously available. Arnold asked Cochran and Alison how it happened. "General, you just have to know the right people!" The commanding general of the Army Air Forces shook his head.[27]

Alison himself denied the story years later and insisted that the order had come through Arnold's office, with no intervention by Hopkins.[28]

Flying machines were not the only equipment Alison and Cochran needed, however. While neither pilot was tolerant of paperwork, Alison proved to be detail oriented, a result both of personality and his engineering days at the University of Florida. He researched everything, from clothing to weapons, food to medical supplies.

Together Alison and Cochran went to see an officer in ordnance, once more explaining that they needed personal firearms for close fighting in jungle conditions, weapons that could be carried in an airplane and perhaps even strapped to a man who had to parachute from a plane. It was difficult, at times, this business of not being able to tell anyone exactly what their mission was, but most career military men also understood that some things could not be discussed. The result in this instance was a supply of folding-stock carbines, just being produced for airborne troops and not yet distributed. A folding stock made the carbine ideal for carrying aboard aircraft. A metal skeleton stock attached to a pistol grip; folding the stock forward reduced the overall length of the weapon from 35.5 inches to 25.5 inches, and it weighed less than seven pounds with a loaded fifteen-round magazine. It would easily stow in nearly any cockpit the Air Commandos might occupy.[29]

It wasn't always so easy. They recalled their own missions, when as pilots they wore a wool A-4 flight suit, which was a glorified mechanic's overall with just two open pockets, one on the chest, another on a lower leg. The leather flight jacket they were issued, the famous A-2, was likewise equipped with just two small flapped pockets. They needed something with multiple and voluminous compartments for carrying a variety of flight and survival gear. Airborne troops wore a special jacket, similar to a bush jacket, with four large expanding pockets, and trousers with large cargo bags on the legs. But the gear was highly prized and jealously guarded by those with jump-wing badges on their chests. In the end Cochran and Alison procured the paratrooper uniforms, and in India and Burma Alison was seldom seen wearing anything else.

Leather boots were judged too prone to rot in wet jungles, so, following Wingate's lead, they lobbied for jungle boots of canvas and rubber. Marines had them, but no one else did. There were more hard feelings over that one. Army Air Force fliers with the coveted marine boots? But they got them.

Cochran and Alison demanded that each man—enlisted and officer, air crew or ground duty—have a .45-caliber pistol plus either a folding-stock carbine or a .45-caliber Thompson submachine gun. Their argument was hard to refute: in the conditions expected, anyone could become a jungle fighter through any number of circumstances. Each flier received a large thick-bladed knife, and the cocommanders ordered thousands of grenades.[30]

Alison, who had flown fighters in China, knew the conditions in which they would be fighting. "When I was in China I had often flown over Northern Burma. Flying over it once, low down, seeing the jungle, the mountains and the streams and the very few roads, you know that the thing that stops movement there, of course, is that there is no easy way on the ground to get around."[31]

The commanding general of the Army Air Forces might be excused for not being personally involved in details such as personal survival equipment. But Hap Arnold had flown over Burma, from New Delhi to Kunming, China, on a tour of the theater in February 1943. His diary records his misgivings as he looked down from his transport plane onto the green canopy of trackless jungle below:

Well, the Japs occupy country extending well into China from the coast. There is always the possibility of Jap planes being abroad. They probably have radar and plot the course of all visiting aircraft such as ours. If we turn back into the wind do we run out of gas in the mountains? Do we jump? If so, when? Will we be captured over by Mandalay? What should we take with us if we have to jump? What will the people back home think if they hear that the Commanding General, US Army Air Forces and the Commanding General, 10th Air Force and others with us have been taken prisoners? What are the best shoes to wear in hiking through the jungle? Can we take emergency rations with us if we jump?[32]

Radios would be the vital link between air and ground, but few systems in the entire theater were extensive or reliable. Cochran called in radio specialists to design an entire communications system and to determine what they needed and how many of each.

And so on down the list. They operated on the principle that if they needed ten items, they requisitioned twenty. They would get little help in-theater, so it was better to have too much than too little.

The only exception was typewriters. Taking Arnold at his word—to hell with paperwork—and falling back on their own animosity toward record keeping, Cochran and Alison made scant provisions for office equipment. In reviewing lists of supplies for the mission, Cochran saw that twenty-four typewriters were on the list of organizational equipment. He crossed through the number and wrote in three. Bullets and bombs were more important than typewriters. When they arrived in India, he found that someone had ignored his directive and shipped eighteen. He was able to live with the change.[33]

With the last of the equipment in the pipelines, and the men already reporting in, it was time to start training.

CHAPTER 10

As the training site for a secret group on a secret mission it was perfect.

Seymour Johnson Army Air Force Base, fifty-three miles southeast of Raleigh, North Carolina (on today's roads), was built in 1941 on the City of Goldsboro's airport in the middle of the piney woods that had long been a staple of the local economy.

Since June 1943 the base, which was headquarters for the Troop Training Command, had also been a center for troops heading overseas and as such was the scene of a constantly shifting population, where few got to know others well and where new faces constantly appeared and then quickly vanished to parts unknown[1].

Project 9 would depend heavily on night use of the Waco glider, and the air base at Goldsboro would allow Cochran and Alison's pilots the space, time, and discretion to perfect a variety of dangerous and precise exercises. In Belgium in 1940 and again in Crete in 1941 the German war machine had proved the glider's worth as a silent intruder. But the plan to use gliders to insert British troops into Japanese-occupied Burma had a major problem: how to get the gliders back out of a small jungle clearing.

Shortly after the base became a transshipment center Cochran and Alison, along with their glider chiefs Bill Taylor and Vincent Rose (see chapter 8), went to Goldsboro to watch the gliders at work.

"People that fly airplanes are fool enough, but anyone that gets into one of those gliders is a damn fool," Cochran said, after observing several takeoffs and landings. Alison nodded in silent agreement. Taylor and Rose looked at each other and grinned, then all four walked out to a CG-4A being hooked to its tow rope. After a short discussion with the glider pilot, they climbed in, strapped themselves to the wooden benches that lined each side of the glider's cabin, and were towed aloft.[2]

Later Cochran said of that decision to fly: "You can't lead anybody unless you know the thing yourself."[3]

While looking at the glider and tug arrangement, they learned of an ingenious device that would allow a cargo plane to snatch a glider from the ground by flying overhead and snagging the towline. The Model 80-X Glider Pick Up System, built by All American Aviation in Baltimore, was a complicated bit of machinery. Central to it was a revolving drum that absorbed much of the tremendous shock created when a stationary glider weighing 5,000 to 7,500 pounds, was suddenly jerked into the air; without the energy-eating drum, a glider's nose hook would be ripped out or a C-47 could be pulled to the ground or the towline would break. The device could be reversed to reel in the towline, had a fail-safe mechanism for instantly severing the line in the even of a catastrophe, and included 1,057 feet of nylon cable with some stretching and shock-absorbing capability, and various pulleys, torque tubes, and hydraulics. All this was concealed inside the fuselage. Externally the towplanes thus equipped were identifiable only by a wooden arm extending from a hawse pipe on the left side forward of the cargo door. All C-47s for Project 9 would be equipped with the 80-X.[4]

So the air task force was taking shape. The aircraft had been approved and were being assigned; the personnel were being recruited, some from overseas posts.

Back at Bowman Field near Louisville, Taylor continued to recruit men for the glider section. He made prospects two unusual promises: the job would be long and tough, and they could expect absolutely no gain from signing on. Enthusiasm was the trait he looked for; anyone not totally committed to helping win the war by participating in a dangerous and secret operation would be immediately disqualified. He also sought four personal characteristics in his glider pilot recruits: technical ability, previous army service, flying experience, and general attitude. He gave no weight to general qualification tests or educational background. In the end the glider section was comprised of seventy-five officers and twenty-five enlisted men[5].

The recruiting process for all personnel often was as unconventional as that for the glider pilots and the rest of Project 9. Albert Eugene Piester was a twenty-year-old aircraft mechanic awaiting overseas deployment at Goldsboro, one of a group of about sixty who had completed a course in Burbank, California, on the P-38. Word went out that interviews were under way for a special project, and he signed up.

"We went into a room with a desk, a captain behind it, who explained that this would be a faraway place, with rugged living conditions. 'You don't have to go, but if you want to, you can volunteer,'" Piester, known as Gene, recalled years later. "Well, we were young, we were ready, and everyone said yes." The men then sat for individual interviews, and the captain asked the usual sorts of questions that might reveal competence and motivation. Then he asked the young mechanic a question that stopped him cold.

"What would you do if you were in a jungle atmosphere and the enemy was near by and you were ambushed while you were out there working on your airplane?" The captain stared at Piester without another word. Piester thought, and thought some more. "I had never thought about that before, you know. We had been trained as mechanics, but now we were talking about real war. What would I do? I couldn't come up with anything. He waited and waited, and finally I said, 'Captain, I don't know what I'd do. I'd just have to figure it out on the spot.' He thanked me and dismissed me."

Piester was sent back to his barracks. Shortly he and one other mechanic, Wayne Bozarth, were told to pack their gear and report to the orderly room. There they were driven by jeep to a far corner of Johnson Field, where they entered a barracks that soon began to fill with other men selected. Rumors were rampant, but no one had any hard information. Then the officers assembled the volunteers, including a large group of pilots housed in another barracks, and told the men: "You are Project 9."[6]

Shortly thereafter all the assembled men were issued combat uniforms, shoulder holsters, and .45-caliber pistols, as well as .30-caliber folding-stock carbines. Project 9 meant business.

Flight Officer Charles B. Turner, a nineteen-year-old glider pilot, was in Louisville awaiting assignment when he was recruited. He recalled that Taylor emphasized flying and at least one other skill. For Turner the ability to double as a glider mechanic paid off. He was selected and would go on to fly twenty-two glider missions and an additional fifteen as unofficial copilot in B-25Hs.[7]

Recruiting for the other sections was equally unorthodox, conducted by either Alison and Cochran directly or one of the ranking key men they had already tapped. Fighter pilots often got a call from an old friend. The project was secret, so no general announcement could be made. Typical was the experience of the fighter pilot Paul G. Forcey.

Early in the war he had gone to Canada, joined the Royal Canadian Air Force and trained as a pilot, then was posted to West Africa. He saw little action there and eventually asked for a transfer to the USAAF. In October 1943 he was a test pilot at Eglin Field in Florida, where he knew Tex Hill, Ed Rector, and Ajax Baumler, former AVG pilots who all knew and admired Johnny Alison. Most of the former Flying Tigers were worn out from their early war in China, but they urged Forcey to apply when they learned who would be leading the Air Commandos. The young pilot was looking for action; he would find it in Burma, where he would be credited with shooting down three Japanese aircraft, the highest score of any of the original 1st Air Commandos.[8]

One group of nine officers came from the 50th Fighter Group at Orlando: Capt. Donald V. Miller, Capt. Holly M. Keller Jr., and first lieutenants Craig L. Jackson, Robert D. Thomas, William R. Gilhousen, Carl Hartzer Jr., Neill A. Bollum, Temple C. Moore, and Irving W. Forde. All received written orders transferring them to Project CA-281 and for temporary duty at Goldsboro "pending movement overseas semitropical climate." Casualties for this group would be especially high.[9]

On 1 October 1943 fighter and glider pilots reported to Johnson Field, and the light planes to Raleigh-Durham Army Air Field.

Although Wingate and others initially saw the light planes as the solution to the problem of evacuating wounded Allied soldiers from behind enemy lines, the pairings of the C-47 and the Waco glider came to be the heart of Project 9.

A civilian DC-3 in military olive drab (with a strengthened floor and the addition of a cargo door), the C-47 Skytrain was a staple of military life: more than 10,000 were in use throughout the war. Almost no one called it a Skytrain; it was usually called a Gooney Bird, or frequently Dakota, the British designation. It efficiently carried men and materiel to bases around the world and every theater of the war. It was a common sight on the Hump route from India to China and just as common across England, North Africa, and the Pacific Islands. It wasn't glamorous, and the youngsters going through multiengine pilot training at bases across the United States hardly ever sought assignment to the twin-engine cargo hauler. Twin-engine Lightnings, maybe, or four-engine Flying Fortresses or Liberators. But not the C-47. But thousands of youngsters received orders that placed them in the cockpits of the Douglas, and most came to respect, if not love, the airplane.

The venerable bird has proved to be one of the greatest aircraft in history, with thousands still flying a half century or more after the last World War II fighters and bombers were retired from service. The C-47, wearing black-and-white invasion stripes, dropped thousands of Allied airborne troops into occupied France, and the plane came to be the symbol to many of the industrial might of America, a flying reminder of the inevitable end to the war.

Ubiquitous might have been a term to describe the cargo ship; *simple* would not have been appropriate. For many a young pilot fresh from flying school and easing into the right seat for the first time, the cockpit must have seemed impossibly complex: hundreds of gauges, levers, buttons, switches, knobs, and handles crammed into the front instrument panel, overhead, alongside, in the pedestal between the two front seats, in the floor space between pilot and copilot, even behind the seats.

As Project 9 began operations in Burma, Cochran and Alison realized they had too many glider pilots and not enough copilots for C-47s. No problem: they assigned glider pilots to the right seat of the Dakotas. All had had some experience in flying powered aircraft, and the duties of a copilot usually were minimal. Len Morgan, a veteran airline pilot and writer who flew '47s during the war, wrote later that many copilots referred to themselves as "non-commissioned ballast."[10] A USAAF training film, *Troop Carrier Airplanes,* sought to alleviate some of the fears of young flyers transitioning to the C-47. It emphasized the familiar preflight inspection—usually referred to as a walkaround—and included checking the condition of tires, hydraulic lines, and overall appearance of the airplane. The film explained the complexities of each preflight sequence, as well as the duties of the copilot, in detail. According to the film, the most important task for the men in the cockpit following the preflight inspection and completion of the Form 1-A was anticlimactic: adjust the seat so you are looking squarely through the center of the windscreen.

Then the film went through the complicated and important start-up procedure in detail, from flipping on the battery switches to checking the hydraulic pressure for the landing gear to determining the levels of fluids and checking the flight controls, props, and radio.[11]

As complex as the C-47 was, the Waco glider was simple. Some aspects of flying the glider were easier than flying the C-47, but having no power plant presented some obvious drawbacks: gliders could not climb and when released had no option but to land. Double tows presented their own difficulties, and of course each takeoff was an adventure that called for precise and prompt responses from the pilot. Two C-47s with experienced pilots were temporarily assigned to the glider section. (They proved so effective that both command pilots were eventually assigned to Project 9.) Glider pilots practiced takeoffs in single tow, then with two strung out at different lengths. They used a primitive kind of autopilot for gliders, consisting of a small wind-driven propeller on one wing that drove a miniature generator that powered a gyroscope linked to the ailerons and tail-control surfaces. It was not intended to take over the functions of a pilot but to make the exhausting business of maintaining position behind the tug a bit less tiring. And they began intensive training in night landings.

The CG-4A was a craft clumsy in appearance, with a flat-sided fuselage more than forty-eight feet long, a blunt nose that tilted up to load and unload cargo, and a wingspan of nearly eighty-four feet. The spartan cockpit had none of the C-47's myriad gauges. But the simplicity of its instrument panel belied its difficulty to fly. The two pilot seats sat alarmingly close to the nose; with no engine little came between the pilots and any objects—airborne or on the ground—with which they might come into sudden and violent contact. A nose-skid called the Corey system was intended to prevent the nose from plowing into soft fields; later a crash-absorbing system of welded pipes, called the Griswold nose, was added to give additional protection to the pilots, but it was not introduced in time for the Burma campaign. A large windscreen provided plenty of visual comfort. The glider pilot had to be able to see his towplane in all conditions.

Two large control wheels—they resembled the steering wheels of prewar commercial trucks—were attached to an inverted V-shaped yoke that was hinged overhead and connected to a series of pulleys. Wire cables to the ailerons, elevators, and rudder were open and visible the length of the cabin. In front of the pilot and copilot was a center-mounted instrument panel with just five gauges: from left to right, airspeed, rate-of-climb, bank-and-turn, altimeter, and a compass. Only the pilot, in the left seat, had toe-operated brakes, but each pilot had adjustable rudder pedals and a spoiler lever. The spoiler was aptly named: pulling the lever raised a flat strip on the top surface of the wing that disrupted the smooth flow of lifting air. When spoilers were deployed, the glider came down quickly. If a glider was too high when approaching a landing, spoilers would help shed the extra altitude and perhaps keep the glider from overshooting the landing field and crashing into trees or other unyielding objects. There were no go-arounds in gliders.

An overhead set of cranks in the cockpit allowed for trim adjustments to ailerons, elevators, and rudder. Also overhead was the release lever for a parachute designed to deploy as an additional emergency brake. It was never to be used while being towed. Between the two seats was a lever with a large round knob that released the nose latches and allowed the entire front section, including the cockpit, to lift and lock in place. This allowed total access to the interior of the glider; a jeep, a howitzer, small bulldozer, or other bulky cargo could easily be loaded and unloaded. When landing while carrying such heavy cargo, the nose latches were released just before landing. A line tied to the cargo could flip up the nose section if a sudden stop propelled the cargo forward. That detail would prove crucial to at least one cockpit crew.

So glider pilots had to wrestle a large powerless aircraft carrying thousands of pounds of gear, soldiers, or cargo; maintain position behind the C-47 towing them despite turbulent air or aerial maneuvering; and land precisely in unprepared fields or clearings, often while being shot at by enemy troops. Piece of cake. But in addition to the obvious dangers, the training manual for the Waco described a few more. One was instrument error. Because the sensors for airspeed and altitude were mounted in the nose, they were in a low-pressure, high-velocity area of the airstream. This meant that the airspeed indicator read faster than the glider was actually flying—by about 10 mph at low speeds. The danger of stalling was thus increased for the unwary pilot. Additionally the low air pressure at the point of the static port caused the altimeter to read high—as much as 200 feet high at 120 mph (calibrated airspeed)—and was another potential disaster for night landings in particular.[12]

Because C-47s were at a premium, and the Project 9 team would have only twelve at some point in the future, training emphasized the double tow. The procedure was tricky, calling for precision, communication, and teamwork between the towplane aircrew and the glider pilots. The training manual laid out standard procedure, which the glider pilots followed rigidly during training at Johnson Field and later. The double tow was difficult enough in the relatively flat and friendly terrain of North Carolina, but it would prove disastrous in the rugged mountains and thick jungle of India and Burma.

In a double tow launch one glider—always the one on the right—was linked to the tug by a towline 425 feet long; the lefthand glider's line was seventy-five feet shorter. As the tug accelerated down the runway, both gliders tended to be pulled to the center; not enough wind crossed either glider's rudder to make lateral control effective, so the pilots had to lightly tap the brakes to ensure correct position. The gliders became airborne before the tug, and each then had to lower its nose and maintain a level constant altitude just feet off the runway, each lined up on a wingtip of the towplane. The glider pilot on the long tow was responsible for avoiding collisions, since the short-tow pilot's rear vision was restricted.[13]

Once the tug and both gliders were in the air, maintaining position while keeping a uniform, continuous strain on the towline was a constant battle. Anyone who has ever been in a car being towed by a chain or rope will appreciate the difficulty. As the towing vehicle slows down or goes downhill, the chain becomes slack; as the vehicle accelerates, the chain pulls taut, sometimes roughly jerking the vehicle being towed. The driver being towed must constantly tap the brakes to maintain proper distance. In a glider, without a throttle or brakes, such jerks could cause loss of control of the towplane or the glider, or they could snap the towline, leaving the gliders with no option but to land. Sometimes a stretched towline snapped back and wrapped around the wings. That was a recipe for disaster.

If they ran into trouble, either the tug pilot or the glider pilot could release the towline. In the C-47 tugs a T-handle mounted on the bulkhead directly behind the copilot was the release for the glider tow. On takeoff the copilot's hand always rested near the handle, while the flight engineer watched through a top blister, ready to relay to the cockpit any sign of distress or disaster. Radio communication between the gliders and their tow was rare; sometimes a two-way radio wire was connected along the towline, but it frequently did not function and the wire often broke, so glider pilots were left to carefully watch the tow for any sign of trouble. If smoke erupted from an engine, or they observed a propeller being feathered, glider pilots were to immediately release from the tug. At night the tug could flash a red light at the glider to signal immediate release, but during daylight tows such warnings were ineffective. A sudden rocking of the wings indicated an emergency; the tug would release the glider within three seconds if that happened, unless the glider released first. To prevent the stretched nylon rope from snapping back toward the glider, it was more desirable for the glider pilots to unhook.

The light signal for danger at night was perhaps the only advantage to flying after the sun set. Night launches and landings were dangerous and often terrifying. Night training in gliders resulted in many crashes and many deaths and injuries. But there was a war on.

Night training continued nonetheless, until Taylor and Rose were satisfied that their glider pilots were highly proficient. Then the training turned to day and, later, night pickups—snatches—of gliders by low-flying cargo planes. The procedure of aerial grabs seemed simple enough on paper, and the training manuals were reassuring: The jolt to glider pilots and passengers of the aerial snatch resulted in "little more shock than the sudden jerk of a starting trolley car." The g-forces involved had been calculated at just seven-tenths of one g and lasted for only 6.5 seconds. This was considered minor, since navy pilots catapulted from carriers underwent about 2.5 g's, according to the glider manual.[14]

However, no one had made night snatches before. Daytime aerial grabs were difficult enough. The procedure required setting up a set of poles about fifty yards ahead of the glider and hanging its towline between the poles in a hoop. The towplane was to fly in a shallow descent, slightly to the right of the glider and initially no faster than 110 mph. The hook operator signaled to the tug pilot that the device was set for pickup, and the tug pilot confirmed readiness with the glider pilot. The weight of the glider and the field conditions now became factors in the speed of the tug plane: A 4,900 pound glider on firm ground meant an approach speed of 130; a 7,500 pound glider on soft earth dictated a tug speed of 140. About one hundred feet from the contact station—the two poles—the tug pilot began to apply more power; at contact he applied full takeoff power until they had cleared all obstacles, then reduced power.[15] For daylight snatches bright yellow signal panels would alert tow pilots when the setup was ready. For night pickups aircrews had to add flashlights to the tops of the two poles; the flashlights were powered by twelve-volt batteries that provided light for as long as six hours. Additionally a series of red lights laid out in a cross marked the pickup zone.[16]

The first flight in a C-47 for Harry McLean, who had trained as an aircraft mechanic and was designated as a flight engineer for the Air Commandos, was a night snatch. The cargo door had been removed and a net secured over the lower half of the opening. His job was to stand by with a boat hook—a bronze curved tip on a long wooden pole—and be prepared to cast off any line that inadvertently went over the top of the horizontal stabilizer.

"The net was waist-high that went across the door, and it was all open above it. I wasn't tethered to anything inside the aircraft, and when we first started down I remember thinking I would float right out the door. Then we started back up [from the lowest point in the snatch maneuver] and I was pushed down by g-forces. I don't think I could have operated that boat hook even if we had snagged the pickup rope wrong."[17]

Even for seasoned fliers, the experience was a novel one. Dick Cole said tug pilots never doubted they had snagged the glider. Even with the dampening effect of the reel mechanism, the airspeed of the C-47 was obviously slowed. The result was a forward jerk by both pilots, similar to the effect on passengers in an automobile traveling at a high rate of speed when the driver suddenly slams on the brakes. It was unpleasant, but the effect signaled a good pickup. Not experiencing this deceleration was a bad sign.[18]

Training went on day and night, and so did the accidents. On 16 October 2nd Lt. Boyd M. Cannon was killed while flying a TG-5 training glider at Wilmington, Ohio. No one witnessed the crash, and its cause was unknown. In another instance a glider flown by Flight Officer R. E. Kuenstler and copiloted by Flight Officer A. J. Bracaliello undershot the landing area, resulting in injuries to both fliers; two passengers escaped unharmed. Another accident, again caused by landing short at night, resulted in a badly broken leg for one passenger, a glider pilot who had to be left behind when the unit shipped out. A third incident occurred when a glider flown by First Officer G. A. Kelly wrapped its wings around a barn when it too released early and landed short.[19] Kelly survived.

The training goal of the glider section had been to certify each glider pilot after completing six simulated and four actual glider pickups. The lack of tugs—only two had been secured for training the crews of Project 9—and the glider accidents meant that in the end glider crews averaged five hours of training and two snatches using TG-5s, not the larger CG-4A.[20] "We just didn't have either the time or equipment for more than a few takeoffs and landings, maybe a couple of snatches. We ended up doing more training in India, of course," Charles Turner recalled. "I was considered a good pilot for snatches, and that meant I would be busy in Burma."[21]

Meanwhile at Raleigh-Durham the training of staff sergeant pilots in the light planes was also proceeding at a frenetic pace. Nearly all the liaison pilots recruited had been trained on L-2, L-3, and L-4 light aircraft. The heavier L-1 was too scarce in the inventory, and most pilots had never seen one up close; the L-5 was so new that few had flown one. They flew constantly, learning a variety of bush-flying techniques that allowed them to take off in the L-5 in substantially less distance than the manual stated. They considered modifications that were not according to Hoyle. Maj. Andrew P. Rebori had designed a kind of bomb rack that was fitted to the wings of L-5s, to which containers with supplies could be mounted, then dropped to targets on the ground. A sergeant pilot even mounted a pair of Thompson submachine guns to the struts of an L-5, to be fired by the pilot with a cable system. The resulting recoil was considered too severe, however, and the nascent system for close air support was abandoned.[22]

Similar training was taking place for the P-51 pilots and the light-cargo UC-64 Norseman drivers. The entire organization was in full-out training mode; when not in a cockpit, the pilots underwent training in jungle fighting, and if they had any spare time, they went to the range to practice with their new folding-stock carbines or submachine guns or pistols. The kinds of training and the intensity with which everything was done meant that few of those chosen for Project 9 had any illusions about the job ahead. And so the days went: a short night or early morn-ing of sleep, followed by flight training, glider snatches, weapons firing, tow rope inspection, night takeoffs and landings.

But after just a month, training came to a sudden end. Orders came in early November to ship out to India. Training could resume there, but it was time to move Project 9 overseas.

CHAPTER 11

In New Delhi, where he had gone ahead of the Project 9 team, Col. Philip Cochran looked around the table at the stern unsmiling faces of the high brass of the China-Burma-India theater of operations. He was thirty-three, a battle-tested fighter pilot, and his orders came directly from the commander of the Army Air Forces. No one at the table out-ranked his boss. Still, Cochran looked years younger than his age, and he was far too self-confident to suit many of the British and American generals gathered at the newly formed South-East Asia Command headquarters. Cochran had brought news of changes to the original Quebec Conference plans to aid Brigadier Wingate and his Chindits, and these changes did not sit well with some of the chiefs of staff to Admiral Lord Mountbatten, supreme commander of SEAC. Cochran was getting his first taste of the in-fighting that Project 9—now called 5318th Provisional Unit (Air)—would encounter.

Mountbatten sat at the head of the long oiled teak table in his head-quarters in the Secretariat, an imposing red-and-gray stone building on Raisina Hill in New Delhi. The building was actually one of two in a government complex, bookends of monumental late British Raj style, three stories high, with arched doorways and topped with *chhatris,* the pierced domes so integral to Indian architecture. In the SEAC office high ceilings held the afternoon heat, and Cochran felt a trickle of sweat run down his back. He held the gaze of the beribboned brass, however, despite his racing pulse. To Mountbatten's right was Joe Stilwell, the

U.S. general and deputy supreme commander of SEAC, glaring through his steel-rimmed glasses. Gen. Claude Auchinleck—who had protested Wingate's plans so vehemently to Churchill—was British commander in India and clearly still disapproved of the whole affair. Gen. Claire Chennault, now commander of the U.S. 14th Army Air Force, appeared mildly amused. Staff officers of Gen. George Stratemeyer wore neutral expressions.

So far as everyone at the table save Cochran was concerned, the original plans for Wingate to move three brigades of Special Force (as his Chindits were known officially) into Burma by land routes were still in effect. Now here was this cocky young colonel telling them that major changes would be instituted, that he would fly Special Force in by glider—and provide resupply and air support for the Chindits. Some commanders seemed to regard this as a misuse, if not outright waste, of valuable assets in a theater always at the dry end of the trough. Additionally the upstart colonel declared that the brigade, then positioned to be ferried to China and thence to walk into Burma, would instead be taken directly into Japanese-held territory by his unit's aircraft from bases in India.

"So that's the updated plan. Any questions, sir?" Cochran directed his query to Lord Mountbatten at the far end of the table. Overhead a ceiling fan with broad woven blades gently stirred the air. It was late November 1943, but the outside temperatures were still in the mideighties. "Is it possible, Col. Cochran, for your unit to move the brigades into position in, shall we say, two weeks' time once we start?" Mountbatten looked directly at Cochran. To the American colonel Mountbatten's pleasant face revealed more than a trace of doubt.

"Sir, we can move them in one week. Or less." Cochran displayed the smallest of smiles, hoping it conveyed confidence. He was acutely aware that he often was accused of being brash, even cocky.

"Boy, you are the first ray of sunshine we have seen in this theater for some time." Mountbatten beamed and looked around at his chiefs of staff. Stilwell remained silent, as did Auchinleck and Chennault.

"Keep us informed, Col. Cochran. Stay in close touch."[1]

Cochran left the Secretariat breathing more easily. He felt for the inside pocket of his tunic and relaxed when he felt the envelope still tucked safely inside. It was his secret weapon, the armament that allowed him to face down everyone at the table. Cochran was a gambler, a pretty good poker player. But he was not playing games now. The entire project depended on Mountbatten's complete support; the letter was insurance, he hoped, that it would be forthcoming. After leaving the Secretariat, Cochran cabled Alison, who was still in the United

States overseeing deployment of the Project 9 team to the China-Burma-India theater. To fulfill his promise to Mountbatten, Cochran would need fifty more gliders. By the next day Alison had already sent them on their way.

But the lack of enthusiasm from Mountbatten's staff was not the only issue, Cochran and Alison quickly learned. Wingate himself was seriously ill, stricken with typhoid after impetuously drinking water from a flower vase at an airfield in North Africa. The pair, full of enthusiasm for the upcoming campaign, visited Wingate in his hospital room in New Delhi. Wingate's adjutant, Brig. Derek Tulloch, said the visit contributed materially to Wingate's state of mind and ultimately to his discharge from the hospital.[2]

Cochran and Alison might have exuded confidence to the patient, but they were concerned about Wingate's health and the future of Project 9, which some were now quietly calling Tragedy 9.

"I remember feeling that if Wingate didn't pull out of this illness that he was in, if he weren't going to be there, all our efforts were going to be for naught," Cochran said many years later. "We would just be assimilated into the theater, and that would be the end of Project 9, because he was the key."[3]

Wingate's appearance concerned Cochran greatly. "When I saw him in India again, and saw him after he had been in the hospital, he looked terrible. He looked atrocious. He frightened me. He looked like death warmed over."[4] Wingate was the key to success of the Chindit operation and thus also to the mission of the Air Commandos. Wingate slowly recovered, but it was many weeks before he regained his strength. The plan went forward. Cochran always believed that Wingate recovered partly because of his renewed confidence that his plan was going to be supported. "I know it built up his spirits. I know it helped him get well," Cochran said, "because from that point on he came back fast."[5]

For at least two years war planners had recognized that air supply of embattled ground forces was a reality that altered the equations of traditional warfare. In 1943, when Stilwell's troops were retreating from Burma, air drops by RAF and USAAF cargo planes had allowed a successful strategic withdrawal. One result of that operation had been the establishment of a unified Allied aerial force, which included the Troop Carrier Command under U.S. Brig. Gen. William Old, who would be boss of all USAAF and RAF troop carrier squadrons. One of his first tasks after the TCC was formed would be the aerial resupply of Field Marshal William J. Slim's 14th Army.[6]

It was obvious from the start of planning for the Wingate operation that the dozen or so C-47s available from the Air Commandos' stable would not be enough for the successful insertion of thousands of British troops, plus additional mules and horses, and thousands of pounds of gear. TCC was thus tasked with the job of ferrying the bulk of Wingate's Special Force into the Burma clearings after Cochran's men had built suitable landing strips.

Cochran had been the first of Project 9 to enter the CBI theater, while the rest of the men followed shortly, in groups from six to twenty in December, 1943.[7] They left a trail of red faces—the angry visages of generals, colonels, and majors who had been bumped from Troop Carrier Command flights by captains, lieutenants, and sergeants. All the men of Cochran and Alison's air task force were armed with priority orders signed by General Arnold himself giving them a seat on any aircraft bound for India, regardless of who had to be left behind. The cargo planes flew in legs—to South America, Africa, the Middle East, and finally India—but the gliders and the light planes had all been disassembled, crated, and loaded aboard transport ships and navy carriers and delivered to the Indian ports of Karachi and Calcutta.

Taylor was the last glider man to arrive in India, in late December, having stayed behind to oversee the deployment of the section. For ten days or so after he landed in Karachi, the men of the glider section underwent ground training, as well as physical conditioning. Before breakfast every morning each man had to complete a half-mile run. British intelligence officers gave lectures that provided a general orientation to the CBI theater, while American officers used the time to speak on a variety of subjects, including health in the new climate, adjusting loads on the cargo gliders, booby traps in the field, and communications procedures. Shortly thereafter Taylor issued the men under his command a memorandum regarding duty hours: all would be considered on duty twenty-four hours a day, seven days a week.[8]

By 1 December the men had been divided into four teams to assemble the aircraft. They made arrangements, through 2nd Lt. H. J. Delaney, to borrow tools from the 28th Air Depot, and soon they were in the aircraft reassembly business.

In a large hangar at Malir airfield near Karachi—the hangar was originally built by the U.S. Navy for an around-the-world dirigible flight—the men of the newly designated 5318th Provisional Unit (Air) went to work. Of the 523 men chosen for Project 9, about 300 were pilots. All had been chosen because they possessed, in addition to superb flying skills, a second and third talent; the pilots were expected to be good mechanics, capable of doing field maintenance, and if they could sing, dance, type, or had carpentry skills or engineering know-how, operate heavy machinery, decipher blueprints, or accomplish any of the hundreds of tasks expected of a self-contained autonomous fighting force, they had been selected. Assuming, of course, that they possessed the suitable ration of enthusiasm for danger. At Seymour Johnson Field Taylor had sent three men packing for "petty incompatibility and general petering out of the voluntary spirit"; three more pilots were promptly selected.[9]

Now, in the cavernous former dirigible hangar, the men pried open the wooden crates into which the aircraft had been packed and began the tedious task of assembling the planes. The work continued into the evening hours, and as darkness wrapped around the hangar hundreds of bats that lived in the high rafters began to dart among the men. When work was slack during the day, the men took to climbing into the upper realms of the gargantuan building to try to capture the sleeping creatures hanging inverted with their wings wrapped around them like capes.[10]

The L-5s and Norsemen had been stowed in crates below the main deck, but the P-51As had been carried on the flight deck of a carrier. They arrived with some saltwater corrosion, in addition to storm damage, and several were deemed unserviceable. A cable was quickly sent, calling for immediate replacements, and they were soon on their way. Sgt. Eugene Piester and his friends went to work on the fighters, attaching the propellers and cleaning off the grease that had been applied to every metal surface as protection against corrosion, a process known as pickling. As they opened each inspection plate, they grinned as they came across the names of the young women who had assembled it.[11] After assembly, the aircraft were flown to an airfield near Calcutta.

Capt. Dick Cole, leading one of the two groups of C-47s flying to India from the U.S., said the status of the group as a secret project was amplified each time the cargo aircraft had stopped to refuel. The glider-recovery mechanism, with its long arm projecting from the hawse pipe, attracted attention and many questions. In response the flight crews painted a question mark, surrounded by a blue circle, on the vertical stabilizer. They also commissioned leather patches for their A-2 flight jackets with the same insignia and began calling themselves the Question Mark Squadron.[12] At Karachi further distinctive paint schemes were added to all the aircraft: five white diagonal stripes wrapping around the fuselage, just behind the cockpits of the fighters and forward of the tail surfaces for the rest of them. The significance of the five stripes has been lost: some argue that they represent the five sections of the aerial group; others have held that the five stripes and the four spaces separating them stood for Project 9.

All the gliders had been sent to Calcutta, a seaport in eastern India. Each had arrived in five crates, containing the wings, fuselage, cockpit, tail assembly, and control wires. Cranes had lifted them from the docks onto large trucks that drove them over horrible roads to Barackpore airfield nearby. Assembling the aircraft was hard, made doubly so because the tools needed to do the job had failed to arrive. The glider pilots worked in teams, lifting the wings into place, stringing the control cables, attaching the landing gear. They found they did not have a tensionometer to precisely stretch the control cables and bracing wires. Taylor had picked Flight Officer Charles Turner for the special assignment because he was also a qualified glider mechanic, and that skill paid off now. Turner came up with the idea of plucking the wires like banjo strings until they sounded right. He had test-flown one of the first gliders assembled, and all the controls felt right; the glider flew as it was supposed to. After landing he listened to the sound of the wires as he plucked them and used the memory of that note to test the others.[13] As soon as the gliders were assembled, they were test-flown and then prepped for tow to Assam in northeast India, which would be their final training base. Included in the shipment of gliders were the tiny three-place training gliders, added to the aerial force as potential small-force insertion vehicles; the TG-5s were used for training, but they never entered combat. They could be towed behind an L-5 or a Norseman, and they provided additional flying time for power pilots as well as glider men.

On Christmas Eve 1943 Alison, Cochran, Taylor, and a few others flew to two grass strips in Assam, at Hailakandi and Lalaghat, to inspect the RAF emergency fields. The fields, just ten miles apart, were 120 miles west of the Burma border and about eighty miles west of Imphal, India. They were dilapidated and overgrown, and they would need some major work to serve the needs of the air task force.It turned out that one of the first officers the freewheeling commanders of Project 9 had recruited on the sly in Washington was the perfect man to make the fields serviceable. Capt. Andrew Cox was an artillery officer with experience on heavy earth-moving equipment and a background in construction. Cox had a regular commission in the U.S. Army Coast Artillery Corps, which meant he could not officially be assigned to an Army Air Corps project. Cochran arranged with Gen. Albert Wedemeyer, SEAC's deputy chief of staff, to have Cox sent to India as part of Mountbatten's staff, and Cox was then placed on permanent detached service to the 5318th Provisional Unit (Air). Cox set to work constructing buildings at Hailakandi and Lalaghat that were necessary for prolonged duty, including new barracks, as well as showers, latrines, mess halls, and administrative centers. Using Indian laborers with elephants as heavy equipment, Cox also oversaw construction of drainage ditches, connecting roads, and ordnance dumps.[14]

The airfield at Hailakandi had been a tea plantation set in a magical landscape. It had no hard runways; the landing strip itself was a large level area that would turn swampy when the rains came in May. This flat basin was surrounded by peculiar hills on which tea plants had grown for a century. The terrain resembled a cookie sheet on which rounded scoops of dough had been placed: flat, then suddenly a hillock erupted from the surface like a blister, with no apparent relationship to the geography surrounding it.

Some serviceable buildings from the tea plantation were quickly converted to the medical needs of the Air Commandos. The tea-processing building became a commissary, and the tea planter's cottage served as the unit's hospital. A sign hung outside: "Sick Inn." A small village had once been situated in the trees surrounding the basin, but the British had moved the villagers out. The Air Commandos now used some of the huts. They pushed aircraft back into the trees, and soon heaps of ordnance dotted the dispersal area.[15] After Pearl Harbor, aircraft were dispersed around an airfield and not gathered in a single area, ripe for enemy bombs.

While the American airmen worked to establish their forward base, Indian women picked tea leaves around them, seemingly oblivious to the war. With large woven baskets balanced on their heads, the women waited patiently in lines to have their harvest weighed and to receive a few rupees for their work.[16]

The runway at Lalaghat was 6,300 feet long, while at Hailakandi the strip was 4,500 feet. Cochran and Alison decided to use the longer strip for transports and gliders and the field at Hailakandi for the fighters and light planes. Most of the Norsemen (UC-64s) were based at Lalaghat. The planes sitting at Calcutta were flown to the Assam strips as soon as they could accept the traffic. Later, when bombers were added to the force, B-25s would be based at Hailakandi.

Activity swirled at both fields. Throughout January, 1944, construction was ongoing and continuous, interwoven with training flights. Elephants lumbered across the area and acted as high loaders, cranes, and heavy trucks. As training for the assault into Burma once more kicked into high gear at Lalaghat, C-47s took off day and night towing gliders. At Hailakandi P-51s and L-5s were constantly in the air, landing, taking off, or taxiing. For the men trying to sleep in their tents nearby, the noise and the dust were constant reminders of where they were and what they were there to do. Eventually Cochran was able to have the 900th Airborne Engineers assigned to the group, under the direction of Lt. Patrick H. Casey, with 2nd Lt. Robert Brackett second in command. They would be vital to the construction of jungle airstrips when the invasion was launched. Rank had few privileges here, with everyone available unloading aircraft or rolling drums of gasoline or manhandling ordnance. When he was not flying, Dick Cole, a captain, was pressed into service to help set up runway lights in the center of the large flying field at Lalaghat, and then he and a communications officer set up the control tower, a small wooden affair that closely resembled a church steeple. At the end of the long days officers and men ate in the same chow hall on the west side of the field, often sitting together at the tables.[17]

Despite Cox's work and the unflagging exertions of the Air Commandos, conditions at the forward bases remained extremely primitive. Hot showers were occasionally available, as the sun heated the water sitting in galvanized pipes that ran above ground from a well to the shower room; once that was gone, showers were cold. But in the manner of young men everywhere, the Air Commandos did their best to make the forward bases tolerable and to enjoy life. Entertainment and respite came from a piano that the group had pitched in to buy for about 800 rupees ($250) in Calcutta. The commandos then drew straws to see who would fly it in a glider to the forward base at Hailakandi—if the pilot broke it during landing, he would have to buy it. The piano arrived intact, and many a tune was coaxed from its ivory keys. Glider pilots Earl C. Waller and Kenneth Georgeson wrote a song about their living conditions, calling it "Basha Blues," and eventually it was played on stations back in the States (a *basha* is a hut). (Waller would fly a glider in the first wave of Operation Thursday, as the Burma invasion was dubbed.)

Basha Blues

Lyrics by Kenneth Georgeson and Earl C. Waller

This is the place they call our home—
A place to rest though our minds may roam.

They call it a basha, Lord knows why;
A primitive silhouette against the sky.
The walls are of bamboo, the roof of hay,
Can't say it's a bad place in which to stay;
It looks picturesque by the light of the moon.
But one thing I dread is the coming monsoon . . .
Our cots are so made you can't sleep "like a log,"
So unskillfully made by our bearer, "Eggnog."
We'll get rid of him and hire another—
By the end of the week we'll be trying his brother.
Our basha can never take the place of home;

It's like drinking a beer that has no foam.
But why worry now? Let's all sing a tune;
Lord help us get back by the coming monsoon![18]

Some efforts at distraction did not end well. One pilot showed up with a bear he had just purchased. He placed it in a bunk where another pilot was sleeping. When the flier awoke, he struggled to free himself from the hug of the bear, but the animal only squeezed him harder. Later several glider men tried to coax it into bed with Taylor, the section leader, but he fled his basha before the bear could hug him. It was riotous and fun for a while. But when one pilot entered his hut and found the bear had destroyed his bed and ripped up all his blankets, he drew his .45 and shot it. For several days the men ate bear meat. It was tough and greasy.[19]

The bashas were primitive buildings by any standard. Walls were of bamboo, roofs were thatched grass, and the dirt floors were covered by woven mats, better than dust or mud but extremely slick. The men slept on four-poster cots; they draped mosquito netting between the posts, then someone tucked it in around the occupant. The men crawled into the cots fully clothed, disrobing inside the netting, and were careful to bring their boots in with them. The bashas were of varying sizes, but a typical sleeping barracks had doors at both ends, an aisle connecting them, with six cots on either side of the aisle.

Harry McLean, a C-47 crew chief, awakened one morning and dressed inside his tent-like sleeping quarters within one of the bashas. He looked for his GI boots and realized he had left them outside on the mat flooring. McLean threw aside the mosquito net and swung his legs over the edge of his cot. He reached for his left boot, turned it upside down, and shook it before slipping it on and tying the laces. He reached for the remaining boot, and as he picked it up a colorfully banded krait slipped out and slithered across the flooring. Kraits are among the world's deadliest snakes; their neurotoxic venom can asphyxiate a human within hours. McLean leaped back into his cot, his heart beating wildly. He never again left his boots outside his protective netting.[20]

The flavor of the Old West was evident at Lalaghat and Hailakandi, despite the exotic bamboo and matting. A frontier town atmosphere permeated the bases, and the lack of military spit and polish reinforced the knowledge that they were forward units close to hostile action. Few officers wore rank insignia, no one saluted, and everyone worked together at the dirtiest, most exhausting, tasks. This apparent lack of military protocol would become a source of some irritation among ranking visitors to the bases.

The grind of work from dawn to dark left little time for personal hygiene or attention to appearance. Wingate had begun growing a beard, as he had before each campaign, and many of his men did the same. The Man, as he was called, frequently visited the air bases. Seeing his beard, the Air Commandos started a variety of facial hair fashions of their own, from full beards to Fu Manchus. Haircuts were a luxury for which they rarely made time, and their clothing was habitually torn and dirty. Headgear was a matter of personal choice: sun helmets, crusher caps, baseball caps, Aussie-style bush hats, fore-and-aft overseas caps, mechanics' caps with the bill flipped up—all could be seen on a small group of men from the same section.

The work went on ceaselessly throughout January. Pilots of small planes flew a variety of drills and maneuvers, trying always to take off in shorter distances and land within a measured block; when they weren't flying, they were working on their own planes, changing the oil, tuning the engines, replacing propellers. At one point Lt. Paul Forcey, the fighter pilot who had first trained in Canada, climbed into an L-5 to settle a bet: he claimed the slow vulnerable liaison birds could face down a fighter and survive. Another pilot in a P-51A with gun cameras but no ammunition did his best to shoot down the little flying jeep, but Forcey was able to keep turning inside the Mustang. The cameras showed that Forcey never was hit by the high-speed fighter. No doubt the confidence of the light plane pilots notched up considerably. Glider men were constantly flying in double and single tows, as well as tweaking the control wires of the Wacos and inspecting their towlines and coiling them at the end of each day to keep them from tangling. Tug crews were busy in a continuous stream of takeoffs and landings, pulling gliders into the air all day long. Fighter pilots flew familiarization flights, and occasional missions over the Chin Hills, to probe the aerial defenses of the Japanese in Burma. When cargo planes with new supplies landed, the Air Commandos—pilots, clerks, ground personnel— all turned out to unload them.[21]

Shortly after the group arrived in India, the RAF determined it would not be able to provide any close air support for Wingate's men. Cochran volunteered the Americans, believing the P-51As would be adequate for the task. Maj. Walter Radovich, a tall hawk-nosed fighter pilot who had known Cochran since the early 1940s, was one of the first pilots to sign up. Rad, as he was universally known, was from Chicago, the son of Yugoslavian immigrants; his older brother Bill was a star football player at the University of Southern California and later an All-Pro guard for the Detroit Lions. Walter Radovich was a fighter pilot to the core, despite having been severely injured in a senseless training exercise. In October

1941 he had been part of a long cross-country training flight that had turned disastrous. Ignoring severe weather, the squadron commander had ordered the thirty fighters to take off; they were battered and scattered. In the end eleven fighters were lost, four men were killed, and Radovich suffered a badly broken leg when he was forced to bail out over San Rafael, California. He was still on limited duty when he met up with Cochran in Washington and was tapped for Project 9.

When the fighters left Calcutta for Hailakandi, fully fueled and armed, it was a tricky business.

"The takeoff was murder," Rad said. "Each of the '51s had six rockets, 1,000 pounds of bombs, and extra fuel. We used all of the runway, and still barely got off. The controls were mushy. We all made it, but that's when we decided we needed B-25s."[22]

Twelve medium bombers (eleven B-25Hs and one B-25J) were secured, and the call for crews went out. Patt Meara was assigned to the 54th Air Service Group, which had arrived in Calcutta months earlier from North Africa. Early in 1944 the 54th's operations officer had announced that five volunteers were needed for hazardous duty. Bored with base routine, and without any further prompting, Meara and four of his buddies raised their hands. In what seemed like minutes he found himself holding a carbine in the backseat of an L-5, with his duffle bag over his lap. The pilot set down at Lalaghat, and Meara looked around at the rough base. He was now a fill-in aerial gunner and would stand in for missions when a regularly assigned gunner was not available. Otherwise he was to be a general laborer of sorts, ready to do whatever was needed.[23]

Maj. R. T. Smith, a tall rangy fighter pilot who had been an original member of the American Volunteer Group, or Flying Tigers, had for a short time been a P-38 squadron commander in California. Because of that twin-engine experience, he was tapped to be the B-25 section leader. Smith had grown up in Red Cloud, Nebraska, where his father was superintendent of schools. The younger Smith had attended the University of Nebraska until his senior year in 1939, when his application for flight training was accepted. Smith completed the rigorous training and was commissioned a second lieutenant in June 1940. A year later he resigned his commission to join Claire Chennault and the original Flying Tigers. Smith was a flight leader in that group and a highly effective fighter pilot credited with at least eight aerial victories against Japanese aircraft. When he returned to the States, he was drafted as a private but was recommissioned as a lieutenant and a month later promoted to major at the age of twenty-four. He accepted designation as bomber section leader when Cochran said he could fly fighters as well.

Smith, whose first name was Robert, had been called "R. T." since his cadet flying days, when three Smiths were regularly called by their initials: B. P. Smith became Beep, and F. M. Smith was known as Fum. No one ever called R. T. Smith Artie but always R. T., with a slight pause between letters. When Smith was in the American Volunteer Group, someone asked what the *T* stood for, and David Lee "Tex" Hill, the storied commander of the Second Pursuit Squadron, replied, "Tadpole." The name stuck.[24]

Cochran and Alison tapped Radovich to be the deputy commander of the new bomber section, but he, like Smith, was not thrilled. Cochran placated Rad by allowing him to retain a P-51 and fly fighter missions as well. In fact the still-green bomber pilots who came with the B-25s were assigned as copilots in the C-47s, and fighter pilots were to fly the '25s after some training in multiengine flying.

The B-25H model Mitchell was a two-engine medium-range bomber with a distinctive twin-rudder design. It was easily recognizable as the general type of bomber flown by Jimmy Doolittle for the raid on Tokyo in April 1942 from the deck of the USS *Hornet*.[25] For the operation in Burma, Cochran and Alison wanted a proven ground-attack aircraft, and the hard-nosed B-25H had demonstrated it was that. It could carry bombs as well as fire four .50-caliber machine guns mounted in the nose, four more from barbettes on the side of the cockpit, and a 75 mm cannon from its nose. It was a formidable weapon.

The cannon had been designed as a tank gun. Its shells were three inches in diameter and weighed twenty pounds each; the fifteen-pound projectile could fire several miles while on the ground. When the cannon was first tried in an obsolete B-18 on the ground at Wright Field, many feared the recoil would tear the bomber apart. It did push the plane back several feet, but it held together. Still, it took many more months of static and aerial tests over Lake Erie before North American (makers of the B-25) and Army Ordnance engineers successfully mated the pair so that the cannon could be safely flown in combat. The first models went to the 5th Air Force in the southwest Pacific in September 1942 and were used to devastating effect against Japanese shipping; later, B-25Hs surprised German and Italian troops on the ground in the Mediterranean.

The cannon, which added about a ton to the weight of a B-25, was mounted in the nose, which was shortened to reduce some of the additional weight, with a magazine for shells located above the breech within reach of an in-flight loader. The pilot fired it by hitting a button mounted on his control yoke.[26]

Charles H. "Chuck" Baisden had been a P-40 crew chief with Smith in the AVG, and he was also a qualified aerial gunner. Tapped to be part of Project 9, Baisden now joined Smith's B-25 flight crew. In his memoir, *Flying Tiger to Air Commando*, Baisden decries the suggestion that the bomber seemed to stop in midair when the 75 mm cannon was fired.[27] But plenty of combat fliers were definitely aware of a hesitation in the forward momentum of the bomber when the pilot fired the fearsome cannon.

Charles Turner, the glider pilot, quickly volunteered to ride along as an unofficial copilot on missions of opportunity, called Rhubarbs, against trains, bridges, and barges in Burma. "It was the only time I had fun. Anytime a glider pilot gets to fly in anything with power, it's a thrill," he said. "We would come in low, firing on a train engine with the front fifties, then the pilot would fire that seventy-five. It seemed like it would stop in midair. I know we didn't, but when all the fifties were firing as well as that cannon, I know we lost two or three knots in air speed. And that train engine, [after] being beat up by the fifties, would just disappear when that seventy-five hit it."[28]

Alison was not overly impressed with the flying artillery piece: "The problem was, unless you had a discrete target, there were other weapons which were better than the cannon. You were supposed to be able to get off about three rounds on a run. I think effectively you might reduce that to two depending on the target that you were shooting at. Certainly, the 75-millimeter round was not nearly so good for area targets as frag bombs."

The accuracy of the cannon for close air support was undeniable, however. Alison described an early mission of opportunity for which he flew the B-25 to familiarize himself with the airborne weapon. "I know one day I was over in Burma and there was a railroad bridge. It had these timber pilings for support, and it went across some small gorge. Just to see what I could do, I backed off, and I picked a piling, and I hit it. The gun was very accurate. It was just as accurate as a machine gun. There was no opposition, and I just drove it down to about 500 feet slant range. When you fired it, it hit exactly where you pointed it."[29] That pinpoint accuracy would prove to be extremely important when the campaign to support the Chindits actually began.

As the operation began to coalesce and grew in size, Cochran was aware of the covetous eyes being cast his way. Too many assets for such a small piece of a big war was the mantra. Better to break up the 5318th and send the badly needed equipment and men to units with a bigger part to play than Wingate's proposed assault. Merrill's Marauders had taken casualties in northern Burma, and Stilwell very much wanted the L-1s and L-5s that Cochran and Alison had brought in. The pressure for an American unit to help another American outfit was enormous.

Cochran's refusal to provide the light aircraft as ambulances to evacuate the wounded caused much resentment.[30]

Cochran and his men were becoming the object of jealousy. Unimpressed Allies were now openly calling the unit Cochran's Circus, which the RAF dubbed Cochran's Young Ladies after a famous London theatrical revue from the 1920s and 30s.[31] It didn't help that everyone knew that the lantern-jawed, steely-eyed hero of *Terry and the Pirates*, Flip Corkin, was actually Cochran himself and that many of his men had become characters in the strip as well. A common farewell phrase—"See ya in the funny papers!"—now had a sharp edge to it for many. Cochran began to be questioned, closely, about what he and his circus were up to. As an Army Air Forces officer, he had certain obligations and expectations, but he also had been given a clear set of instructions, orders that kept him and Project 9 out of the organizational charts. Cochran did not report through the usual chain of command, answering instead directly to Arnold and secondarily to Mountbatten. The lack of accountability through regular channels further incensed some ranking career officers.

Resentment grew. Who were these guys, that they could come in with all their new equipment, refuse to aid American units in need, and not answer to anyone? In late January 1944 the situation became critical, and Cochran knew it was no ordinary visit when Mountbatten's HQ radioed that the SEAC commander would be paying a visit to Hailakandi. Cochran dispatched a flight of P-51s to escort him; it would be a bad beginning if the supreme commander for Southeast Asia were shot down by roving Japanese fighters while on his way to visit the new American unit.

The Dakota, a C-47 with RAF markings, touched down on the dusty strip and taxied to the ramp. Wearing a Royal Navy cap and a beribboned bush jacket, Admiral Lord Mountbatten stepped down from the transport. Cochran, Alison, and the rest of the small group gathered to meet the supreme commander saluted him; Mountbatten returned a quick salute, then shook hands all around. Several members of his staff nodded solemnly to the assembled Americans. A cursory inspection of the remote air base followed, with the theater commander asking questions. He appeared engaged and interested but perhaps slightly distracted.

Mountbatten had a special feeling for the group, now unofficially known as the Air Commandos, a term used by Hap Arnold because he knew the British Commandos were an object of particular pride for the admiral. The Project 9 group had also begun to call itself the Air Commandos, and they knew Mountbatten viewed them as an elite unit; because he had been in on the initial idea at Quebec in August 1943, he also had a paternal interest in their work.

Cochran's men were aware of the admiral's interest, and they looked on him as a peculiarly British character, a titled lord and potentially a benefactor, if such an animal could exist in the military hierarchy. They referred to him as Louie the Lord and were in fact a bit impressed by his bearing, his title, and his authority.[32]

Cochran himself was dressed in his usual forward-base combat uniform: a crusher cap well back on his head and a khaki field jacket; his pants were rolled up well above the ankles. He was a caricature of the laid-back American. Alison was equally informal, in his inevitable jump pants and a khaki shirt, sleeves rolled up. He seldom wore a cap and did not today. All around, men continued their frenetic work pace, mindful of their visitors but with an eye on the operational clock. They still had a great deal of work to do.

Mountbatten pulled Cochran aside. "Can we get somewhere where we can talk privately? I don't want anyone else to be with us." He looked around. "Perhaps a car?"

Cochran knew what was coming. "Sure, we'll do that. We'll get a jeep and go down to the end of the runway."

The SEAC commander nodded. "That will be good." Just a fraction of a pause. "Do you have a driver you can trust?"

The American colonel grinned and motioned to an enlisted pilot nearby. "Get the jeep, Joe, and bring it over here and come on with us." The young man nodded. He bore a striking resemblance to Cochran. "Lord Louie, this is my brother, Joe, one of our liaison pilots." Joe grinned and gave a half-salute. The admiral laughed and touched the bill of his braided cap in return.[33]

The three drove to the end of the grass runway, which now was becoming more dirt than grass as the Mustangs and Norsemen touched down repeatedly in the same area. Joe Cochran stopped the jeep on a perimeter track, climbed down, and discreetly walked about fifty feet away to inspect a runway light, leaving the two officers alone.

Mountbatten was clearly uncomfortable, and he broached the subject immediately. "I don't like this," he said. His eyes took in the airstrip and the casual figure of Joe, who now appeared to be intently inspecting the field's surface. "I have to tell you that my staff has been after me, and they have very strong and compelling arguments of why you should be brought into the formal organization and be run through the regular chain of command, the 10th Air Force command, through the tactical air part." He paused and looked at Cochran, searching his face as though trying to decipher his first reaction. Cochran, primed for the visit, put on his best poker face. He waited for the admiral to finish.

"They have many reasons that are plausible," Mountbatten continued, "and before I make up my mind, I thought it was fair that I talk to you." Cochran nodded, and Mountbatten repeated himself. "They have good reasons, and you probably are aware of some of them." Mountbatten, in the front seat, had twisted around to face Cochran in the tiny rear seat of the jeep.

Cochran, keenly cognizant that the future of Project 9 and the Air Commandos was in the balance, was walking a tightrope thin as a single thread. He had to be forceful but respectful. He needed Mountbatten on his side. If the supreme commander of the theater opposed Cochran, then the Air Commandos would just have to pack their tent and return to the States to face General Arnold. Cochran did not want to do that.

"I'm aware that there are those who think we should be assigned to a regular command," he told Mountbatten. "But those who are advising you that way are doing you a disservice." Cochran named several staff members whom he believed had the admiral's ear and had urged assimilation of the irregular force. He said the officers in question did not know the entire situation, and therefore their advice should be disregarded.

"I don't want to stop something that's a success and start another one," Cochran continued. "I will admit we bother other people, but I would think until we get through with this task, that they can put up with us, and I'll ask them to put up with us rather than change the whole doggone thing just because we are a bother. I hope you can see it that way." Cochran read Mountbatten's face. Evidently he had not yet heard a case convincing enough to silence his staff.

Just then a Mustang with two bombs beneath its wings began its take-off roll as a second P-51A revved up its engine. The two officers watched intently as the first fighter slowly gained speed, heading for their end of the runway. Both men welcomed the diversion. They watched as the pair slowly receded into the horizon beyond the trees.

"Now, I'm going to have to do something that's a little impolite," Cochran told the admiral. The faintest look of disapproval showed in the eyes of the king's cousin. Cochran went on anyway.

"When I left General Arnold, he warned me that this was going to happen to me, and I didn't understand what he was saying at the time. But now I know. He forewarned me, and he put me on my guard against this." A tiny frown had appeared on the face of Mountbatten.

Three more Air Commando units were to be formed following the present operation, Cochran explained. If he were to report to Arnold that the first unit had been dissolved, and the fighters sent one way, the light planes somewhere else, the gliders and bombers dispersed to other units, no additional Air Commando forces would be formed, of that he was certain.

"You are going to have to pardon me, but I have this letter that General Arnold gave me, and I would like for you to read number three in paragraph two." Cochran, with advance warning of Mountbatten's visit, had armed himself with the letter. He removed it from an inner pocket and handed it to Mountbatten. It was the "Dear Dickie" letter that Cochran had carried like a loaded pistol to be used against brigands and highwaymen.

The letter stressed that the Air Commandos must retain their autonomy, free from the usual chains of command and free from any interference from other units. Apparently no copy of the letter survives, but Cochran said it had four points: the Air Commandos will retain their autonomy; they will not be absorbed into any other commands; they will have a single task, that of supporting Wingate; they will operate for six months only. Mountbatten read the letter, then reread it. He looked up expectantly, clearly relieved.[34]

"Those are my orders," Cochran said, "and now you are going to have to do something pretty doggone drastic to get me to accept being dissolved." Cochran's normally smiling open face was a solemn mask.

According to Cochran, Mountbatten beamed. "You have lifted the entire thing off my back, and I am so tickled. I can go back with this and tell those guys to hell with it," the admiral declared.

The Air Commandos had survived by the narrowest of margins. The letter from Arnold to Mountbatten had turned the tide, and all talk of dissolving the unit and dispersing its assets died as quickly as it reached Mountbatten's office in New Delhi.[35]

(Above) March 1944. *Left to right*: Taylor, Scott, Alison and Calvert.

(Top right) March 1944. B25Hs at Hailikandi; note the 5 diagonal stripes of the First Air Commandos.

(Bottom right) 6 March 1944. Crashed gliders at Broadway, part of the carnage revealed the next day.

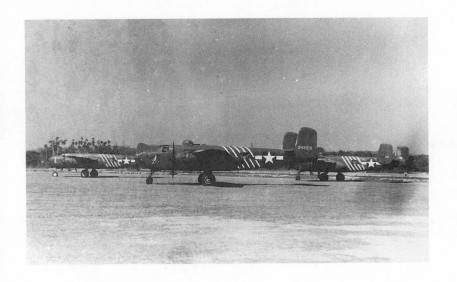

(*Above*) March 1944. Flight surgeon Cpt. Murphy, with bandaged hand, arrives at Broadway after a 14-day trek when his glider broke loose.

(*Right*) 24 March 1944. *Left to right*: Cochran, Wingate, and Radovich. This is probably the last picture taken of Wingate. Later that day he took off in a B-25 and was killed when his plane crashed.

(Above) Wingate *(standing, pointing)* reviewing a map of Burma with Alison (*right of map*) and company for Operation Thursday.

(Left) Col. Cochran, with his usual, casual mien.

(*Above*) March 1944. Calvert talks with Wingate as the general boards a C-47 for the flight to Chowringhee.

(*Right*) March 1944. Alison, Scott, and Taylor beside a glider.

(Above) Operations office at Lalaghat.

(Right) 6 March 1944. A small bulldozer begins preparing the field for the arrival of large aircraft.

(*Above*) A B-25H drops incendiaries near Mawlu.

(*Right*) Flight Officer Jackie Coogan, in charge of tow ropes, inspects the apparatus.

(Above) March 1944. Even Wingate smiled a bit at the success of THURSDAY. *Left to right*: unidentified, Alison, Calvert, unidentified, Wingate, Scott, unidentified.

(Right) Maj. Dick Cole (*left, kneeling*) with his crew.

(Above) March 1944. *Left to right*: Lt. Col. Olson and CWO Bruce Evans, who walked out of the jungle after their glider broke loose.

(Left) March 1944. Wingate & his faithful .303 army rifle, en route to Broadway.

(*Above*) March 1944. This C-47 carrying troops to Lalaghat was intercepted by an enemy plane and hit several times.

(*Top right*) 5 March 1944. Cochran, standing before two large drawings of the fields, briefs pilots before Operation Thursday.

(*Bottom right*) 10 January 1944. *Left to right*: Cochran, Mountbatten and Wingate inspect a glider.

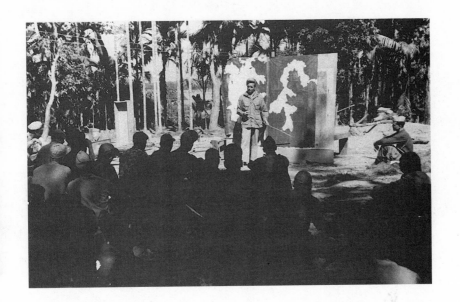

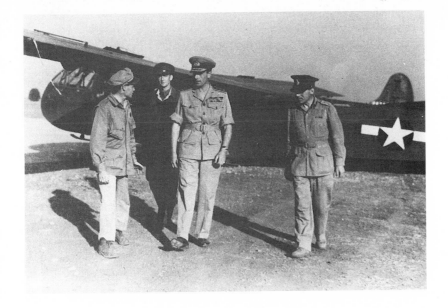

(*Above*) 10 January 1944. At dusk, Cochran (*3rd from left*) briefs C-47 and CG-4A pilots on the night exercise.

(*Top right*) March 1944. Light plane pilots erected shelters over their foxholes at Broadway.

(*Bottom right*) March 1944. Wingate and his American aide rest in the plane's mule stalls en route to Chowringhee.

(Above) 5 March 1944. TCC pilots receive their briefing at a tent complex before the invasion of Broadway.

(Right) C-47 #2100446 tows a CG-4A glider.

(*Above*) 10 January 1944. Tow rope is attached to "Gaty's Special," a CG-4A glider.

(*Top right*) 4 March 1944. Cochran points out one of the fields that will be used.

(*Top bottom*) 6 March 1944. Alison visits wounded glider pilots who have been placed in the shade for protection.

CHAPTER 12

With the political questions largely settled, at least for the moment, it was time to get the British and Commonwealth troops of Special Force together with the American flyboys and convince everyone, including the two American colonels and Wingate himself, that this somewhat madcap adventure would indeed work. But trust and teamwork would have to be developed; the divide between the Allied troops and the Yanks was far wider than the distance between London and Washington, or even the thousands of miles from the United States to Assam. More than a literal world separated the Americans from their erstwhile Allies: vast differences in background, experiences, and outlook were obvious to all. These differences were exacerbated by the complexities of language and the obvious differences in pay. By British standards the Yanks were outrageously overpaid. Worse, in the eyes of the king's men, the Americans flouted it. They always seemed to be ostentatiously flashing their money at every turn.

Part of the issue was the very real difference in how, as well as what, the governments of Britain and the United States paid their fighting men; it was not just appearance but an obvious disparity that often rankled the Brits. Coupled with the historic pay gap between officers and enlisted ranks, the differences were vast. Most Chindits were enlisted infantrymen, one of the lowest-paid specialties in the British Army, where pay was based on military specialty as well as rank. A disproportionate number of Americans in Project 9 were officers, and as pilots they received an additional allotment of 50 percent of base pay for flying duty and another 10 percent for overseas deployment.[1] Many had never made that much money before, and the effects of this sudden wealth, combined with the stress of flying and of being in a strange and potentially dangerous locale, caused some to overcompensate by spending money freely and perhaps talking a bit too much.

Cochran, Alison, and many of the section leaders of Project 9 were aware that the usually reserved British officer class thought that Americans were too often loud, blustery, and full of braggadocio, to put it kindly. On the other hand Americans often viewed the British as effete, ineffective, and unimaginative. For these troops to work together, their impressions—or deeply held convictions—would have to be overcome. Indeed at one point to promote camaraderie and good relations with Allied troops, Capt. Bill Taylor, head of the glider section, issued orders to the Americans to refrain from talking about money, Texas, or the United States.[2]

Then there was the psychological resistance to boarding a motorless aircraft piloted by these overpaid Yanks. As the assembly of gliders progressed, some were towed into the areas where the Chindits were training. Alison recalled an incident that revealed that suspicion of the Americans was still widespread early in the program.

A British officer was drilling a party of Gurkhas during a glider familiarization exercise; it was the first time the Nepalese troops had seen a glider. The young, fully kitted-out Gurkhas were practicing boarding the CG-4A quickly, with the officer timing how fast they were all in place, belted in, and gear safely stowed. The drill continued with timed disembarking with their equipment, orderly but rapidly, and this sequence was repeated numerous times until the officer was satisfied with their performance. After several evolutions of the maneuver, the Gurkhas stood down for a short rest. The consternation among the Gurkhas was obvious, and a short excited conversation ensued among them. Finally one soldier, selected by his squad as a spokesman, approached the officer who was standing nearby; offering a crisp palm-forward salute, the soldier requested permission to speak.

"Sir, I think you should be aware of something," he announced to the lieutenant. "This airplane that the Americans have brought—it has no motors!"[3]

Cochran's brash assurances to Mountbatten's staff in New Delhi that gliders could land troops and equipment, including mules, in jungle clearings had salvaged the Wingate plan. Now it was time to prove it.

A week after flight training for gliders and tows began on 29 December, plans were completed for a joint exercise, one involving American fliers, Commonwealth troops, and Indian landing fields. A clearing between Gwalior and Lalitpur, south of New Delhi, had been chosen for its resemblance to the jungle clearings that would be used in Burma. The area had mountains, hills, and forests similar to those in western and northern Burma and would present a realistic setting for the exercise.

Wingate had never given up his fondness for using mules to haul equipment through the jungles, and part of the requirement for measuring the success of the operation would be delivering mules as well as men to the glider landing fields. That requirement sent Cochran's men scurrying to devise a means of carrying the animals without fear that they would panic and kick the glider apart from inside. They consulted some British muleteers, who sagely suggested construction of stalls inside the gliders to accommodate the animals. The muleteers even offered up some plans, and Cochran's men dutifully constructed a set that could be installed in a glider with reinforced flooring. The weight, however, was excessive, and the glider men began thinking of other solutions. How about drugging the mules, something that would keep them sedated for a couple of hours? The obvious downside was how to get them out quickly, especially under fire, if the sedation had not worn off. Finally one young flier suggested the obvious: Why don't we try flying with one to see what happens? So they loaded a couple of mules aboard a glider, secured them with ropes and slings so they could not move about and disrupt the balance of the aircraft, and told an attending trooper to shoot the animals if they began to panic. During the takeoff and flight the mules were calm, quietly chewing their feed, even leaning as the glider banked, climbed, and descended. That solved that problem, but another one was that the control cables for the rudder and elevators ran along the top of the glider's cabin and were completely exposed. Afraid that the mules' ears would become entangled with the cables, the men tied the mules' ears together with strips of cloth.[4]

Wingate worked on his plans for the glider assault test maneuver. He stationed a force of his West African troops near the field as defenders; a contingent of Black Watch troops, tough Scotsmen, would ride aboard the gliders as the attacking force. When Wingate was ready, he notified Cochran, who was in New Delhi. Cochran cabled Taylor, the glider section commander, to prepare for the maneuver, but the wire was delayed. Taylor received it with just enough time to assemble twenty-four gliders in double tows and head for the main airfield at Lalitpur. When he arrived in a steady drizzle and lowering clouds, Cochran rushed up to him. Wingate had ordered the attack to begin immediately. Taylor looked at Cochran as though he had lost his mind.

"No way. We just arrived, we're all worn out from the trip, and we haven't had any briefing," Taylor declared.

Cochran relayed a request to postpone the exercise to Wingate, but the brigadier refused. Stress was part of the job; short notice would be the norm in combat. Now was the time.[5]

Thirteen soldiers of the 42nd Highland Regiment—the famed Black Watch—who had never seen the interior of a glider before, climbed aboard in high spirits, eager for the adventure. Cochran, who was not glider rated, volunteered to fly as copilot in the first pathfinder glider with Taylor, to point out the field. They took off in the rain, ducking through patches of clouds, and soon Cochran pointed out the field. Taylor released the glider and realized quickly that they were higher than they should be. He lowered the nose of the glider but then had to approach at a high speed. The Waco skimmed across the muddy field, finally stopping just short of the trees. The British soldiers jumped out and made for the safety of the jungle, as they had been taught, to secure the landing site. Cochran looked out and saw a figure coated in mud leaping across the clearing and falling several times. It was Wingate.

"Phil, you've done it!" The normally taciturn Englishman was panting, but his face was alight with enthusiasm. He and his staff had driven to the clearing to observe the test.[6]

Cochran understood at that moment the doubts that had plagued the British genius of guerrilla warfare. Keeping the Chindit idea viable despite the doubts and opposition of the planning staff was one thing. But to quietly harbor misgivings and then to witness the undeniable proof that the plan could succeed was something else. Wingate was vividly alive, drawn in by the skill of the Americans, awed by their calm self-assurance. The remaining gliders came in silently and disgorged their troops, all heavily armed, who dispersed to the edges of the field to provide protection against the resisting West African defenders. Some gliders carried heavy equipment, and a couple delivered mules. Wingate watched it all with growing enthusiasm.

The next morning proved to be equally interesting. The gliders, all twenty-three of them (one had mistakenly landed elsewhere), were stuck fast in the mud, and the ground forces had been unable to free them. Aerial snatches were arranged, and an expectant crowd formed to watch this miracle. The tugs were told by Taylor to set their reels for a heavier load to allow for the grip of the mud and to approach at a higher airspeed. Soon the waiting throng could hear the rumble of engines coming from the direction of Lalitpur and then saw a C-47 roaring low over the field. A hook snagged the glider's towline strung between two poles, and a couple of seconds later the Waco slid across the mud before rising and taking flight behind the tug. A murmur of excitement swept across the onlookers.

"When is it my turn?" Wingate turned to Cochran, a rare smile softening the brigadier's sharp features.

It was quickly arranged. The Chindit commander, along with a somewhat reluctant aide, climbed aboard the glider piloted by Taylor, with Cochran again acting as copilot. Just seconds before the tug hooked their towline, Taylor looked behind him and to his horror saw Wingate standing at the open door of the glider. He was yelling in a high shrill voice: "Tell the RAF that I have not only seen it, I have done it!" He was back and buckled in just before the snatch. Once airborne, Wingate pulled a book from his pocket and began reading. It might well have been the 8:20 to Paddington. Taylor was furious with Wingate, and Cochran had to firmly deny the pilot's request to execute some extreme maneuvers.[7]

Wingate's poking a sharp stick in the eye of the RAF, many of whose officers in India had pooh-poohed the idea of using gliders in the way envisioned by Project 9, must have been gratifying to the Americans. Cochran's Young Ladies, indeed.

The glider men had perfected the snatching of gliders, even those mired in mud, during daylight hours. But actual insertion and extraction would occur under cover of darkness, in much more demanding and stressful conditions. The Air Commandos needed to demonstrate their prowess at night, and Mountbatten came down for that one. Military protocol called for receiving him with some ceremony, so the men lined in neat ranks and files, and Cochran and Alison greeted him with their snappiest salutes. The SEAC commander dutifully walked through the lines of men, inspecting them in an offhand way, occasionally stopping to say a few words to one and then another. Mountbatten wore a khaki Royal Navy cap and a tan uniform complete with shoulder boards and ribbons. His sleeves, which he had rolled up to his elbows, were his only concession to the heat. He chatted amiably with Cochran and Alison, and then an aide whispered something in his ear. His lordship grimaced, but the aide was insistent.

"I should address your men, I suppose." Mountbatten tried not to frown as he said it.

"We would be honored, of course, sir." Cochran and Alison began looking around for a suitable dais, and the aide stepped up once more. Perhaps the hood of one of the jeeps would allow the assembled men to be able to see the admiral? Cochran ordered all aircraft to stop flying and to shut down their engines to enable the supreme commander to be heard. Mountbatten stepped up to the front bumper of the jeep and then onto the flat hood of the little utility vehicle. He held his hands awkwardly in front of him and began an impromptu address to the American and British personnel.

Cochran, in his usual khakis rolled past his ankles, tan crusher cap, and an airborne jacket, looked up intently. Next to him stood bareheaded Johnny Alison, likewise wearing the airborne uniform and sporting a Colt .22 pistol in a shoulder holster. A faint buzz caught their attention, and the American colonels looked at each other as it grew louder, distracting the audience from the inspirational words of their supreme commander. They both saw it at once: a P-51. They had forgotten that, before Mountbatten arrived, R. T. Smith had taken off in his fighter, a P-51A christened Barbie. Tadpole Smith was a consummate fighter pilot, which meant he could be impetuous and high spirited.

Smith, peering down from his cockpit at the crowd of soldiers, and seeing a uniformed figure on the hood of a jeep, deduced that Cochran was addressing the group. He couldn't resist. He pulled up, winged over, and came in low and fast, heading straight for the jeep at something more than 400 mph. He pulled up at what must have seemed only inches over the head of Mountbatten, the blast from the propeller causing the theater commander to grab his cap. Cochran, never a stickler for military protocol, was appalled by this egregious breach of protocol, not to mention basic safety and common sense.

"That damn fool just arrived, Lord Louis. He was away and didn't know you were here." What kind of court-martial would he have faced if one of his pilots had decapitated the commander of the South East Asia Command? Mountbatten was gracious but clearly angry with his aide for placing him in such a position.

"That's all right," the admiral said. "I shouldn't be talking on a flying field."[8]

When Smith landed, Cochran ordered him to the operations basha and laid into him, fiercely berating him for nearly beheading the SEAC commander. Cochran's Irish temper was in high gear, and he had an enviable vocabulary of pejoratives and expletives that seemed to breed descriptions of ineptitude never previously heard in the English language. At last he began to taper off, and Smith was finally able to offer an explanation, of sorts.

"I'm sorry, Phil. But I didn't know it was Mountbatten. Honest, I thought it was you!" With that Cochran launched into a second chapter of verbal abuse, a litany of colorful invective that left Smith standing ramrod straight and staring into the distance. Later that evening Smith was seated beside Mountbatten for dinner. The cousin of the king of

England apparently bore no ill will toward his aerial tormentor; Smith always described him thereafter as a "good egg."[9]

Mountbatten at the time was forty-three, and most of the flight crews were in their late teens and early twenties. Smith, a major and veteran fighter ace, was not yet twenty-six. The war had produced field-grade officers whose fresh young faces were jarringly discordant with the rank insignia on their epaulettes. The officers' club at a field in San Juan, Puerto Rico, displayed a sign over the bar that summed up the new reality: "No liquor will be served to Lieutenant Colonels between the ages of 18 and 21 unless accompanied by parents."[10]

That night brought new worries. The weather had turned sour; a light rain had stopped, but low clouds obscured the moon, and the Americans feared that they would not have enough light to find the clearing and bring in the gliders. Without a convincing demonstration that a night landing was possible, the entire project might still be canceled. Wingate and Mountbatten drove to the clearing a few miles away, while Cochran flew an L-5. Together they waited in the intense darkness for the sound of the tugs, the first indication that the exercise was proceeding. Right on schedule, the towplanes roared by, and then, straining in the blackness, Mountbatten, Wingate, and Cochran could see vague shapes descending onto the clearing. As if scripted in Hollywood, the first pathfinder glider came to a stop just in front of the gallery of spectators, and Black Watch soldiers silently and swiftly piled out and took up positions at the edge of the trees. The second glider carried flares, and when it too landed safely the soldiers quickly laid out a diamond of lights to identify the landing zone; a mile away another light signaled the glider release point.

Cochran, his nerves clearly on edge, sought out Taylor. "Sure you have the lights right, sport?"

Taylor was fatalistic. "If not, it's too late to do anything about it." Both looked toward the sound of additional tugs pulling the main force of gliders. In just a few minutes twenty-two gliders were safely on the field; two had suffered a towline malfunction at takeoff but had landed safely at home base.

Mountbatten was impressed and enthusiastic. He was unable to quite fathom that so many gliders had come down silently in the field in front of him, so the Americans took him on a tour, counting the gliders as they went.[11]

The landing had been nearly perfect. But they still needed to show that gliders could be snatched in the dark. Meanwhile melees had broken out between the Black Watch invaders and the West African defenders, both sides enthusiastically entering the spirit of the event as though it were an international sporting contest. Fistfights that led to black eyes and bloodied noses were common. In the end the observers declared the invading force had won and stopped the mock but serious battles.

Next the glider men set up poles and lights for the night snatches. The first tug swept in low, hooked the towline on the first pass, and pulled the glider out as though it was something they did every night. The observers, including Mountbatten, were electrified and spilled out onto the field. The Americans herded them back into the trees, and the pickups continued, each as seemingly effortless as the first. Soon excited staff officers were begging for rides out on the gliders, and an aerial shuttle was established to the field at Gwalior. Mountbatten, Cochran, Wingate, and Alison lay in the wet grass and brainstormed through the night about the upcoming campaign. Earlier plans had called for one brigade of Chindits to be taken in by air. After the night's demonstration they changed it to two; Stilwell still insisted that the third should be a ground-only operation in support of his efforts in extreme northern Burma.

It was set, then. Mountbatten was solidly on their side, and his staff officers were enthusiastic about the capabilities of the American air task force. Project 9 was getting a green light from all quarters.

At Gwalior the next morning Cochran prepared to fly out in the L-5 he had brought in to the field. Mountbatten approached him as he was doing his preflight check. Could the admiral hitch a ride? At the first stop Mountbatten explained that he was a licensed pilot, although he had not flown for several years. Might he get in a bit of stick time? What does a colonel say to a theater commander who makes such a request? Cochran climbed into the backseat, and Mountbatten sat in front.

The takeoff was awful. They ground-looped immediately and on the next attempt ran off the runway and scraped a wing. Aware that the safest place to be is off the ground, Cochran guided the admiral through the takeoff and then for the next hour and a half allowed him to herd the small plane through the air in roughly the direction of New Delhi. The landing was nearly as bad as the takeoff, and Cochran feared they were going to flip over.

A few days later Cochran received a letter of apology from Mountbatten for his sloppy flying.[12]

CHAPTER 13

Twenty-year-old Sgt. Harry McLean opened the brown cardboard package of bar chocolate from a D-rations box, removed the cellophane wrapper, and carefully shaved curls of the unsweetened survival staple into a heavy china mug. He sprinkled several spoonfuls of Klim—dried milk, spelled backward—over the chocolate shavings, then poured boiling water over the mixture, stirring it until it was smooth and the last tiny islands of undissolved dehydrated milk had sunk into the brew. Finally he added a single spoonful of carefully hoarded sugar to the mixture. GI chocolate lacked the sugar that made it palatable; it was to be eaten slowly, over a half-hour or so, and was engineered to taste like a boiled potato so soldiers wouldn't raid their ration kits and wolf down the chocolate bars.[1] Army brass had not figured on American ingenuity, however. Now McLean made his way carefully toward the cockpit of the C-47, where Col. Philip Cochran sat in the copilot's seat. Cochran, McLean had learned, was a chocoholic who craved the ersatz hot chocolate concoction that the young flight engineer could make from ingredients aboard the aircraft.

Cochran was looking through a binder of papers. A headset was pulled over his crusher cap, which, as usual, was pushed well back on his head. The young colonel looked up when McLean came through the cockpit door and grinned broadly when the engineer extended the cup of hot chocolate milk.

"You're the best, sport," he shouted over the roar of the engines. "You're the reason I always fly with you guys." The pilot looked over and smiled wryly.[2]

Commanders of Project 9 frequently shuttled between Karachi, Calcutta, Gwalior, and New Delhi to meet with the SEAC staff or coordinate with their RAF counterparts. Air travel made conferences with Mountbatten, requisitions for parts, or picking up new arrivals infinitely easier. Roads were rough, tortuous, and agonizingly slow; the railroads were better but could entail interminable delays, turning hours into days. As flight crews waited for their commanders' meetings to end or paperwork to catch up with parts or repairs to be completed, the fliers often had time to wander through the cities and take in the sights.

On a tour of the region in February, Gen. Hap Arnold had seen his own share of the sights of India. His diary entries clearly show his lack of appreciation for the culture:

> More men with diapers. . . . We are a sanitary race, we recognize athlete's foot and cholera but we can't change the Indian way of life. We need water; we hire someone to dig a well; water is reached 100 feet down. A platform is erected with a pulley, a leather or skin bag attached to a rope provides the means to haul up the water. Can we go ahead with that? Not yet. We must make a track, an inclined plane from the pulley dome at an angle of 30 degrees. Then we get two sacred bulls and a driver. The two sacred bulls are attached to the rope; now we are ready to get water. The leather bag is down in the water well. The oxen start pulling the rope. To make it easier the driver climbs aboard the rope, the leather bag reaches the platform. Now here's the secret to the whole system. An old man in diapers catches the bag and empties the water over his feet into a cement enclosure and it runs into the water system for our men to drink. I must admit in fairness that the water is chlorinated before they drink it.[3]

Many of the young Americans had never been outside their own state before joining the army; for most assignment to India was their first trip outside the United States. War was a big adventure when you weren't actually being shot at, and they took advantage of their opportunities to explore. The contrast between their home lives and the crowded, noisy, malodorous corners of Calcutta or Karachi or New Delhi could not have been greater if they had awakened and found themselves on the moon. They wandered the teeming streets, sticking together, conspicuous in their khakis and brown leather flight jackets, eager to experience the wonders of these cities with such musical names. As the fliers wandered slowly through the bazaars, their senses were constantly assailed by the rich pungent aromas of spices, the earthy smells of goats and chickens, the acrid biting smoke from small fires slowly cooking varieties of curry. Conical piles of brilliantly colored cumin, saffron, za'atar, and sumac were visual delights in open-air stalls; metal workers, sitting cross-legged on tiny stools, tapped out intricate designs on brass and silver ornaments; kilim rugs with their geometric designs were piled on sidewalks to entice passersby. Men in white turbans tied loosely around their heads clutched the Americans' arms: "Please, Sahib. Many good things here." The nauseating stench of human waste blasted the young fliers' senses as they walked by certain alleyways in the maize-like shopping districts. They would stop to watch a dancing bear wearing a necklace of brass bells, while a young boy beseeched them for rupees. As he sat on a colorful woven mat, a dark-skinned man in a red turban blew into a pungi, a strange flute-like instrument fashioned from a gourd, and from a basket in front of him slowly rose a cobra, its hood flared. The viper swayed hypnotically, seemingly in tune with the haunting melody escaping from the flute; yet another cadre of boys worked the crowd, seeking to charge admission to this thrilling sight and emphasizing the danger to the snake charmer. Once one of the keen-eyed flyboys noted that the cobra's mouth seemed to have been sewn shut, and he asked if the snake had been drugged. The boy seemed genuinely shocked by the suggestion. The wide-eyed Yanks moved on.

Further down the market street, the Americans stopped to inquire about some heavy wickedly curved kukris, the machete-sized knives of the Gurkhas that were capable of beheading a dog—or a human—with a single blow.

Equipped with their language booklets, the Americans felt confident as they bargained in Hindi like tourists.

"Namaste," they began. "Ye kitne ka hai?" A young pilot hefted one of the larger kukris, pulling it from its leather-covered wooden sheath. The shop owner grinned a gap-toothed greeting.

"Namaste, sirs." The single word exhausted his command of English. Without further discussion, he named a price.

The American fliers leafed through their booklets. "Iska kya daam hai?" They said, feigning incredulity. The awkward negotiation went on for several minutes, with a final price one-fourth of that originally quoted and apparently breaking the heart of the merchant. He sold two of the native-produced knives, painstakingly hand-filed from old truck springs, and considered his day a success. The pilots left happy, looking forward to posing fiercely for photographs to send home.

A couple of minutes later they were drawn toward an open-air leather shop, where a thin ragged man operated a foot-powered sewing machine and painstakingly turned out layered-leather China-Burma-India patches, perfect for their horsehide flying jackets. They promised to return with a drawing of their unit patch as well, and the man grinned toothlessly and bowed repeatedly as he gave them his business card. The next stop was a photography studio; photos were a perfect souvenir to send to family and friends back home. Sometimes the young men hammed it up, seeking perhaps by their flippancy and clowning to ease the fears of parents. A frequently reproduced photo of a trio of glider pilots—flight officers Sam Altman, Frank Randall, and Troy Shaw—shows them in their decorated flight jackets, clowning for the camera with their hats turned sideways, large cigars clamped in their teeth.[4]

They made their way through the crowded street, stepping to the side as a man pushing a rickety wheelbarrow slowly plowed his way through the mob. As he passed, the fliers glanced idly into the cart to see what he was carrying, then looked at each other in horrified silence, unable to speak. The man, afflicted with elephantiasis, ignored them as he continued on his way, pushing his ham-sized genitals before him. A few minutes later thick sweet smoke wafted through the street as they approached a crowd near a pile of sticks and tree limbs, where flames crackled and licked their way upward. The crowd was wailing; after several minutes of silent wondering, the fliers spotted a ragged bundle in the fire and only then realized that the bonfire was in fact a cremation. They quickly and silently departed.

Everywhere, it seemed, were beggars, thin and wretched old men, women, and, worst of all, children, who held out their hands in silent despair. A blind man, sitting on a pile of rags, stretched his emaciated limbs and blessed them; his irises were milky white. At one point, where the crowd had thinned and they walked several abreast, they were startled by what they first thought to be someone rushing them from behind. All turned at once to face their attacker: a dark-skinned man with powerful shoulders and arms was propelling himself along the sidewalk, using the stumps of his legs only to balance before launching himself on his hands once more. He stopped when they did. The Americans pooled their remaining cash and were able to come up with a pair of two-rupee notes, small paper bills half the size of American dollars. The legless man smiled and, standing on his useless stubs of legs, placed his hands together and bowed. Unprepared for such overt poverty, the Americans were helpless. They were besieged by a small army of waifs screeching for more, their small open hands accusing in their emptiness. The young fliers, ashamed, held up their own empty hands and lifted their shoulders. They headed back to the airfield.[5]

The leaders of Project 9 recognized the importance of creating a sense of team, of showing the world that their men belonged to an elite organization. Cochran had written to Milton Caniff, the artist who drew the *Terry and the Pirates* comic strip, asking him if he could design a patch for the glider group. Caniff sent a drawing of a patch that was to become one of the most colorful and recognizable insignia of the war: A mule's head, with a Gurkha kukri in its mouth and a pair of wings behind its ears, was superimposed on a *G* (for glider) with a *1* prominently in the center. The numeral was unmistakeably the naked torso of a brown-skinned woman in profile, amply endowed. By now the men were openly calling themselves the 1st Air Commandos, and the patch, although still unofficial, began showing up on the fronts of leather flight jackets, along with CBI insignia on the sleeves and American flags on the back. Most patches were carefully stitched in pieces of leather by enterprising craftsmen in the area, and the jackets became prized possessions and great souvenirs. When Cochran showed the design to Wingate, the Chindit leader was so taken with it that he wanted to make it the official badge of the entire Anglo-American team.[6]

The fighter section designed its own badge, as well. A black horse, bearing five white stripes, sported white wings under which were slung red bombs. A red rocket tube was strapped to the side of the horse, and the entire figure was superimposed on a red *1*. The C-47 section had been the first to display a distinctive insignia, the question mark symbol they had painted on their aircraft following the numerous queries about their modified cargo ships on the long flight to India. Many tug pilots still wore a white leather patch with a dark blue question mark on their leather jackets.[7] Leather name tags with the flier's name in English and several native languages were also popular flight jacket accoutrements.

But the time for exploring and shopping for souvenirs was brief. Everyone understood the pressing need to be ready in a matter of weeks. A veritable mountain of physical work and training stood between the Air Commandos and readiness for the coming historic mission.

Among the glider pilots was Flight Officer John Leslie Coogan, better known to most as Jackie Coogan, who in the 1920s and '30s had been a mop-headed angel-faced child actor starring in more than twenty Hollywood movies. The son of vaudevillian performers, he had caught the eye of Charlie Chaplin, and Coogan's first big role was as Chaplin's little sidekick in *The Kid* (1921). Now twenty-nine Coogan was a broad-shouldered, balding, and brash military glider pilot who often regaled other pilots with tales of sex with starlets. He had been married for less than two years to Betty Grable, the iconic GI pinup girl, and he sometimes startled newcomers with a handshake and a vulgar greeting. Many considered his loud comments about the various starlets in the films shown in the evenings to be crude; they did not appreciate his constant bragging about his sexual prowess with some of the biggest names in Hollywood.[8]

Sgt. Patt Meara had volunteered for the Air Commandos from a service unit in India, and would be a replacement aerial gunner and all-around heavy hefter. Meara met Coogan while both were unloading a cargo plane, introduced by a mutual friend. The sergeant stuck out his hand to the flight officer instead of saluting; handshakes predominated over the more class-conscious salute during the Air Commandos' stint in India.

"Congratulations, you have just shaken the hand that holds the penis that effed Betty Grable," Coogan boomed, laughing loudly. Meara, as he recalled, stared in awe at his hand, vowing to never wash it.

As he had grown out of his preadolescent cuteness, Coogan had encountered hard times. His parents had squandered the several million dollars he had earned. He sued them but managed to recover only about $125,000. The pillaged account had caused a national scandal and had resulted in a California law—the Coogan Act—that required a percentage of the earnings of child actors be placed in a trust. It also established working hours and school requirements. But Coogan found that doors of movie moguls that had once opened to him as if by magic were largely closed now; his last movie—with Betty Grable—was released in 1939.

As he told it, he had gotten into flight training almost by accident. Knowing the United States would be at war eventually, he had joined the army in March 1940, assigned as a private to the medical corps despite having a private pilot's license. After Pearl Harbor he had applied for a transfer to the Army Air Forces but never heard anything. While on leave, he stayed at a motel near Palm Springs and heard a commotion at the pool. Investigating, he discovered an older man being loudly castigated by a younger guy who was wearing an obviously expensive tailored suit. Coogan said something, the younger guy said something back, and the muscular Coogan threw him into the pool, suit and all. The older gentleman turned out to be Gen. Ralph P. Cousins, commander of the West Coast AAF Training Command, who was then recruiting for the fledgling glider corps. Coogan applied, completed flight training, and then volunteered for Project 9. There he made a name for himself, both for flying into jungle clearings behind enemy lines and for a pronounced proclivity for pranks.[9]

At Lalaghat construction continued while gliders and tugs made continuous takeoffs and landings. As the gliders landed, the pilots waited until a truck was available to pull the powerless aircraft back to the runway takeoff position or, if it was the final flight of the day, a revetment. The wait could be several minutes or much, much longer on a busy day. Coogan landed his glider one day and waited impatiently for the truck to appear. It was hot, well over a hundred degrees. Coogan, who could be impetuous, spotted an elephant nearby that was being used as a heavy construction vehicle. Instead of waiting for the truck, Coogan reasoned that the pachyderm could pull his heavy glider to the staging area. What could go wrong?

Coogan convinced the mahout, the elephant handler, to bring his mount over to the glider, and in short order they had tied a towrope from the nose of the Waco to a harness rigged around the elephant. Coogan entered the cockpit, to be able to brake and control the glider during the tow, and at first it worked like a dream. Coogan would be first done for the day, and a new page in glider towing would be written for posterity. Alas, the elephant had been trained to lift and to push but never had been used to pull anything. It was nervous, for something was following it, and it increased its gait. The pachyderm's eyes were wide and fearful as it looked behind. Something large and menacing was following it close behind, so it went faster yet. Soon the panic-stricken elephant was trumpeting his terror and galloping toward a line of trees at the end of the field, impervious to the commands of the mahout, now holding on for his life. Coogan watched in horror as the trees grew closer and the elephant's speed grew faster. Braking was no help at all.

It ended badly. The elephant, seeking the protection of the forest, charged between two large trees, breaking the towline but also shearing off both wings. The glider was a total write-off. Cochran was unhappy with Coogan but took no action against him.[10]

The movie-star-turned-glider-pilot irritated many of the other pilots. Most resented his crude comments about Hollywood pinup gals, and at least one pilot—Charles Turner—did not appreciate being hit up for loans that Coogan seemed never to repay. But they agreed that Coogan was a good pilot with an ample supply of courage.[11]

For all the Air Commandos the unending, back-breaking work was not the worst of it. Both bases—Hailakandi and Lalaghat—were miasmic swampy areas that were among the few areas flat enough for airfields. If their proximity to Burma had not been so important, other fields might have been better. But the location was prime and had been the first consideration. However, malaria was endemic and the Air Commandos began dropping from the illness. Normally five to ten days in a hospital and the right medicine—quinine, now in short supply, or the synthetic alternative, Atabrine—would allow the patient to emerge from sick bay and return to work. Atabrine tablets were distributed to all the American troops in India and Burma, as well as the Pacific islands, but they were extremely bitter, and they tended to turn skin and eyes yellow. Troops hated them, and medical types were in a constant battle to get the troops to take the medication daily. Many did not take the tablets at all and suffered no ill effects. Dick Cole was representative of this group; religious in using his mosquito netting at night, he never took Atabrine and suffered no bouts of illness.[12]

Not all were so lucky. Maj. Robert Page, the flight surgeon and chief medical officer who had placed his name first on the volunteers list back at the Pentagon, recorded that the light plane pilots, sleeping in tents in miserable conditions, were among the most severely afflicted. One case, involving an enlisted pilot, proved fatal. The man reported to Sick Inn with a temperature of 105. He was quickly admitted and given a dose of quinine. His temperature dropped to 102 and remained so for the next twenty-four hours. However, the following afternoon it shot back up, and additional medications were administered. On the fourth day the man leaped from his bed, shouting incoherently; he was restrained, and morphine was given him as well as quinine. Early the next morning he again became agitated, shouting and babbling. His breathing became labored, and he was given oxygen. He died at 8 in the morning. An autopsy revealed that he had contracted malaria of the brain, causing widespread hemorrhaging.[13]

Page noted that 18 percent of light plane pilots in the Air Commandos had contracted malaria and that an engineering outfit on temporary assignment to the unit had suffered an 85 percent rate the previous malarial season. He pointed out in his report that the malarial season was June to September and that the Air Commandos could expect much higher rates of the disease if they did not take immediate precautions.[14]

Flying accidents, despite or perhaps because of the intense training schedule, continued to take a toll on aircraft and pilots. But a tragic crash that involved British Chindits who were now training with the Air Commandos could have threatened the goodwill that had been so carefully built up. The Brits had eventually become fans of the cheerful and tireless Yanks, largely because of the skill with which they flew the tugs and gliders that were to take the first wave of Chindits into Burma; the Americans were equally taken with the tough guerrilla fighters who were to operate on the ground far behind enemy lines. On 15 February, during a night training flight featuring double towed gliders, it finally happened. That midair collisions had not occurred before was both a testament to the skills of the glider pilots and to remarkable good fortune.

That night their luck ran out. The double tow was always a tricky maneuver, requiring precise control inputs and a keen awareness of distance between the towed gliders. It was imperative that the Waco on long tow not override the line and approach the glider on short tow. Seventy-five feet sounds like a comfortable distance to be apart, but at night it was extremely difficult to judge when the aft glider was creeping up on the short-tow Waco. Lt. Kenneth Wells's glider eased up and clipped the glider flown by Lt. Donald Seese. Seese and his copilot, Flight Officer Troy Shaw, struggled to get the glider down safely despite severe damage to one wing. Wells was unable to recover; his glider crashed straight into the ground. Wells, Flight Officer Bishop Parrott, and Pfc. Robert Kinney were killed, as were four British troops, part of Dah Force under Lt. Col. D. C. "Fish" Herring's command.[15] Cochran sent condolences to Herring and his men, fearful that the fatal crash would adversely affect the relationship between the two groups. Trust and a close working atmosphere were vital to the success of the upcoming mission.

The next day Herring sent Cochran and the Air Commandos the following note: "Please be assured that we will go with your boys any place, any time, anywhere." The note was posted on a bulletin board in the operations basha. The gracious communication not only reaffirmed the faith of the Brits in the American fliers, it furnished the motto for the Air Commandos: Any place, any time, anywhere.[16]

CHAPTER 14

The time for the assault was growing closer, and the fighters, bomb-ers, and light planes already were flying combat missions. On 3 Febru-ary Cochran led a flight of five P-51s on a sweep into Burma. It was more a familiarization flight than a combat mission, but they were in-deed over Japanese-held territory for the first time. It gave the pilots an idea of the terrain and of potential targets, and it inspired some con-versations about improvising new tactics. While bridges, trains, trucks, and the like were always targets of opportunity, Cochran and his com-mandos were also devising new ways to disrupt the Japanese lines of communication. Someone—Maj. Olin Carter believed it was Cochran himself—suggested attaching a heavy weight to a substantial cable to tear out telephone lines.[1]

Cpl. James Eckert, a young aircraft welder who had been "volun-told" to the Air Commandos after arriving in India in December, had been assigned to Hailakandi. At first he found not much work for his skills, but in January he was tapped to help construct the new weapon that Cochran envisioned. Eckert sat in with several pilots and maintenance officers to design the new device, then was sent to Calcutta aboard a UC-64 to secure the material they needed. He spent the night with his old outfit, then headed back the next day to Hailakandi. A major storm bounced the '64 around the sky for three and a half hours, and when he landed Eckert was woozy. He knew there was a reason he had not volunteered for flying duty.

Eckert and the enlisted men in the welding shop fabricated a device that attached to the bomb racks of a P-51: they wound a 300-foot steel cable between the two racks on the left and right wings and fitted a third hard point to the bottom of the fuselage aft of the wings and attached a heavy steel weight to it. When the pilot hit a button installed in the cockpit, a solenoid would open and the weight would drop, pulling the steel cable with it. Maj. Bob Petit took off one morning to test the device; in a few hours he was back and flew over the airfield to drop the cable. It got hung up, and he made six passes over the field before the cable and weight would release. Eckert and his buddies worked on the release mechanism until they perfected it, and Petit once more made a trip into Burma, flying at near treetop level from west to east, ripping out telephone lines and disrupting Japanese lines of communication to the central and northern regions of the country. When he landed, he had tree branches stuck in his wings.[2]

Maj. Olin Carter, an Air Commando fighter pilot, later described a new technique for bombing bridges that he said Cochran also developed: "We'd come in low, and just over the bridge we'd climb to lose airspeed, do a wing-over, and come down absolutely vertical, releasing the bomb very, very low. The 1,000-pound high explosive bombs had a 120-degree cone of debris, so you'd get hit unless you were quite low. Then we'd haul out of there just over the trees. We could put two 1,000-pound bombs inside a 40-foot circle every time."[3]

The gliders also experienced combat before the planned assault. On 28 February Maj. William Cherry, commander of the cargo section, was towing a Waco flown by Flight Officers John H. Price Jr. and John E. Gotham. They were carrying a small patrol of British troops. Bad weather forced Cherry to fly east of the Chindwin, well inside Burma, and when the weather continued to disintegrate Price released the glider and attempted to land on a sandbar in the river, near Mindin. The glider was severely damaged, and Price was badly injured. Cherry returned the next day, hoping to snatch the glider off the sandbar, but it was too damaged to fly. The men burned the glider and set out on foot to walk the 130 miles back to India; along the way they bumped into two Japanese soldiers, whom they killed, and floated several miles down the Chindwin in a native boat. After two weeks they made it back to India.[4]

Part of the complicated plan for the Chindit incursion called for one brigade, under Brigadier Bernard Fergusson of the Black Watch regiment, to enter Burma on foot, leaving from Ledo in the far north of Assam ahead of the airborne brigades. His task would be to capture and hold the two airfields near Indaw and await arrival of additional British troops to exploit the situation.[5] Fergusson, an erudite Scotsman with a monocle who would write several books after the war, traveled by light plane to Ledo numerous times to meet with Gen. Joe Stilwell. They agreed that Stilwell would arrange for Fergusson's Chindit column to use a portion of the Ledo Road to begin its incursion; in return Stilwell wanted the Chindits to capture the town of Lonkin, an action that would seriously disrupt communications of the Japanese 18th Division, Stilwell's main adversary.

In a later account of their first meeting, Fergusson wrote that he feared that his monocle and waxed mustache might put off the American general. Vinegar Joe, who could look as sour as ever a human could, peered at the British officer as though pained by what he saw. He explained what he wanted, using a map as a visual aid and stabbing at the town of Lonkin with his finger. Finally he asked Fergusson what he thought of the plan. The brigadier replied that he liked it very much indeed and thought he could do everything Stilwell wanted.

"I like the sound of that," Stilwell replied. He said he would write a letter to Gen. Haydon L. Boatner, his chief of staff, telling him to start the plan in motion and to support Fergusson and his troops. A year later Fergusson learned how Stilwell had worded the letter. It was typical Vinegar Joe: "Help this guy. He looks like a dude, but I think he's a soldier."[6]

Fergusson's column headed out in early February, helped in the early stages by Stilwell's forces along the Ledo Road. By 29 February the column was at the Chindwin River, where the swiftly flowing water was proving difficult to cross. Fergusson radioed for boats. In a few hours two Dakotas flew low over the troops, each towing a Waco glider. Fergusson watched, entranced by the scene, as the first glider descended, "broadwinged and silent as a hovering albatross."[7] It seemed to float motionless, then appeared to pick up speed before touching down in a cloud of dust. Men quickly dragged it out of the way, and the second glider landed. Men lifted the gliders' noses and swiftly unloaded the cargo: inflatable rubber boats, along with paddles, long poles, and small outboard engines and fuel. That night Fergusson's force began crossing the river.[8]

Flight officers J. S. "Mickey" Bartlett and Vernon "Needlenose" Noland had flown the two gliders. The second glider was damaged in the landing and could not be snatched that evening. Bartlett and Noland set up the poles and extended the line for the aerial snatch of the undamaged glider, and they heard Dakotas approaching as they waited in the cockpit for the familiar g-force push into their seat backs. Instead they listened in horror as heavy objects thudded and pounded across the glider. No one had told them another base had scheduled an airdrop of supplies, and many bundles landed squarely on their Waco. But the glider was undamaged, and later they were successfully snatched from the sandbar by a specially equipped Dakota.[9]

The pilots of the light planes had also been testing the combat waters. In February the section had been further divided into four units; A went to Ledo to support Fergusson's 16th Brigade; B went to Taro in northern Burma to provide direct support to General Stilwell; C went to Tamu, also in northern Burma, to prepare for Wingate's invasion; and D, a contingent of just ten light planes, was sent on temporary duty to support the advance into Arakan in southwestern Burma, another element of the plan to take Burma from the Japanese. This was where the concept of using light planes on front lines—and beyond—was first tested. Few could have foreseen the outcome.[10]

Arakan was a potential disaster for the Allies. British and American forces, joined by Chinese, Indian, West African, and loyal Burmese units, were on the offensive in various parts of Burma, but the Japanese forces were neither idle nor complacent. They had carefully planned major thrusts to neuter or conquer India and knock China out of the war. The calendar was very much on their minds as well: Japanese commanders knew full well what the monsoon season would mean to ground operations. So while the Air Commandos and Wingate's Chindits were eyeing the first week of March as an optimal time to launch their invasion, Japanese leaders were actively engaged in their own operations. The Japanese landed the first punch.

British commanders in India were convinced that a major Japanese advance into that country was only a matter of time. Field Marshal William Slim had carefully built up his army after its shattering defeat and retreat from Burma in 1942 and regarded Arakan as the ideal area from which to begin retaking Burma to ease the threat to India and China. The state of Arakan was in the extreme southwest of Burma, an area far beyond where the Air Commandos were planning action, but it turned out to be the region of first combat for the American group. Slim's intelligence officers were able to confirm that a substantial buildup of Japanese forces was occurring in Arakan; its long coastline ensured easy transport of troops denied them by the tangled jungle and steep hills of the interior. At the end of November 1943 Slim's forces advanced into Arakan from their positions south of Chittagong in far southeastern India. Japanese resistance was fierce; they had built fortresses overlooking the only road in the area and were dug into underground spaces as much as thirty feet deep.

At a position near the Ngakyedauk Pass road, the advancing British took advantage of a broad valley to establish a maintenance and supply area, known in the parlance of the army as the administrative box. In a region with exotic musical names, the prosaic label stands out. But it would become famous as one of the most important battles on the Burma front.

The Japanese counterattack was part of a much larger strategic operation, as it turned out, but the Battle of the Admin Box would go down as one of the bloodiest, nastiest battles in a bloody nasty theater of war. For two months the attacking British units, including the 5th and 7th Indian Divisions and the 81st West African Division, slugged it out in fierce close combat with the Japanese defenders. Despite the eventual importance of defeating the Japanese throughout Asia and the Pacific, many Allied units had been recalled from the theater and sent to Europe as part of the buildup for the cross-Channel invasion of France. Meanwhile the Japanese had been transferring units to Burma in preparation for their planned breakout into India and China.

About the middle of January 1944, after six weeks of hard fighting, Field Marshal Slim embarked on a tour of the Arakan region, hopping from unit to unit by air. There he witnessed one of the heartbreaking ironies of war, death by friendly fire. Hurricane fighters were in the air to escort the field marshal's plane, and they orbited over the base to provide protection against enemy aircraft. One young pilot inexplicably fired upon his best friend ahead of him, sending the fighter plunging to Earth and killing the pilot.[11]

Two weeks later the Japanese launched their counterattack in force. The weak point in the British lines was the administrative box, plump with fuel and ammunition in a shallow valley easily dominated from the surrounding hills. Hand-to-hand fighting ensued, and the Japanese attacked in wave after wave. But the British, Indian, and Gurkha troops refused to withdraw, and hundreds on both sides were killed. At one point the wound dressing station of the 7th Indian Division was overrun just as doctors and staff were preparing for surgeries. Two days later Japanese brass arrived and ordered the prisoners killed. Six doctors were lined up and shot through their ears; all the wounded were bayoneted. Indian orderlies were forced to carry litters with wounded Japanese back to their lines and were then shot as well. When word of the massacre reached other British troops in the area, it only steeled their resolve not to be taken prisoner. What had been fierce fighting became maniacal combat.[12]

By early February Japanese forces had surrounded and cut off the British force. A contingent of Air Commando L-5s was sent to the region as the fighting intensified, and they now began to show what the small aircraft could accomplish. Japanese aerial forces had been part of the buildup; Slim reported seeing Japanese formations of more than a hundred fighters and bombers. But the stalwart American sergeant-pilots ignored the enemy fighters patrolling the area and flew countless treetop missions into the region to evacuate wounded Allied troops. Between 10 February and 6 March these fliers airlifted more than 700 sick and wounded from the front lines to a field named Reindeer, near Ramu, that was large enough to accommodate C-47 hospital ships. None of the small planes was shot down. Some pilots flew more than seventy sorties in support of the operation, often flying six or more sorties a day. A report from the Joint Intelligence Collecting Agency at the time was effusive in its praise for these pilots: "The exploits of this group of light plane pilots, commanded by a Sergeant, in rescuing wounded within gunshot of Japanese positions and flying them at tree-top level under the noses of Japanese aircraft then active in that area were such Air Marshal Baldwin, KHB, DSO, commander of the 3rd Tactical Air Force, paid them a personal visit of congratulation."[13]

Brigadier General Old led a squadron of cargo aircraft to drop much-needed supplies to the beleaguered and encircled Commonwealth troops. The weather was stormy, and other planes had turned back, but Old knew that the ammunition and supplies he carried were crucial to the survival of the soldiers below. He plowed through the weather, located the isolated British troops, and dropped the ammo and gear directly on top of their position. He received the Silver Star for this mission; the Allied troops eventually fought their way out and turned what seemed like a certain Japanese victory into a stinging defeat. Writing of the mission a few months later, RAF Squadron Leader H. B. Dickson was full of praise for the effort. He quoted an unnamed officer on Old's staff: "'Troop Carrier Command's operations over Burma have proved conclusively that with air superiority there is no such thing as encirclement.'"[14] In the end the Allied forces pinned a punishing defeat on the Japanese. Slim called it "the turning point of the Burma campaign."[15]

Meanwhile the Air Commandos and the Chindits continued with a rigorous training regimen and aerial combat missions. They were occasionally able to make their own breaks in the grueling routine. Sgt. Eugene Piester, whose recruiting officer at Goldsboro had asked what he would do if he were attacked by Japanese while working on an airplane, became a P-51 crew chief. His pilot was Maj. Olin B. Carter, a former P-38 instructor pilot in San Diego who would fly eighty-two missions in Burma.[16]

The P-51s were kept fueled and armed, ready for combat at a minute's notice. Each morning, in preparation for any mission of opportunity into Burma—where the fighter guys prowled the rivers searching for Japanese barges, as well as the occasional railroad train or highway bridge—a lone P-51 would take off at first light to scout the weather over the intended targets. Fog frequently hid the rivers and valleys from the eyes of the pilots, and the weather scout pilot reported conditions that he encountered. The mission depended upon the lone scout's radioed report.

One morning the pilots and crew chiefs were waiting to hear from the weather plane when the word came: ground totally obscured by fog. No mission this morning. Carter walked over to Sergeant Piester and nodded toward his P-51, christened Little Kitten.

"Gene, you think we could both fit in that cockpit?" Piester knew the fighter pilot had in mind a bit of entertainment, and he grinned.

"We could try."

The pair walked to the Mustang and climbed up the wing next to the cockpit. Carter reached down into the cockpit and pulled out his parachute, which formed the seat cushion for the pilot. A bare metal seat was all that remained. Carter threw the parachute onto the grass beside the fighter and motioned for Piester to get in. The crew chief sat as far back in the seat as he could, and Carter followed, sitting between Piester's outspread legs. He pulled back the control stick, moved it from side to side, and said he thought they had enough room. The pair passed the lap belt around both and cinched it tight. Carter started the engine, and Piester suddenly remembered the armament.

"Hold on. We have a 500-pound bomb under each wing!"

Carter reached for the bomb salvo lever and dropped both bombs on the grass below their wings. He advanced the throttle, and Piester was pushed back into the seat. In seconds, it seemed, they were airborne. For several minutes Carter cruised the area around the field at Hailakandi, with Piester straining to see over the edge of the canopy. Suddenly another P-51 swooped down on them, then rocketed away in a climbing right turn. Lt. Joe Setnor had been test-hopping his own P-51 after some repair work. He recognized Carter's plane and could not resist bouncing him. For the next twenty minutes or so the two Mustangs rolled and twisted through the sky above Assam, the pilots trying to outmaneuver each other for bragging rights later. Piester, still unable to see out to the sides, looked up through the top of the canopy. All he could see was jungle where the sky should have been. At last he yelled to Carter that it was probably time to land.

They did, and a slightly dizzy crew chief then set to work refueling Little Kitten and reattaching the two 500-pound bombs that rested peacefully in the grass.[17]

As March neared, everyone knew the invasion was only days away. There would be little time for fun after that.

CHAPTER 15

On Valentine's Day 1944 the Japanese made the Air Commandos pay for their forays into Burma, strikes that until now had gone largely unanswered. The fighter and bomber missions begun on 3 February against the famed military might of the Rising Sun had proved something like a one-sided boxing match, with U.S. warriors scoring points against a lethargic unresponsive opponent. But the mission on this day almost two weeks later, against a supply depot on the northern edge of Mandalay on a bend of the Irrawaddy, would engender bitterness among the fighter pilots, call Cochran's leadership into question, and threaten the morale and can-do spirit of the Air Commandos.

Operations by the fighter section, headed by Grant Mahony, had started with panache and the invincible cocky attitude that is vital to fighter pilots everywhere. Mahony himself was a seasoned veteran, a handsome dark-haired Irishman with a reputation for deep and abiding hatred of the Japanese. A 1939 graduate of the University of California, Berkeley, with a degree in forestry, Mahony joined the Army Air Corps immediately after commencement and trained at Kelly Field in San Antonio. As a young lieutenant in the Philippines, he was awarded the Distinguished Service Cross on the recommendation of Gen. Douglas MacArthur following a hazardous night reconnaissance flight in bad weather; the information he provided led to a highly successful bombing raid the next day. The following week two enemy fighters jumped him; his guns jammed, and he dived to escape. The Japanese pursued him, and he was aware that they were firing wildly and into a concentration of their own troops. He had the presence of mind to climb and dive again in the same location, again noting that the fighters were firing into their own positions.[1]

In 1942 he became commander of the 76th Fighter Squadron, 23rd Fighter Group, 14th Air Force, a successor to the American Volunteer Group, or the Flying Tigers. He was named to Project 9 in November 1943 and immediately put in charge of the fighter section.

On 13 February Cochran received an intelligence report that indicated a large Japanese supply depot was situated just north of Mandalay, on a bend of the Irrawaddy River. The Japanese were using metal-roofed warehouses as staging points for military materiel in northern Burma, near the Laudaung Railroad Station. Could the Air Commandos take them out?

Cochran, frustrated with the China-Burma-India theater and admittedly still a bit unhappy about not leading a fighter group in Europe, committed his fighter force to attack the target; moreover he would lead it. This decision, as it turned out, was the first of several with disastrous consequences.

It was a clear day, forecast to be the same over the target. Cochran briefed his pilots and displayed some recon photos of the area, emphasizing the bend in the Irrawaddy as an identifier. The warehouses to be hit were part of a larger complex of metal-roofed buildings; the exact targets would be difficult to pick out.

At 0820 thirteen P-51A Mustangs took off in pairs from Hailakandi; each fighter carried two 500-pound high-explosive bombs and full racks of .50-caliber ammunition for the four Browning M-2 machine guns mounted in the wings. They would observe radio silence until over the target. The Mustangs, all bearing the five white diagonal stripes of the Air Commandos, arrived over Mandalay in about an hour and quickly located the area of the target.[2]

And then Cochran made the most egregious tactical error of the day: he was looking down at the target, not up. He had failed to specifically assign a high cover for the attack. The Air Commandos would pay for that oversight.

Peering at the densely packed buildings in the area of the river bend, and trying to match what he saw with the intelligence photos, Cochran finally identified what he thought was the large storage depot in a cluster of similar buildings.

"All right, I've got the target spotted," he radioed to the other pilots. "I'm going down to mark it; if anyone sees something else they believe is the target, then we'll talk it over and decide which is which." He pushed forward on the stick and began a dive on the buildings below. He pulled the bomb salvo lever and his two 500-pound bombs tumbled from their hard points under the wings as he pulled back hard and increased power to climb. Other pilots, apparently all watching the ground, radioed that they were certain that Cochran had the right target.[3]

From the south came a flight of ten Hayabusas, the Nakajima Peregrine Falcons that the Americans dubbed the Oscars. The Japanese pilots had been keenly searching for American raiders. For two days now the 50th Sentai had patrolled the railroad line between Indaw and Kawlin to guard against the depredations of the 1st Air Commando Group that had suddenly and recently appeared from the west. Today the Japanese fliers undoubtedly felt they had been handed a gift: a formation of American fighters circling over northern Mandalay with no top cover; as the Japanese formation approached, the Americans gave no sign that they had seen the Japanese fighters. They drew closer, and still the Americans did not react. The formation of Hayabusas maneuvered so they could drop on the invaders out of the sun, the classic tactic for engaging enemy aircraft. Warrant Officer Isamu Sasaki watched the flight leader, and when he started down, Sasaki pushed his stick forward and felt the lightness of his body and the grip of his safety belt as it pulled into him. He concentrated on positioning himself on a single American fighter. He had learned through many aerial clashes that focusing on one aircraft was the secret to success; merely heading downward into a formation was not going to bring down any enemy planes. Sasaki was a gifted and fierce fighter pilot who would finish the war with thirty-eight victories. He had been with the 50th Sentai since the taking of Rangoon. Later, when the B-29s began their bombing campaign, he would shoot down six of them, three in a single mission.

A Mustang was in his gunsight, and Sasaki pressed the trigger. Behind him Warrant Officer Yojiro Ohbusa did the same thing. Ohbusa was also a Japanese ace and would finish the war with nineteen aerial victories. Both Sasaki and Ohbusa (whose name is sometimes spelled Ofusa) would be awarded the Bukosho, equivalent to the American Medal of Honor, for their fierce attacks against B-29s over the Japanese homeland.[3]

In a matter of seconds a Mustang flown by Capt. Donald V. "Red" Miller was on fire, and another flown by 1st Lt. Carl Hartzer Jr. exploded. Both men were from the group of nine recruited from the 50th Fighter Group in Orlando. Neither Sasaki nor Ohbusa knew the names of the men they shot down that day, but each was credited with a victory. As was common on both sides, excitement and confusion masked the actual damage inflicted: the victorious Japanese pilots reported downing eight Americans in that engagement, while the Americans later claimed three Oscars damaged.

Hartzer apparently was killed immediately. Miller was able to bail out of his stricken Mustang but was captured by the Japanese and imprisoned in Rangoon. He was married, with a young son. Mary Miller received the usual terse telegram, the visit from Western Union that so many had learned to fear during the war. It was not encouraging: "The Secretary of War desires me to express his deep regret that your husband Captain Donald V. Miller has been reported missing in action since fourteen February over Burma. If further details are received you will be promptly notified."[4]

A few weeks later Miller's father, F. E. Miller, received a letter at his home in Menominee, Wisconsin, from Grant Mahony. It was a bit more upbeat and included some details of the combat. The mission, Mahony said, had been "extremely important," and the men had all been thoroughly briefed. Moreover each pilot "carried adequate fire arm protection (and) . . . new parachutes, equipped with jungle emergency packs out of which they could live for a reasonable period of time."[5] Additionally, Mahony informed the elder Miller, each flier was given "some secret items (of which I can not tell you) to aid them in guiding them back to friendly territory." He said that it was believed that a bullet from a Japanese fighter had damaged the cooling system of Captain Miller's Mustang. "Your son was heard by all the pilot's [sic] to say that he was having trouble with the plane and would head away into the hills to bail out. As far as we can tell he was not hurt. Due to enemy action some of our pilots were unable to follow him."

Mahony went on to say that elaborate procedures were in place to aid pilots in escaping from behind enemy lines, but of course he could not reveal what they were. But he ended with this: "I wish there was something more that we could do to lessen your anxiety or buoy up your hope. I know nothing further to tell you except in my squadron in China over a period of ten months, seven of the pilots went down in enemy territory and all seven returned safely and in good health. Our prayers are for his safe return home at an early date."[6]

The Japanese never reported the capture of Captain Miller. His wife and parents did not know that he was alive until the recapture of Rangoon in May 1945.[7]

Climbing back up with his flight of four pilots, Cochran looked up at last. Suddenly the sky was filled with Oscars, the Ki-43 that so closely resembled a Mitsubishi Zero that Cochran believed he was looking at the famed fighter used by the Japanese navy's air forces. The Japanese planes all bore a red lightning flash on the tail identifying them as members of the Fighter Sentai 50, a seasoned and highly skilled unit that boasted many top pilots.

"They were all over us, and they had us. They had us low in climbing, and they were above us, and they knew what to do. They weren't any kids. And we had quite a skirmish over dear old Mandalay," Cochran said later. The formation of Mustangs was scattered across the sky, and the radios were filled with the excited shouts of pilots, some of whom were seasoned combat veterans, and some of whom were facing their first contact with enemy fighters. Cochran quickly realized that they needed to extract themselves from the fight as soon as possible. Their sole assignment was to protect Wingate and his troops; in seeking out targets such as bridges, railroads, marshaling yards, and supply depots, they could make the case that they were in fact carrying out that mission. But now the best course was to break out and fly for Hailakandi.

"Fighter to fighter never does anything. We had valuable fighters and valuable pilots, and this wasn't our true mission," Cochran said many years later.[8] "So I yelled, 'Down and out. Every one of you!' I could hear the guys on the radio." Cochran, like the other ten fighter pilots, was twisting, turning, rolling, climbing, and diving, desperate to keep from being shot down. Inside the cockpit of the Mustang, Cochran felt the familiar dryness in his mouth and could feel his heart racing as he swiveled his head side to side, checking above him, craning around to get a glimpse of what was behind him. He pulled the stick back hard and felt the blood drain from his head. His body felt 400 pounds heavier as centrifugal force combined with gravity and pressed him deep into the seat. Over the radio he continued to hear his pilots shouting, "One on your tail! Dive!" to each other, and he assumed that no one had heard his command to break off the combat and streak for home base. He could hear shells slamming into his fighter.

"Get out of here! Now! Everyone break, down and out!" But still the whirling lethal aerial dance continued. The howl of Allison engines mixed with the roar of the Nakajima Ha-115 Japanese engines, all the noise punctuated by the staccato bursts of the Brownings as a Japanese fighter flew in front of a gunsight.

Cochran began calling his flight leaders. "Where are you? How many you got? Are you headed home?" He was trying to count noses, and it was impossible in the confusion.

"I'm north, I'm out of it and headed home," came a report.

"You all right?"

"No, got some holes in me."

"You're going to make it?"

"Yes, I'm going to make it."

"Stay north. You know the areas that are safest."

Cochran called R. T. Smith, using his name. "R. T. Smith, where are you?"

The reply chilled Cochran's blood. "I'm having a hell of a time. I'm all shot up, my engine is missing, and I'm overheating."

"Hang on to it! Hang in there and get it in there. Any enemy around you?"

"No, I'm free of it. I'm all right."

Soon came a query as to Cochran's location. "I'm over the target. I'm trying to get you guys to go home. Get out of here!"[9]

As the Mustangs broke off the engagement and headed west for Hailakandi, the Japanese fighters followed, diving, firing, inflicting wounds. Cochran had incorrectly identified the attackers as Mitsubishi Zeros, but the mistake is understandable. The profile of the Oscar is similar; moreover both were highly maneuverable, lightweight fighters. Unencumbered by any protective armor or self-sealing fuel tanks, the Oscar was agile and extremely lethal in the hands of expert pilots. It originally was equipped with only two 12.7 mm machine guns firing through the three-bladed propeller; later versions were also armed with 20 mm cannon. The Ki-43 Oscars were capable of a top speed of 329 mph and could climb to 16,400 feet in less than six minutes.[10]

The Mustang would become the premier fighter of the war, capable of flying more than 2,300 miles, with a top speed of 437 mph, and a service ceiling of more than 43,000 feet. But that was the P-51D and later models, which had a bubble canopy and the famed Merlin engine. Cochran's men were flying the first version, the A model, with a 1,330 horsepower Allison V-12 engine. It was a fine fighter, rugged, fast, capable of carrying an impressive load of armament, but it could not compete with the Oscar in a contest of close-quarter aerobatics. The Japanese fighter, like the Zero, could turn inside a Mustang all day long.[11]

Cochran immediately recognized two things about this fight: the Air Commandos had been jumped from above, and the Japanese pilots were seasoned, accomplished fliers. At one point three Japanese fighters were on him over the target, and he worked desperately to avoid their guns as he called out for his men to dive and run.[12]

For those still in the air confusion continued to reign. Faulty radios might have contributed to the garbled communications. At some point in the whirling madness, one pilot called out for Cochran, but the Air Commando leader did not hear the query. He did hear another pilot—perhaps Lt. Paul Forcey—respond: "No, I think Cochran was in that airplane on fire that went down, and I didn't see anyone get out of it."

Cochran immediately came back: "I'll be damned if that was me. I'm still here, and I'm not in a very good position. I'm over the target, and I got three of them on me. I'm running, but I am still at it. That wasn't me that went down."

Radio transmissions are, in a word, strange. They tend to bounce and skip across the atmosphere, obstructed by hills and mountains or ricocheting off clouds, picked up by transient vapors or slapped down by vagaries of wind or moisture. On this particular day a friend of Cochran's was flying more than 200 miles away with a formation of P-47s. Col. David D. Terry Jr. of Baton Rouge, Louisiana, picked up a brief snatch of excited conversation from the melee near Mandalay but then lost the rest of the transmissions. What he heard was that his friend Phil Cochran was lost, shot down in a burning plane from which he did not escape.

When Terry landed back at his base in northern India, he reported in his debriefing what he had heard on his radio. Word quickly spread, and journalists at the base soon reported it to newspapers in New Delhi. In no time it was on the wires, unknown to Cochran.[13]

Back over Mandalay Cochran and his band of Air Commandos were still trying to get back to Hailakandi. Most of the flight had obeyed Cochran's command to dive and head back to their airfield, but with fractured communications and pilots transmitting over each other, Cochran was convinced that they were ignoring him and engaging what he believed was a superior force of highly maneuverable Zeros. He remained in the area of the target, desperately striving to stay out of the gunsights of as many as three Oscars intent on shooting him down. It slowly dawned on him that the radio chatter had ended, his fighter section had turned for home, and he now had to run a gauntlet of Japanese fighters strung out between him and Hailakandi.

He made a beeline for home and quickly encountered the first of the several Japanese fighters; it tried to turn into him, but Cochran had his throttle open and quickly left the Oscar behind. But another immediately got onto his tail, and the embattled American colonel tried to coax more speed from his P-51A by continually making small dives. The Japanese pilot fired, ineffectively, and Cochran held his throttle open.

"I just had it to the firewall. . . . I was running like a scared rabbit. I admit it, it isn't terribly brave. You don't do that in the storybooks. You turn around and start fighting this fellow. But that wasn't in my mind at the time. I had made enough errors that day, and had enough discouragement in what we had done, that I was going to use my speed and live to fight another day."[14]

For Cochran speed was all he had left. He had given away all his altitude in an effort to gain more speed, but still the Japanese fighter pilot stayed with him, and now he was roaring across Burma at treetop height, popping up over a particularly tall teak tree and then dropping back down, trying to make himself as small as possible in the cockpit. The Mustangs, even the early models, were fast machines and should have been able to outrun the Oscar. But on this day it seemed to be in slow motion.

The P-51 "was a pretty fast airplane. But I'll tell you, I was terribly disappointed in its speed that day," Cochran recalled. "It wasn't anywhere near as fast as its book said it was, because I had it wide open. I was shoving with my feet getting out of there."[15]

Eventually the Mustang began to gain ground—and air—on the pursuing Japanese fighters, and at long last Cochran climbed over the Chin Hills and circled to land at Hailakandi at about 1130. He was tired, disgusted, and still shaking from the overdose of adrenaline that had been released into his body. But he still had a fight ahead of him, this time with his own men. They were angry, outraged even, at his order to run. To a man they believed they should have engaged the Japanese fighters over Mandalay, and they were ready to have it out with their commander. But there was plenty of blame to go around, in Cochran's view.

He held a meeting, and criticism flowed freely. The young pilots were disgusted—with themselves and with Cochran—and they were mourning, in the hard-shelled nonchalance of combat fighter pilots, the loss of two of their comrades. Miller and Hartzer were friends, buddies with whom they had trained since the beginning of Project 9, and now they were gone. Cochran, wisely, let the pilots have their say, accepting criticism where he thought it was deserved, and then he turned the conversation around. Sure, he had made plenty of mistakes, but some were on the shoulders of the fighter pilots themselves. Cochran blamed himself for the decision to lead the mission—mistake number one. He accepted the blame for not having specifically assigned a top cover and then criticized both the fighter section leader (Mahony) and the fighter section pilots for not having automatically assumed the tactical position of high cover. He pushed back on the anger at not standing to fight the Japanese when they were bounced: disadvantaged by altitude, caught unprepared, and believing the enemy outnumbered them and was flying the Zero with its near-mythical maneuverability was no time to try to snatch victory from defeat, he told them. Cochran also berated them for not immediately obeying his command to dive and run, although it seems that both Hartzer and Miller were shot down on the first diving pass by the Japanese.[16]

It would not happen again. The Air Commandos would suffer more losses as they struck again and again inside Japanese lines over Burma.

But the pilots had been bloodied and beaten, and they were disgusted with themselves. They would do better. They resolved to never again be caught off guard as they had been today.

Some pilots, including R. T. Smith, flew another mission that same day. He made it back to Hailakandi safely. Although his fighter was severely damaged in the encounter with the Oscars, Smith's flight record for February 1944 shows four flights on the fourteenth: the P-51 raid of three hours, fifteen minutes, with the notation "combat with Zeros"; and three entries for a B-25H. The last included a flight of thirty minutes each way from Hailakandi to Imphal and return, and a two hour and 45 minute combat mission. 1st Lt. Daniel A. Sinskie, assistant operations officer for the group and a B-25 pilot, verified the flight log. The entries are testimony to the grueling flight schedule that conditions in Burma demanded of the Air Commandos.[17]

The mission to the warehouses near the Laudaung Railway Station had repercussions. The report from Colonel Terry's debriefing reached headquarters, and soon a corporal handed Cochran a teletype that can only be described as strange. It was addressed to Cochran, 1st Air Commandos, from Stratemeyer, HQ: "Verify or refute Cochran's death today." Since it was addressed to Cochran, of course it was delivered to him. It was a Mark Twain moment: "Reports of my death are greatly exaggerated." Cochran, being Cochran, immediately sent a report back. "Hell no, I am not dead. Signed, Cochran."[18]

But he also learned that his death had been reported in his hometown of Erie, Pennsylvania, and he immediately cabled General Arnold that the story was untrue. Air force officers also were dispatched to the home of his parents in Erie to assure them that their son was safe.

It was Cochran's last combat mission. When Wingate and Mountbatten heard of the mission, they quickly arranged for a USAAF order grounding Cochran from further missions over Burma. He knew too much, they reasoned, to risk capture by the Japanese. Such an event would likely end the Wingate operation into Burma.[19]

CHAPTER 16

Tonight you are going to find out you've got a soul.
——Col. Philip Cochran

The message from RAF Air Marshal Sir John Baldwin arrived at Lalaghat and Hailakandi early Sunday morning, 5 March 1944: "Weather is suitable. Carry out Operation Thursday."

Plans had been under way for days, but the cable confirmed that with good visibility the invasion would begin that evening.[1]

Darkness would descend early, but a waxing moon was expected to provide adequate light for the tug pilots to navigate and find the fields deep inside Burma where each would release his two gliders filled with British guerrilla troops and heavy equipment for constructing rough airfields. The focus of the Wingate expedition was to coordinate other offensives against the Japanese in Burma: "Cutting the Japanese lines of communication with North Burma, permitting the possible entrapment of the Japanese forces in that area and, as a consequence, securing the advance of the Ledo Road to China."[2]

A glance at a topographic map of the area reveals that the aerial invasion would not be easy, even if the operation began at dawn with the full light of day as a guide. The site code-named Broadway was 267 miles from Lalaghat and only a rough, relatively open clearing in thick jungle. It lay in rather marshy land between two steep ranges of hills: the

Gangaw on the west and an unnamed range on the east. The crests of the hills rose more than 1,000 feet above the jungle glade. On a topographical map of the area the contour lines are close together and wander like the crayon scribbles of a two-year-old. The second landing site, a clearing codenamed Piccadilly, was equally far and just as formidable. The hills in northern Burma are rugged, gouged with steep crevices and covered with nearly impenetrable undergrowth beneath 75- to 100-foot trees that block any view of the sun. Freshets and larger streams cascade from the upper levels, tumbling to the lower elevations to create swampy fogged-in clearings in the otherwise unrelenting vista of trees. Northern Burma would not be anyone's choice for a battleground; less so would it be considered suitable for aerial operations. But it was where the Japanese were. And the Air Commandos would take the Chindits there to fight them.

Capt. Dick Cole turned from the cockpit, ambled down the sloping floor of the C-47 cabin, and stepped down onto the hard-packed earth of the flying field of Lalaghat. He was certain that the two-engine tug was ready for the mission. Flight crews had filled the big olive-drab bird to capacity with fuel, made the preflight checks, started it, taxied it into position, and then thoroughly rechecked everything. It would do its job. Hairless Joe, named for a character in the *Li'l Abner* comic strip, had performed well in grueling conditions since Cole had flown it to India from the States. Now he had done all he could to ensure that he was equally prepared. Cole had chocolate bars in his flight suit pockets and had double-checked his flight maps and a stack of instrument procedures for fields in China.[3]

He looked at the line of a dozen C-47s lined up wingtip to wingtip along the east side of the unpaved runway. The Cole tug was third in line; Capt. Bill Cherry would fly the first one, and Cole's old friend Capt. Jacob Sartz would command the second tug. Cole surveyed the west side of the strip, where Waco CG-4A gliders were similarly arranged. The tugs would pull into takeoff position at ten-minute intervals, and crews would push two gliders into stations behind each tug. Staggered lengths of nylon rope would connect the three aircraft, and at a green light signal from a biscuit gun, the cargo planes would start their takeoff run. Cole glanced at his watch. The first aerial invasion of a country would begin in an hour.

Cole was eager but not anxious; anxiety was not part of his makeup. A year of flying the Hump in C-47s in some of the worst weather conditions in the world, using maps that were notoriously inaccurate, with few navigation aids and risking interception by Japanese fighters daily had inured him to the rigors of combat aviation. While flying into winds that often howled at more than a hundred miles an hour, in icy clouds that could turn deadly turbulent in an instant, many young pilots and their crews had suddenly smashed into an unmarked peak. Others had gone down somewhere in the high valleys of the Himalayas and seldom were heard from again. Others disappeared into the jungles of northern Burma, which were inhabited by fierce—and reportedly headhunting—Naga tribesmen. The Hump pilots landed at Kunming, discharged their cargoes of aviation fuel and the supplies Chiang Kai-shek's army needed, then turned around to fly back and repeat the exercise the next day. It was one of the worst jobs of the war, but Cole had survived. He had first run into Johnny Alison at Kunming while Alison was flying P-40s with the 14th Army Air Force.

The Hump was dangerous, to be sure. But Cole already knew something about danger, and about dicey takeoffs for that matter, before his year of flying the Hump. Less than two years previously he had strapped himself into the right seat of a B-25 bomber, sat with his hand near the landing gear lever, and rolled down the heaving deck of the USS *Hornet*. Lt. Col. Jimmy Doolittle, in the left seat, coaxed the first of sixteen Mitchells into the spray-flecked air on one of the most memorable missions of the war: they would bomb the imperial capital of Japan and shake the confidence of the Japanese. The raiders had had to launch early, after being spotted by a Japanese trawler, and consequently had flown much farther than they had planned. After bombing a variety of targets in Tokyo, most of the sixteen bombers had crash-landed in China or the crews had bailed out; one landed in Russian territory, and the crew was interned. The Doolittle crew had climbed to 8,000 feet over China that night in the midst of a thunderstorm, then jumped into the black hole and came down through a thick layer of clouds. Cole's parachute settled over the top of a pine tree on the side of a vertiginous mountain. He wrapped himself in the silk canopy and waited for daylight. The next day he climbed down and was reunited with the rest of his crew; for several weeks, with friendly Chinese guiding them, they walked, rode horses, and hid aboard boats while Japanese troops scoured the area for the fliers who had dared bomb their capital. Finally the raiders were airlifted to Chungking, where Madame Chiang Kai-shek personally decorated him with the Chinese Army, Navy, and Air Corps Medal, Class A.[4]

As the Air Commandos awaited Baldwin's order, the airfield at Lalaghat had become a raucous circus, with C-47s flying in from sunup to sunset for two days with British soldiers, Gurkhas, mules, and supplies from Gwalior. The roar from their radial engines drowned out conversation with each takeoff to bring in more troops, more supplies.

Men, their tension displayed in boisterous talk, exaggerated laughter, and schoolboy pranks, had spent hours sharpening knives, cleaning guns, checking equipment. They wandered out to the gliders they would ride that night, looking them over, perhaps wondering if they would die in the winged freight car or if it would provide a safe and silent ride. Trucks drove up and down the field, distributing meals. Officers called their men to attention to inspect their uniforms and gear, items that had already been checked and rechecked a dozen times. As dedicated as novices counting the rosary, glider pilots ran through preflight checks of their aircraft and inspected the towlines laid out in neat files near the flight line. Cochran was frazzled and spent much of the time moaning that they should have launched the invasion the day before. Alison was calm, almost beatific, as he quietly gave last-minute orders and approved late additions and changes.

The brass were there, all but Mountbatten himself, who was nursing an eye injury. The ranking British officers were conspicuous with their red tabbed collars—gorget patches, in the parlance of the king's army—and included Field Marshal Sir William Slim, overall commander of the British 14th Army; Baldwin, and Maj. Gen. Orde Wingate himself. American commanders included Gen. George Stratemeyer and Brig. Gen. William D. Old, head of Troop Carrier Command.

In the grand tradition of centuries of British commanders, Wingate had issued a prebattle communiqué, a stirring written encomium designed to instill a sense of gravitas and history in the men about to embark on this aerial expedition: "At this moment we stand beside the soldiers of the United Nations in the front-line trenches throughout the world. It is always a minority that occupies the front line. It is a still smaller minority that accepts with good heart tasks like this that we have chosen to carry out. We need not, therefore, as we go into conflict, suspect ourselves of selfish or interested motives. We have all had the opportunity of withdrawing and we are here because we have chosen to be here; that is, we have chosen to bear the heat and burden of the day."[5]

Wingate was not Shakespeare, but the brigadier's speech was well received. At least Wingate was always in the midst of the mud, blood, and danger; he was no Alfred, Lord Tennyson speaking for the doomed Light Brigade from the comfort of his parlor back in England.

The American flight crews were also encouraged, in words that were perhaps less formal but that carried as much weight for them. The mission briefing had been typical Air Commando, an informal and improvised distribution of information they needed. Cochran and Alison had hand-drawn a map on a bedsheet to show the approximate locations of the clearings code-named Broadway and Piccadilly, for the famous streets in New York and London. The cocommanders had given the flight crews the procedure for gaining altitude, the route to fly into Burma, the emergency procedures if towropes should break. They would fly in at 8,000 feet, return at 9,000. The briefing was a hallowed tradition, part numerical rundown, part locker-room huddle, a fine-tuning of what was expected of young aerial warriors as well as a ritualistic blessing by higher powers.

Despite his Yankee upbringing and natural aversion to the theatrical, Cochran recognized the need for words of encouragement. After briefing the flight crews, he gave a pep talk with a Catholic choirboy accent.

Waving a pointer as he stood in front of the improvised map, he finished the briefing with a question. "Now is there anything anybody doesn't understand? If there is, let's get it straight now." The pilots sitting and kneeling in front of him had no questions. He launched into his pep talk.

"Okay, now just before I came over here, I had a final meeting with the British ground troops that you're going to take in there tonight. And I talked to the guy that's got the red flare that you know is going to be shot off if there's too much interference with the first few gliders that land. He tells me that flare's in an awful deep pocket, and it's going to take somebody an awful lot of finding to get at it." The pilots looked at each other and smiled. "So, if those guys have that kind of heart, and they got that kind of guts, it's up to us to get them in there so they can do their job and get them in right."

Cochran looked out at the assembled pilots, the handpicked crews in whom he had so much confidence. "Now tonight, your whole reason for being, your whole existence, is going to be jammed up into a couple of minutes, and it's just going to balance it there and it's going to take your character to bring it through. Now nothing you've ever done before in your life means a thing. Tonight you are going to find out you've got a soul." He paused for a half-second. "Good luck."[6]

This was sobering talk from the usually flip Cochran, but even Flip Corkin gave sage advice to young Terry Lee, advice that went down well with readers and stirred the blood of young soldiers.

The twelve C-47s and two dozen gliders lined up along the sides of the runway were ready to be pushed into position. Now there was little to do but wait.

The pilots stood in groups, talking, smoking, watching the sky as the light slowly faded. They wore wool flight overalls or khakis, with the tools of war slung around them in a various ways. Many wore their .45 around their waist on a web belt, with large knives, first aid kits, and ammo hooked in the numerous grommets designed for the purpose.

Others wore the aircrew shoulder holster; a few had slipped the lightweight leather holster down around their waist, lending a vaguely Wild West cast to their mien. Cherry, the lead tug pilot, was festooned with weapons—a .38-caliber revolver in a shoulder holster, a .45-caliber pistol in a belt holster, another small pistol in a pocket, a large jungle knife at his waist. A folding-stock carbine was stashed in the cockpit of his C-47. He told anyone who asked that he had gone down once unprepared; he would never be unprepared again. The other tug and glider pilots were also heavily armed, with emergency rations stuffed into every pocket.[7]

It was too warm on the field to wear their leather jackets gaudily decorated with leather unit patches, American flags, and blood chits, but many pilots had slung a jacket over their shoulder. It would be cool when they flew across the 7,500-foot Chin Hills to the east.

Cochran, Alison, and Wingate were huddled in a nervous group, with Generals Stratemeyer and Old watching impassively. Field Marshal Slim stood nearby with several staff officers. The Air Commandos would begin taking off at 1700 (5 p.m.).

A P-51 had landed a few minutes earlier, virtually unnoticed in the bedlam. The pilot quietly sought out Cochran to hand him a large package of aerial photographs. The photos, the pilot said, had been given to him a few minutes earlier when, a bit lost, he had landed at Hailakandi. Shortly thereafter a small plane had circled the field at Lalaghat and touched down. As soon as it taxiied to a halt, a lone figure leaped from the fuselage and ran to the gathered officers. Cochran recognized Capt. Charles Russhon, the unit photographer. Russhon—known to all as Rush and to readers of *Terry and the Pirates* as Vanilla Joe—was tall and outgoing. He sported a dark bushy mustache and had worked in Hollywood before the war. He had talked his way into the Air Commandos by telling Cochran that a photographic and film history of the invasion would be necessary—and mentioning his work in Hollywood but neglecting to note that his background was in sound, not film. Cochran hired him, and Rush learned camerawork on the job. He frequently went on bomber missions to provide aerial photos of target areas and to help in mapping the largely unmapped regions of northern Burma. Now he was breathless and clearly agitated.

"Hey, Boss! You've got to look! They've caught on to us!" Rush grabbed the photograph from Cochran and laid it on the grass. Cochran peered at the image, puzzled at first, then stunned by what it revealed. The photo clearly showed logs, probably teak, strewn everywhere across the clearing. Any glider or aircraft attempting to set down would be destroyed, no question. The field, Russhon explained, was Piccadilly.[8]

Cochran now had a dilemma. Wingate, full of caution, had ordered that no one was to fly over any of the landing sites in the week before the invasion. He did not want to draw Japanese attention to the area. Cochran had not agreed with the decision but had acquiesced until Russhon had badgered him with the plea that he needed a good photographic record of the fields before the campaign. Having the latest photo-recon intelligence before sending in his pilots made sense to the fighter pilot in Cochran, so that morning he had finally agreed that a single bomber, with R. T. Smith at the controls, could make a couple of passes over Piccadilly and Broadway. Russhon had taken the photos, returned to the tented darkroom set up at Hailakandi, and quickly developed the film. When he studied the prints, he was aghast. He could not radio Cochran at Lalaghat for fear of being overhead, and no planes were available. Then the P-51 pilot landed while trying to find Lalaghat; Russhon gave him directions and pressed the pack of photographs on him with the urgent plea to get it to Cochran as quickly as possible. Russhon then commandeered a jeep for the rough twelve-mile journey to Lalaghat, but just then an L-1 landed. Rush directed the pilot to take him to Lalaghat without delay.

Cochran had not expected to report the results of the recon flight to Wingate, but now there was no putting it off. Cochran walked over to where Wingate was standing with several of his staff. When Cochran showed him the photograph, the brigadier was irate.

"Who did this! Who flew over the landing area when I gave orders not to do so?"

"General, I gave the order. I just had a hunch." Cochran looked Wingate in the eye. The Man softened and smiled slightly. He understood hunches, the metaphysical warnings that he had often felt himself in previous campaigns. Cochran continued: "Now the question is, do we go in or not? The Japs may have blocked this field and sent all their soldiers to Broadway."[9]

Months of training had gone into this project, tons of supplies had been transported into Assam to support it, men had died in accidents and combat, bad blood had developed when aircraft were not available to other Allied units in-theater. Now it might all go to waste.

Wingate, in his ever-present tropical helmet, stood looking down at the ground, his hands on his hips. He pulled at his beard, a gesture Cochran recognized as a signal of deep concentration. It was agonizing for Cochran and Alison, who saw their mission from Arnold disintegrating. General Stratemeyer was silent, observing the scene carefully, and Field Marshal Slim likewise remained apart.

"Phil, what do you think?" Wingate looked at Cochran. His voice was soft.

Cochran and Alison had spent several minutes discussing the odds that the Japanese knew about Broadway as well as Piccadilly. Wingate had used the latter clearing in the first campaign, when a C-47 had landed and carried out some of his badly wounded troops. The timing of the logs across the clearing could have been serendipitous, a precaution by the Japanese in case a similar raid was planned for the dry season, now just starting. Or perhaps the logs were the work of Burmese teak workers seeking to dry the wood before sending it to market. The American colonels agreed that the odds were slim that Japanese troops were waiting in deadly ambush at Broadway. The mission should go ahead. Cochran and Alison had worked together long enough, and were in such accord, that they needed little conversation.[10]

"We think we should proceed in to Broadway."

"Right." Wingate nodded crisply. Who made the final decision to go remains a matter of debate today. They had plenty of good reasons to proceed: the moon was favorable now, and a month's delay until the next good night meant a sharply curtailed campaign season before the monsoons began; the men were at a finely tuned state of readiness, which a stand-down would devastate; lengthy delays would increase the chances of discovery by the Japanese; one Chindit column under Fergusson had already departed from Ledo on foot and would be unable to sustain itself in the Burmese jungles for four weeks or so. Although the risk of ambush by the Japanese at Broadway was slight but real, the combined weight of the factors mitigating against delay left them with little real choice.[11]

Cochran called his pilots together, both tug and glider drivers, and briefed them on the new plan. His breezy demeanor was typical Cochran. He climbed atop the hood of a jeep and held up the crude bedsheet map of Broadway.

"Say, fellers, we've got a better place to go." The pilots clustered around the map, saying little. Alison stood next to Cochran, holding the rolled-up photo of the logs strewn across the landing area at Piccadilly. Neither commander mentioned the reason for the change of plans as they went through the details of the mission.

So now the eighty gliders that were to have been split between Piccadilly and Broadway would all go in to Broadway. Earlier Cochran and Alison had sparred about which of them, if either, would ride a glider into the landing zone. By their natures and experience both desperately wanted in on the action. Wingate, however, had insisted that one had to remain behind to direct the aerial forces. Alison made the better case for going: he had more experience in gliders, and Cochran was, after all, the official commander. He would be needed to direct the overall aerial lift.

Loading of the gliders resumed. The Chindits were in high spirits, eager to get on with it. They flashed grins and thumbs-up signs to the Yank airmen, who grinned and winked back. They were a colorful lot. Most Chindits wore baggy shorts, long stockings with heavy boots, and Australian-style bush hats. Occasionally one would take a long pull on a beer, then grin and hand the half-empty bottle to a ground crewman, who grinned back. Pilots watched closely as the men filed aboard, each trooper loaded with a .303 rifle, ammunition, provisions, personal gear, and first aid equipment. Their weights had been calculated beforehand; each Chindit had been warned to bring only prescribed gear. Distribution of the weight inside the cabin was essential to balance and control. But in nearly every case the Chindits carried more ammunition and more provisions than allowed because they did not trust that additional supplies would arrive. The additional weight would prove crucial and in some instances disastrous. Cochran had approved additional loading, increasing the weight of the gliders by as much as 1,000 pounds. But subsequent checks revealed that some gliders had been overloaded by as much as 2,000 pounds.[12]

Nodding to Cochran, Alison turned to his glider. There was no point in a formal farewell, since it would only exacerbate the wound to Cochran's pride at being left behind. Alison had carefully stowed in the cockpit of the Waco his personal gear, a folding stock .30-caliber carbine, a bag of grenades, and his ever-present .22-caliber Colt pistol. He wore a sweater against the chill of altitude, and he now donned his paratrooper jacket, the four pockets loaded with additional gear, and slipped on the shoulder holster with the .45 and extra magazines.

Alison had nearly had to stay behind. Cancellation of the Piccadilly force initially left him without an assignment, since he had been tagged to lead that mission. Lt. Col. Arvid "Oley" Olson had been named leader of the Broadway force, and Alison bumped another glider pilot in order to serve under Olson for the mission. Taylor, leader of the entire glider section, had also been slotted to fly in to Piccadilly. He too exercised the prerogative of rank and bumped another pilot to be able to fly in to Broadway. Taylor's would be the first glider to attempt the landing, and it would be towed by Captain Cherry.

The hastily reconfigured mission to Broadway resulted in some miscues as pilots and troops quickly reloaded gliders. Most Wacos in the first wave would carry troops and their equipment; Olson's carried the main radios, the vital communications link with Lalaghat and the commanders; a small bulldozer was aboard another glider. The plan was to land silently, quickly secure the clearing, and make a primitive airstrip that would accommodate C-47s bringing in additional troops and supplies.

Bill Cherry taxied into position, crews attached towlines to two gliders, and the tug slowly moved forward, taking up the slack. The pilots of the Dakota and the Wacos waited for the green light from the biscuit gun. In the lead glider with Taylor was his copilot, Tech. Sgt. Perry Garten of Kansas City, Missouri, line chief of the glider ground crews. In Cherry's second towed glider were 2nd Lt. Neal Blush of Whitefish, Montana, with Cpl. John Kinner of Iron River, Michigan, in the right seat. At 1812, just seventy-two minutes after the original launch time, Cherry got the go signal and applied full power. Imperceptibly at first, the three aircraft linked by a dual umbilical cord began to move reluctantly across the grass runway. It was a tough slog. The gliders were grossly overweight with too much gear packed forward of the center of gravity. The nose of Taylor's Waco began to dig into the dirt of the Lalaghat airfield. Ground crew saw the problem and ran to hold down the tail as long as possible. The three birds at last struggled into the air, and at 500 feet Cherry began the procedure established to bring the tug and the gliders back over the field at about 4,000 feet, at a minimum climb rate of 150 feet per minute. If they could not achieve that altitude and rate of climb, the lift over the Imphal plain and Chin Hills would be extremely problematic. They needed to reach 8,000 feet, which gave them a bare 500 feet to spare over the tallest peaks of the Chins.

The pathfinder force of Wacos and their loads of Chindit troops were to secure the landing area at Broadway. They were to be followed a half-hour later by the main force of gliders. The second wave of Wacos would contain additional fighting troops, as well as an engineering section for construction of the primitive airfield.

Dick Cole watched out the left cockpit window of the C-47 for the green light. It was warm, with only a slight breeze. His goatskin flight jacket was draped over the curved metal back of his seat; it was nonregulation, a navy jacket with a fur collar. When he was flying the Hump, he had gotten it by trading the A-2 jacket he had been issued, with his name badge and Thunderbird patch of the 34th Bomb Squadron, the one he had worn on the Tokyo raid. The navy jacket was warmer around his neck at high altitudes. He wore a wool flight suit and stout boots; his .45 was strapped in a shoulder holster, and a large Ka-Bar fighting knife was on his belt.[13] A straight-stock M1 carbine was propped behind him. The war against the Japanese was a brutal one; few Allied troops had any illusions about the treatment they could expect if they were forced down in the jungle in Burma and captured. Cole, perhaps more than the others, could expect no mercy if the Japanese learned his identity. He pushed away any thoughts of that and concentrated on the job of getting the two gliders on the runway into the air, over the Chin Hills, and into the clearing known as Broadway.[14]

The towropes had been secured, and Cole had inched forward to take up the slack. As was his habit, he felt for the propeller controls without taking his eyes from the light gun, assuring by touch alone that they were full forward in the high RPM position, that the mixture controls were in auto rich, and that the tail wheel was locked. To Cole the cockpit was a familiar and comforting place.

Green light! Cole eased the throttles forward, counting a long five before they would be fully open, and at the same time he pushed forward on the control yoke. He could feel the vibrations of the powerful Pratt and Whitney radial engines as the fuel-air mixture ignited in the cylinders, and the growl became a roar as the levers reached the full-power positions. The tug was sluggish and seemed to move in slow motion; the field was dry, but it felt as though they were attempting to take off through thick gumbo. They had made many takeoffs with single and double gliders in tow, but tonight the Wacos seemed to have been filled with crates of lead. The marker lights of the runway went by far too slowly for this to be a normal takeoff. Beside him in the right seat 1st Lt. Ralph C. Bordley sat with a hand poised to pull hard on a T-handle mounted on the bulkhead that formed the aft wall of the cockpit; this would release the gliders if the takeoff or climbout went bad.

He felt the drag of the gliders slacken when one, then the other, lifted into the air behind the tug; they always were airborne before the tug, and he trusted the glider pilots to hold their crates level and just slightly above the vertical stabilizer of the Douglas. At last the tail of the C-47 came up, and their airspeed crept upward with agonizing slowness. Cole looked down the runway while Bordley watched the airspeed indicator and scanned the engine gauges for the first sign of trouble. At 90 mph Cole began pulling back on the yoke. The tug seemed reluctant to give up the comfort of the earth and become a creature of the sky.[15]

A combat plan becomes little more than a hope as soon as the operation starts. Unforeseen problems are expected, an acceptable rate of attrition is built into the plan, and alternatives are carefully spelled out. But it is impossible to plan for every possibility. Operation Thursday was no exception. A couple of Wacos were released over Lalaghat when their tug developed electrical glitches; others were released over Imphal when the Dakota pilots realized that their fuel consumption was much too high and they would never reach Broadway.

The problems continued. The moon had given the glider pilots plenty of light to enable them to stay in formation behind their tugs and avoid each other. They had turned off all position lights, so they were flying in low tow formation to allow the glider pilots to see the blue exhaust flames from the Dakota engines. After crossing the Chindwin, however, a heavy mist filtered out the moonlight and began to obscure the exhaust stacks. The gliders began to surge forward, then jerk hard against the towlines as they slowed. It was a recipe for disaster.

In the cockpit of the third tug Cole struggled to keep the C-47 on course for Broadway. From the time he had pushed the throttles forward to take off, he had been acutely aware that something was very different from the dozens of tows he had handled during training at Goldsboro and Lalaghat. The twin-engine Douglas never would be mistaken for a fighter, but now it was far less responsive than at any time he could recall. It was like riding an elephant after training on a horse.

Tonight the C-47 was wallowing, that was the only word for it. Clearly the gliders were far heavier than during any practice tow. The Douglas was laboring.

They had finally climbed to 8,000 feet and passed over the Chin Hills. The Douglas, even in a shallow descent, was obviously still working hard, and now, as the two gliders fought to keep from riding forward on their towlines, Cole and Bordley looked at each other as their tug was jerked and jinked by the gliders. The constant jerking had stretched the towlines and snapped the communications wires. Cole looked at the clock on the instrument panel. It had been about an hour since they launched from Lalaghat; they had about an hour and a half to Broadway. Instinctively he scanned his instruments. The engines were running slightly hot; the oil pressure was down slightly as well but not alarmingly.

In back the flight engineer was stationed in the ventral blister, carefully watching the gliders under tow. Lexan domes had been installed on all the Project 9 aircraft specifically to allow visual observation of the gliders. After the radio wires broke, constant visual contact was crucial. They hit rough air, and the C-47 bounced through the dark Burmese night.

Suddenly the wallowing ceased. The C-47 was instantly more responsive and less like a draft horse slogging through mud. Cole knew the gliders had broken away even before the flight engineer called, obviously upset. "Oh, crap!" Cole and Bordley said in unison. They craned their necks to look below and behind but saw no sign of the gliders, which now were descending into the black jungle that stretched as far as they could see. Cole turned to his copilot: "Don't touch that T-handle.

We don't need any more trouble." Some line might still be attached, and Cole didn't want anyone second-guessing what had happened.[16]

Back at Lalaghat, Cochran knew there was serious trouble when Cole radioed in: "I lost my gliders." Aboard one was Oley Olson, who was to command the aerial force at Broadway; Richard Boebel, group intelligence officer, was aboard the other. Soon others were calling in, reporting similar ominous events. The overloaded gliders had snapped their towlines and plunged down into the void. Seventeen gliders were lost, nine east of the Chindwin in Japanese-controlled Burma. The brass decided to stop the double tows, and as soon as Cole landed, he fueled up and headed out to the flight line to hook up once more to a glider. This time he was easily able to take the single Waco to Broadway without incident.

Cochran waited anxiously for more news. It was all bad. Olson's glider, now lost somewhere in the Burmese jungle, had carried the main radios that were to provide communication with Lalaghat. Alison's glider carried a backup radio. Code words had been established. If things were going well and there was no Japanese resistance, the message would be "pork sausage." If things were rough and going badly, the message would be "soya link," the name of the artificial meat despised by the British troops. A backup signal was a red flare. If incoming tugs saw a red flare coming up from Broadway, they were not to release their gliders and were to pass the word by radio.[17]

Tug pilots returning from single tows to Broadway reported few issues with the revised formula. Still, they had no word from anyone on the ground. He continued to fret, pacing at the HQ shack, driving his men crazy.

Then word came in from the C-47 pilots: red flare at Broadway. They were coming back with gliders in tow. Then, around 2:30 a.m. Cochran's radioman came in with a long face. They had finally heard from Broadway. He handed Cochran a two-word message that nearly stopped his heart: "Soya link."

CHAPTER 17

It was like going through hell a second at a time.
　　　　—Flight Officer Earl C. Waller, glider pilot

Johnny Alison peered through the gloom at the blurred image of his tug's right engine exhaust. The trick was to keep the blue flame in the same position on the upper left of the Waco's ample windscreen; it was the only visual clue that he was holding his proper position in the trinity of Gooney Bird and two Wacos. Slightly ahead and to his left he could just discern the other glider on double tow, a smudge in the darkness.

The takeoff had been hair-raising. Other pilots considered Alison to be a "good stick," a birdman with natural instincts who flew intuitively and could master anything with wings. They were right to an extent, but the assessment failed to consider the endless hours of practice and experience, the countless takeoffs and landings in a variety of single- and multiengine aircraft, the aerial acrobatics he had assiduously performed until he was satisfied that he had it right. A certain sameness accompanied the piloting of powered planes—usually they differed only in the numbers, the critical speeds at which performance of certain phases of flight or maneuvers is safe. All took to the sky with the same basic inputs from the pilot, leaving the earth at a particular speed, cruising at a set speed and within prescribed engine performance parameters, and landing within a narrow range of airspeeds (airplane drivers learned to consider such things as weight of the airplane, loading within the bird, and temperature, among other factors).

A glider was different, and a Waco CG-4A was vastly different, than any of the fighters, bombers, and cargo planes that Alison had flown so well. The takeoff was totally dependent on the tug pulling the glider. A hiccup in an engine could prove disastrous not only for the towplane but for the glider as well. The towlines were carefully inspected before each launch but still could break when exposed to severe jerking. If loaded with cargo too far forward, the nose skid would bore into the ground; if too far aft, the glider would nose up, stall, and crash. The glider pilot had to quickly force the craft into level flight just a few feet above the runway to avoid pulling up the tug's elevators, which could result in a premature takeoff and potentially fatal stall.

Alison had flown a glider only a few times, enough to become familiar with the basics but not enough to be comfortable. In fact the day before the launch of Operation Thursday Alison had taken off twice at the controls of a Waco, released, and landed at Lalaghat. That constituted his entire glider piloting time.[1] The strange heavy controls felt awkward and slow. The arrival of dusk, the time of strange half-light that is neither night nor day, had degraded visual clues. Added to the stress was the proximity of both other aircraft in the takeoff triangle, the forward glider on the dual towline and the C-47.

When the biscuit light flashed the green signal at the tug pilot, the veteran Hump flier Jacob Sartz, Alison could feel the one-inch nylon towline begin to stretch. (It was actually 15/16ths of an inch.) Somewhere from within the bowels of the Waco came a slight screech followed by a deep-pitched moan, as from a living creature in pain. A slight jerk, and he could feel the ungainly bird begin its first tentative forward movement. Alison held back the large wheel, felt the solid rudder pedals under the balls of his feet, and then stopped himself from reaching for the throttle lever. Of course, he said to himself. No throttle in a glider.

The C-47 was moving now, but something was wrong, Alison was certain. The nose seemed to be lowering, and he sensed the raising of the tail despite his holding the yoke to the rearward stop, the wheel almost touching his chest. He looked to 1st Lt. Donald Seese's glider on short tow and could see that its nose skid was digging in, and, yes, the tail was rising. The launch crew suddenly ran to both gliders and pulled down their empennage, or tail assembly, holding on to the tail surfaces and running as far down the runway as they could manage. The two gliders eventually lifted off, nearly simultaneously, and Alison pushed forward on the yoke to hold it just feet off the grassy surface of the Lalaghat airfield, just above the straining tug. He was sweating.

For the next half hour they climbed, both gliders fighting to hold their positions behind the tug, all three turning left every ten minutes, the gliders varying their bank to maintain formation. It was physically hard work, and Alison could feel the strain in his arms and back. The thin light was fading quickly; from the altimeter he knew the trio had passed over the field at Lalaghat at 4,100 feet. They swung left once more and headed east toward the Imphal plain and the Chin Hills, the last barrier to the interior of Burma. If they continued to climb at their present rate, they would have enough altitude to clear the highest hills.

Alison felt like he was herding, instead of flying, the elephantine cargo glider through the caliginous void. The nearly full moon was now partially—and at times completely—obscured by a thickening mist, a swirling dampness that clung to the windscreen and gathered in tiny rivulets that ran up the Plexiglas in the 100 mph relative wind. Judging distances was difficult, and watching the exhaust stacks of the tug gave only position information, not distance. The constant staring was a strain on his eyes and his nerves.

In other gliders the flight was equally wearing on the straining overworked pilots. Flight Officer Earl C. Waller had known since takeoff that this was not going to be a by-the-book repeat of the numerous training flights made by the Air Commandos since arriving in India. It was obvious from the start that the glider was much heavier than it had ever been, far heavier than the pilot's manual recommended. But who was going to stop this operation now because of a few extra pounds? On the ground the oleo struts of the main landing gear were compressed to the stops, he had noted, and the heavy tires, although fully inflated, appeared nearly flat. The takeoff roll was slow and sluggish, and the C-47 tug had lifted off a second before either glider, something that had never happened before. Once airborne the Waco flew like a whale.[2]

It did not improve while flying into the mist-shrouded Burma night. Waller remained on low tow to be able to focus on the blue exhaust flames of his tug, but the strain compounded the stress. After clearing the Chin Hills the tug and two gliders began the long gradual descent into the narrow valley that cradled Broadway.

"Soon something unusual started to happen. The towropes seemed to stretch like a large rubber band and the glider would surge forward causing the rope to loop back over the top of my right wing. I called for spoilers to take up the slack; there was great danger of the rope hooking the wing and tearing it off. This remained the entire flight. It was like going through hell a second at a time," Waller recalled more than thirty years later.[3] The loss of a wing would be certain death for all aboard. No one in the gliders wore parachutes, including the pilots.

The flight would get worse for Waller and his passengers, twenty Chindits and a medical doctor.

Alison passed the Chindwin River, barely visible in the moonlight as a gauzy silver thread. It was easier to see down through the mist than ahead, but there was nothing to see. In the tug Sartz had reduced power, beginning a slow descent to bring them down to their release altitude by the time they were at Broadway. The glider surged, eating up distance from the towplane, and Alison raised the spoilers to bleed off the airspeed. Despite everything he tried, the glider jerked harshly as the slack in the towline was taken in.

Below, all was blackness, a stygian void. Alison tried to think of other things, but finding anything comforting to focus on was difficult. He thought of his new bride, and of her photograph tucked into his shirt pocket. Shaking his head, he forced himself back to the mission. The hurried reorganization of the night launch and the gnawing doubts about whether Japanese troops would be awaiting the gliders at Broadway were unsettling. Still, he was a seasoned combat pilot, accustomed to being rudely awakened in the black of night for an unscheduled takeoff, used to facing deprivation, danger, and death in a variety of forms.

Quiet. Gliders should be silent birds, winging their way through the skies sans the loud internal combustion engines that propelled powered aircraft. But Alison could definitely hear, faintly, the symmetrical bass thrumming of the tug's two radial engines. He could also hear creaking from the wood-and-metal airframe of the Waco as it strained and protested against the weight and the wind. Occasionally he could hear the thumping of the doped fabric as it slapped against the welded tubing of the fuselage; it sounded like someone beating on a door to be let inside.

For the passengers aboard the Wacos, the ride was a combination of relief, anxiety, and outright fear. James Warner Bellah, riding in Alison's glider, was an American lieutenant colonel assigned to Mountbatten's staff and attached to the Air Commandos for the Broadway operation. Bellah had been a pilot in World War I and was a professional writer between the wars, mostly pulp fiction westerns. In an article that appeared in *U.S. Air Services* (and later abridged in *Reader's Digest*), Bellah recounted the flight across Burma: "Everyone was in full field kit and armed to the teeth with carbines, tommy guns, knives and grenades—a pirate crew, Wingate's army and Cochran's air commandos, in mottled camouflage suits, with broad-brimmed, rakish, paint-dabbed jungle hats, most of them with a growth of rank beard."

It was quiet aboard the gliders, according to Bellah, with no boasting or babbling as they flew over the dark canopy of the jungle far below.

"Soon all we could see was the blue blob of exhaust from the tow ship's starboard motor. All we could feel was the breathing of tightly packed men and the animal shudder of the glider as it swung into the prop wash and out again, weaving on its long snaking tow rope. All we could hear was the thundering noise of our thrust through the air, for gliders are as noisy as power planes."

The potential danger from Japanese aircraft or groundfire was on everyone's mind. "If the Japs had even one good night fighter pilot we could all be done in like sitting birds, for we were sneaking in without fighter cover and in unarmed ships—counting entirely on audacity and surprise.

"The moon was bright and high over Burma. We crossed the Irrawaddy River and passed within a few miles of a Jap air field. All of us who could plastered our faces to the windows searching for tracers or pursuit aviation. But they let us through that bottleneck—they must have thought us a night bombing mission."[4]

Alison glanced at his government-issued wristwatch, the radium hands and numbers faintly visible in the blackness. It was 2010, ten minutes past eight in the evening. Two hours after takeoff and an hour since crossing the line into Burma. Sometime in the next half-hour, they should receive a light signal from the tug; the communication wire wrapped around the towline had broken shortly after takeoff. He would pull the release lever and drop the towline to descend to Broadway. There would be no go-arounds if they were at the wrong clearing or if they were too fast or too high—or, worse, too low. And there would be no going back under any conditions: the C-47s would not have enough fuel to tow the gliders back to India if they encountered enemy fire at Broadway.[5]

They approached the broad Irrawaddy River near Katha and, once past it, turned north toward Mogaung. The Irriwaddy took a giant turn to the east, and they crossed over it once more. They were close now, over a small valley between two ranges of hills. No villages were anywhere nearby, and the absence of lights on the ground meant that only a black blanket stretched below them.

"Target in 20 minutes," Alison shouted back to the troops in the cabin. He could feel them moving about on their benches to belt themselves in. Bellah reported that each Chindit chambered a round in his Enfield, the bolts snicking sharply.[6]

Suddenly from the tug came a flashing green light, aimed at Alison's cockpit. Below he could see a faint easing of the blackness; the mist had begun to thin, and the opalescent glow of the moon revealed what must be a clearing. The tug began a slow left turn over the clearing, followed by the two gliders. Somewhere ahead of them were the first two gliders, carrying Taylor and Neal Blush, as well as two dozen fully equipped assault troops.

They were level at a thousand feet, and Alison watched the tug intently for the steady green light that meant release. He reached overhead toward the lever, keeping his hand close to but not directly on the handle. He didn't want a sudden lift or drop to cause his hand to jerk the release handle early. That might mean disaster. At the proper release point they should be one mile from the clearing, and a steady speed of 70 mph—and no more than 80 mph—would assure them a safe landing after a constant descent, not unlike sliding down a bannister.

When first practicing glider landings, the group had started with releases at 3,000 feet, but this had proved problematic because of the need for the largely inexperienced pilots to judge speed and altitude at various times during the descent. So a landing profile was established. "We figured the slant range of a glider if it were cut loose at 300 feet at 120 miles an hour, and the glider would go just so far, and then it would be on the ground," Alison said. They extrapolated the distance to glide from various altitudes at a constant airspeed of 120 and determined that the glider would safely hit the landing zone each time.[7]

There it was, the steady green light. Alison's copilot, Capt. Donald Tulloch, the medical officer, shouted to the British troops to prepare for landing, and Alison pulled hard on the tow release handle. He immediately turned 30 degrees to the right, as the forward glider on the left simultaneously turned left. The maneuver was to ensure they did not tangle with each other or the tug. He turned back left after a few seconds to stay lined up with the clearing, all the while struggling mightily to hold up the nose of the Waco. The glider manual called for a tactical glide speed of 70 mph as indicated on the airspeed instrument, so each pilot had to decrease the airspeed on final approach by pulling back the yoke to raise the nose, thus reducing the speed. But the nose of the glider wanted to drop despite everything he tried, including cranking the overhead trim tab wheel to the aft stop. He watched his airspeed indicator, illuminated in red light by a 12-volt battery, and tried to steady the glider at 70. No way. The nose continued to drop and the speed built to 80, then 90, and continued to increase. What the hell was going on?

He peered intently at the landing zone, which was only a slightly paler shade of black. Then a faint small flickering light was visible, followed by another, and another. "They've got the smudges lit!" he called out.[8] The dimly outlined landing area was now steady in his windscreen. If it appeared to move up on the glass, it meant he was landing short; if it dropped down, they were too high. If they landed short in the jungle, all they could do was hold on; if they were too high, they could deploy the spoilers to kill their lift or shove the nose down and land fast. Both maneuvers gave up altitude they could not get back.

Closer now. Alison strained to see the first two gliders, but all he could see was various shades of darkness. He was aware of the closeness of treetops and swept over them into the safety of the jungle clearing. Hold it, hold it, hold it, now pull back the yoke to prevent landing squarely on the nose skid. The Waco should touch down and roll to a relatively smooth stop, even at the increased airspeed. He could hear the soughing of elephant grass brushing the leading edges of his wings, an unexpected sibilance that was now the only sound. Even the normally noisy jocular Chindits behind him were deathly silent.

He felt the wheels touch and pushed forward on the yoke to force the skid into the earth, but the glider continued to whistle through the tall grass; Alison was blind now to what lay ahead. The makeshift strip was rough, like riding a bicycle down a railroad track, with creosote-soaked ties slamming against the wheels in an irregular jolting rhythm.

The bouncing teeth-jarring ride ended as the nose skid finally bit into the ground, plowing a thin furrow that marked the path of the rollout. Total silence embraced them. The quiet lasted only seconds, as the Chindits quickly leaped from the glider and raced for the edge of the jungle. All, including the flight crew, waited for the sounds of incoming fire, but absolute stillness blanketed the clearing. Alison unbuckled his safety belt, looked at Tulloch, and shook his head, grinning. He grabbed his carbine and musette bag and turned to exit through the cabin, using the same side door as the Chindits.

He was quickly met by Taylor and British Brigadier "Mad Mike" Calvert, a veteran of the first Chindit campaign who was head of the initial assault team. Taylor pointed mournfully to his glider, smashed nearby. Alison had been lucky: the clearing at Broadway, which had seemed so flat and friendly in aerial photos, was a morass of ruts, many of them a foot and a half deep, caused by locals who used elephants to drag teak logs through the clearing. The heat had baked the mud hard as concrete; logs were strewn haphazardly about; the grass hid tree stumps. Deep watering holes for elephants and water buffalo also awaited the unsuspecting gliders. The fields were nearly perfect glider traps. That Alison's Waco was not wrecked was more luck than skill, he knew.[9]

They waited for the glider carrying Oley Olson, who was to command at Broadway. It should have been no more than ten minutes behind them, but they waited twice that time before realizing that something had happened. Olson was not coming. Alison, who had lost his command at Piccadilly, now took over at Broadway. But before he could issue his first order, a shot shattered the stillness of the night, and everyone flattened against the ground. The Japanese had been waiting for them. For several heart-pounding minutes they searched the dark tree line for movement or muzzle flashes. At last word came that a British trooper, hurrying to secure the perimeter of the clearing with his finger on the trigger, had accidently squeezed off a round from his Enfield. Alison, Taylor, and Calvert grinned at each other, relieved but peeved at the unknown soldier.[10]

The problems with the landing field had not gone away, and with the addition of more wrecked gliders the hazards were mounting exponentially. The first of the main wave of gliders was now approaching, and Alison ordered more smudge pots to be lit and placed in the diamond shape that would mark the landing zone. Another pot was to be placed a mile south of the zone to mark the release point for the gliders. Taylor himself ran through the grass and trees, carrying the pot to set it in position.

The steady influx of gliders proved deadly and chaotic. They all appeared to release too late and were landing beyond the safe area and crashing into trees or smashing into wrecked gliders already on the field. The signal pot was moved farther south. Still the gliders were coming in high and fast. The mayhem continued. Smashed broken gliders littered the field, eerily lit by gauzy blue moonlight, and still more continued to arrive. It would be many hours before they realized how grossly overloaded the gliders were, necessitating a vastly higher airspeed to land.

For Waller, well behind Alison, the night's flight was much longer than he had planned. For each tug and its twin gliders in tow, the flight was essentially a solitary flight into the unknown; they left Lalaghat to climb above the Chin Hills, then make their way to Broadway without benefit of a lead navigator or a formation of tugs to hold to. In the darkness the pilot of Waller's tug missed the clearing at Broadway and was forced to execute a 180-degree turn with his gliders and search for the clearing. Instead of a two-and-a-half hour flight, it stretched to nearly four hours.

Waller watched the tug intently, fighting off stress-induced vertigo, keeping that blue exhaust flame in sight. Suddenly the C-47 banked sharply left to avoid the steep hills surrounding Broadway. Waller was on short tow, and as he turned the glider nearly on its left wingtip to stay in position, it stalled and he was forced to release to recover from the loss of lift. When he recovered, he was over the clearing. He slipped the glider violently and called for full spoilers. His airspeed was 120, far too fast, but he was out of options.

"We hit the ground on the right spot but sheared off the left gear," he recounted later. "Here's where the luck came in. The accident threw the glider to the left sharply, otherwise we would have hit a wreck heap of smashed gliders." Shortly after, the second glider on tow with Waller came in and sheared off the tail of Waller's Waco.[11]

For the men on the ground Broadway was a disaster, a scene of terror and confusion. As those who were unscathed ran to help the men who were trapped in their smashed gliders, some suffering from horrible and painful injuries, the gliders continued to come in silently and smash into those piled up in the clearing. "It was hazy, the moon was getting low on the horizon, and you couldn't hear the gliders coming in. A glider would touch the ground and you could hear the rumble, but even then you couldn't start to run. Men were trying to get the wounded out, and there was no sense in running until the glider could be seen and you could tell where they were going. It was terribly harassing," Alison reported a few weeks after the landings.[12]

The primary radio, which was supposed to be the lifeline for the Chindit campaign, had gone down with Olson somewhere in the Burmese jungle. A second radio had made it into Broadway aboard Alison's glider but had been damaged on landing. Alison felt a deep sense of frustration. Unable to call Cochran to hold off on sending more gliders, Alison had to watch helplessly as they continued to arrive every few minutes and collide violently with those already jammed into the clearing. The rough terrain, teak logs, and deep ruts were ripping off the undercarriages of the gliders, and without wheels they could not be moved. Incoming gliders, announced only by a slight whistle of wind over their wings, continued to careen into the wreckage of those already on the ground.

Alison ordered the smudge pots moved, to divert the new arrivals, but everywhere the results were the same. The clearing, which had seemed so perfect from several thousand feet, was a glider killer. Alison searched in vain for the red flares to call off further glider releases, but finding anything in the jumble of equipment in the cabin of the Waco was impossible.

Still the gliders continued to arrive. More than three dozen were now in the clearing, all but two or three smashed beyond repair. At last, early in the morning hours, came a bit of good news. The secondary radio had been repaired. Alison immediately ordered a message sent to Cochran and Wingate: Soya link. Soya link. Soya link. The code was intended to alert the commanders to stop glider operations until the mess at Broadway was cleared. Then the radio died again. But at least those back at Lalaghat would understand the message, he hoped. The tugs and gliders would be called back.

It appeared, for the moment, that no more gliders would arrive. Alison, Taylor, Calvert, and the men—except for the frantic, overworked medical team under Captain Tulloch—could get a bit of rest. They had settled in, sick at heart and weary beyond all words, when they heard the sound of aircraft engines. Alison, who had grown accustomed to the arrival after dark of Japanese planes, immediately believed they were going to be bombed. As the plane grew closer, however, they all recognized the familiar deep thrumming of a C-47's Pratt and Whitney engines. Was this the start of a new wave of gliders? Calvert again searched frantically for a flare to warn them off, but none could be found quickly. They sent someone to douse the smudge pots, but that too was unsuccessful.

The cargo plane turned and left the area. They listened intently and soon could hear the eerie sibilant whistle of an approaching glider. They gritted their teeth as they awaited the inevitable crash. It soared over them, and they heard the horrifying sounds of the large glider slamming into trees somewhere in the darkness. It was impossible to tell exactly where it had crashed, and the jungle was dense and impossibly dark. Several men headed out in the general direction of the crash site but returned with no news after an hour's search. No doubt the dead could wait until first light. "Let's go to bed. Things always look better in the morning," Calvert advised the despondent Alison. They turned in for a couple of hours of fitful sleep.[13]

The glider, as it turned out, was carrying a small bulldozer, which was vital to clearing a runway for the cargo planes that would be landing with additional troops and supplies. It smashed into the jungle, where two large trees ripped off the wings; the fuselage, now a missile, hurtled farther into the thick overgrown forest until the tenacious undergrowth stopped it. The bulldozer was ripped from its tie-downs and shot forward, a two-ton block of iron that could crush to pulp the two pilots in front of it. And would have, if Flight Officer Gene Kelly had not rigged a safety line from the dozer to the nose release handle that stuck up between the pilots' seats like the shift lever of a Model-A Ford. As the dozer shot forward, it triggered the line that pulled the lever; the entire cockpit flipped up, with Kelly and Sgt. Joseph A. DeSalvo still belted into their seats. The heavy machine flew out of the glider and landed ten yards in front on its side. The two glider pilots remained in their seats as the nose and cockpit slammed back down. DeSalvo suffered a broken thumb, Kelly was unhurt. Uncertain whether Japanese were prowling the jungle, the pair remained silent and spent the night sitting in the broken glider. When they were found early the next morning, Kelly was calm and matter-of-fact about the bulldozer.[14]

Many others were not as lucky. Fifty-four gliders had been sent to Broadway; thirty-seven reached the clearing, and all but two or three were smashed and splintered. Twenty-four men were dead; many others were seriously injured. In the dim light of early morning, while the overworked medical team cared for the injured, Alison pondered the next phase of the operation. The plan called for quick construction of a primitive landing strip that would allow C-47s to ferry in the bulk of troops and supplies; without the C-47s the entire operation was in doubt. The engineering officer who was to oversee the construction, Lt. Patrick H. Casey of the 900th Airborne Engineers, had been killed in the melee of the night landings. Operation Thursday was unraveling rapidly.

But as Calvert had predicted, things began to look better with the full light of morning. As Alison and the British officer took stock of the misery around them, they turned at the sound of a chugging diesel engine nearby. The bulldozer flown in by Kelly and DeSalvo was found to be undamaged. It had been set upright and a clearing cut out of the thick tangled jungle. Now 2nd Lt. Robert Brackett, second in command of the engineering detachment, was at the controls.

Looking around at the dismal clearing, with its wrecked gliders, tall elephant grass, and a morass of deep ruts, stumps, and watering holes, Alison asked Brackett: "Do you think you can make an airstrip here?"

Brackett gazed mournfully at the unpromising landscape, slowly shaking his head. He looked at Alison with an unhappy expression, but his answer was positive. "Yes, I think we can."

"Well, how long is it going to take you?" Alison looked keenly at the young officer.

"Well, if I have it done late this afternoon, will that be soon enough?"

The delighted and astonished Alison laughed aloud. Get started, he said.[15]

By 0630 Calvert had reestablished radio communication with Wingate and requested light planes to fly the badly injured to hospitals. The radio again went out, leaving Wingate—and Cochran—still uncertain as to what had occurred at Broadway. They knew there were casualties but not the circumstances.

Eight P-51s flew over early that morning to assess the damage and determine what had happened. Olin B. Carter, one of the fighter pilots, described the vista at Broadway: "I looked down on a scene of utter destruction. Not a single glider was intact. The original plan was to snatch the gliders out, but not a single one was in a condition to do that."[16]

Cochran, miserable and downcast, sent Maj. Walter Radovich to Broadway to see first hand what had happened. Radovich, carrying a spare radio, flew an L-5 at treetop level. He buzzed low over Broadway, expecting to be shot out of the air at any minute. He landed, and the spare radio was quickly set up. Radovich looked around. After the first brief radio transmission that morning, Maj. Andrew P. Rebori had dispatched several L-1s from Tamu, and six of the most badly wounded men had been airlifted to hospitals in India. The other pilots were ordered to stay to provide air supply and recon, and to wait for the C-47s to arrive to evacuate the rest of the wounded.

Lieutenant Brackett was as good as his word. Using the small bulldozer, and dozens of Chindits pressed into manual labor, he had the airstrip ready to receive the Dakotas by late afternoon. Men used dynamite to blow out tree stumps, shovels to fill gouges and ruts, and tree trunks tied to harnesses as improvised graders. It was back-breaking work, but no one complained. Brackett was one of the largely unsung heroes of Broadway. He was killed in Burma two months later.

That evening the first C-47 landed at Broadway, bringing additional troops and supplies. When it took off just hours later, it carried the remaining wounded Chindits back to a hospital in India.

CHAPTER 18

Back at Lalaghat, Cochran felt immense relief when radio reports from Broadway detailed what had occurred and why Alison had sent the original "soya link" message. Cochran had spent hours in an agony of suspense and self-doubt, imagining the worst had happened to his friend Alison and the entire glider-borne assault team.

Nonetheless the total picture was bad. Nearly all the gliders had been destroyed, rendered unavailable for future missions. Two dozen men had been killed—four Air Commandos and twenty British and Indian troops—and dozens more injured, all in accidents, none by enemy action. Nine gliders had broken their towlines and were lost somewhere in the jungles of Burma; eight others had landed in India. A mission involving ten of the Air Commandos' UC-64 Norseman light cargo aircraft, sent out to drop additional supplies, had been a disaster. The Norseman fiasco resulted from a hasty and incomplete briefing of the flight crews following the change of plans that eliminated Piccadilly as an objective. The UC-64s were supposed to drop supply bundles to the Chindits. Told to simply fly in formation several pilots lost visual contact with the leader, Lt. Col. Clinton Gaty, because of the poor visibility. One landed on a sandbar in Burma, and others became lost and turned back to India. In the end three of the aircraft were lost after their pilots bailed out, and only two bundles of supplies made it to Broadway.[1]

Despite the catastrophically high number of casualties, Cochran learned days later of some good news involving the gliders that had broken their towlines and landed in the Burmese jungles.

Aboard one glider that went down short of Broadway was Capt. Weldon O. Murphy. He was acting as copilot aboard the glider and was to serve as medical officer at the stronghold. His glider was designated to serve as a hospital ship, and it was equipped with stretchers as well as a full load of Chindits and battle gear. Murphy recorded the events following the crash landing of his glider, and the chief medical officer and flight surgeon, Maj. Robert C. Page, included Murphy's account in a comprehensive medical report. Murphy noted that he and the pilot had been apprehensive during the flight. Their Waco was scheduled to land early at Broadway, but their worry was less about the possibility of combat and more about the constant surging of the glider and the loss of elasticity in the nylon rope. Two hours after takeoff the surging "became sufficient to break the communication wire between the tow ship and glider."[2] When that happened, the towline flew back into the glider's right wing, badly mauling the trailing edge. Things quickly got dicey.

"Now there were two damaged gliders tied together in the air," Murphy recounted. "There was an eminent [sic] danger of spinning. The rope was quickly released. Our badly damaged right wing was raised by constant banking to the left. The ship glided to a safe landing on a sand bar located in the midst of Japanese-occupied territory on the East bank of the Irrawaddy River opposite Katha."[3]

No one was injured in the unscheduled landing, and they quickly evacuated the glider and slipped into the surrounding jungle. Accompanying them was the RAF flight lieutenant who was to have been the ground-air liaison at Broadway; he insisted that they destroy the virtually intact glider. Seventeen men were aboard Murphy's Waco, and they stood ready in the inky darkness to provide the RAF officer with covering fire if he were attacked. Murphy, armed with a Thompson submachine gun, eased off the safety as he nervously waited for the RAF officer to return. Suddenly the sandbar was illuminated by a bright blaze, as flames licked at the doped fabric of the glider. The fire quickly consumed the covering and the wooden wings of the glider, leaving only the blackened skeleton of its fuselage.

They were eighty miles from Broadway. The men resolved to walk to their original destination rather than try to return to India. For the next eight days they trod stealthily through the jungle, avoiding trails and villages, speaking only in a whisper, eating a third of a day's ration per day, and never stopping for more than four hours. Despite frequent use of mosquito repellent at each rest stop, they were covered by insect bites after two hours. Ticks were a continuous irritant, and they constantly checked themselves and each other for signs of the blood suckers..

Despite their predicament and the constant danger of discovery, Murphy recorded that the group's morale was quite high, and he noted numerous instances of self-sacrifice. One man had difficulty keeping up with the others; Murphy learned that he had no salt tablets and had not wanted to ask others to share theirs. That was easily remedied. After several days of hard going, another man was completely exhausted; he had started out with only a single day's rations and had not eaten anything in two days, because he did not want to deprive others in the squad. They quickly supplied him with rations from their own kits.

As medical officer Murphy was especially aware of hygiene, insisting that they remove their wet boots and socks each time they stopped to rest. He administered ointment to facial scratches from the branches and sharp-edged leaves of jungle trees, and he watched carefully for signs of malaria, which had proved to be such a scourge with Wingate's irregular forces in their first campaign. But prudence and good practice were sometimes difficult in the circumstances. The men were supposed to treat water with chlorine tablets before drinking it; all were aware of this catechism.

"On several occasions after we had been long without water it was difficult to abide by the rules," Murphy reported. "Particularly when a stream suddenly came into view and each man had to quietly wait his turn to slip down the embankment to fill his canteen. The water he carried with him was chlorinated—the water he drank now was more likely not."[4]

Despite stretching their emergency food, they did not have enough. As they walked through the thick jungle, broken occasionally by small clearings, they came across a pond in which they clearly could see fish darting below the surface. They were tantalizing, frustrating, and torturous to see, and finally Murphy acceded to the request of his starving troops: they tossed in a couple of hand grenades. The resulting concussive force of the explosion killed nearly sixty fish, which they consumed on the spot.[5]

Finally, on 13 March, Murphy and his band of tired, dirty, and hungry troops arrived by foot at Broadway—just in time to be strafed and bombed by the Japanese, who had at last found the stronghold in the jungle. For the first time in his medical career Murphy had to treat an officer wounded by enemy action. That night Murphy, the glider pilot, and the wounded officer were evacuated to Hailakandi.

Murphy had previously viewed the primitive conditions at Hailakandi with distaste. A week in the Burmese jungle had changed his perspective.

"Here I found C rations good, crude beds comfortable and the countryside which before seemed only partially civilized, quite home-like."[6]

The glider containing Lt. Col. Arvid "Oley" Olson, who had been slated to command at Broadway, also suffered a broken towline (this was one of two towed by Capt. Dick Cole). The glider pilot quickly turned back west and managed to land near the Chindwin River close to friendly territory. Olson injured a foot, making walking difficult. He made a crude crutch with a forked top that he wrapped in bandages for padding and limped out. After several days of walking his party arrived safely back in Assam.[7]

The second glider in double tow with Olson did not fare as well. Maj. Richard Boebel, group intelligence officer, was aboard; he later related the story to the journalist Lowell Thomas. Boebel, an aspiring pilot who had washed out of flight school, had jumped at the chance to leave his desk job in the States and see action. Now, he was rethinking that decision. When the towline broke, it wrapped itself around the wing of the glider, and the pilot had pushed the nose forward and headed for the ground. He told Boebel that he planned to pancake the glider into the tops of the jungle canopy, a maneuver that had been explained—but of course never demonstrated—by his instructors at the glider flying school. Boebel was unconvinced. In the moonlight he spied a nearby flat field. The pilot was certain that Japanese would be guarding it but reluctantly agreed to try a landing there.

The pilot was right. After a noisy landing marked by crunching and cracking sounds as the damaged glider skidded to a stop in a rice paddy, its seventeen occupants piled out. Four Americans, five Burmese riflemen, and eight British troops looked around warily. They were greeted by gunfire and flopped down.

A Burmese captain whispered to Boebel that it must be a small force, perhaps a patrol, since the firing was only scattered rifle shots. As Boebel nodded in agreement, a machine gun began spraying bullets around them, and the men decided to leave quickly.

"We didn't know it, but we had landed near a Jap military headquarters [the Japanese army's 31st Division Headquarters]. So the glider pilot had been right. The Japs, hearing us crash, were shooting in the direction of the sound. None of us was touched," Boebel said later.[8]

Boebel, like many of the Air Commandos, was perhaps overarmed: he was carrying a folding-stock carbine, a Thompson submachine gun, a .45-caliber pistol, and a small personal handgun. The arsenal made running difficult, but he was not tempted to leave any of his weapons behind.

Three incidents seared into his memory marked their trek to safety: a monstrous python, a near murder and mutiny, and the courageous death of a glider mechanic.

A Burmese python is among the largest reptiles on Earth, as long as twenty-three feet. While not venomous, they are capable of suffocating large mammals—including humans—by wrapping around them and constricting the victim's ability to breathe. They swallow their prey whole and are excellent swimmers, able to stay under water as long as thirty minutes at a time. While on the journey home, Boebel's group had stopped to rest, scattering through the jungle so they could not be easily ambushed. Boebel, sitting and leaning against a tree, heard a rustling and was instantly alert, his senses keyed, his heart racing. He watched in horrified fascination as a python, five inches in diameter, slowly crawled toward him. Should he shoot it and risk detection by Japanese? Pull out his jungle knife and try to cut off its head? The snake was a perfect symphony of camouflage, a beautiful undulating composition of design and color for which he had no appreciation at all. In the end he held his breath as the serpent, about twelve feet long, slithered over his legs and disappeared into the surrounding jungle. His comrades were equally horrified when he shared the story with them. They might have been more traumatized had they known of the huge family of venomous snakes, nearly forty species in all, that lounged on tree limbs throughout the jungle and whose bite could kill an adult male in a matter of hours.[9]

After a few days in the fetid jungle, several British Chindits came to Boebel one evening and matter-of-factly informed him they intended to kill their commanding officer, a lieutenant colonel who was by all accounts insufferable. Boebel acknowledged that the man treated everyone shabbily: he insisted that a Chindit act as his orderly, addressed everyone in a condescending tone, consumed more than his share of rations, ignored the Burmese troops, and generally lacked leadership skills. The Burmese captain was the true leader of the party, intimately familiar with the jungle, and Boebel and the Chindits all recognized this reality.

The Chindits said they intended that a terrible fatal accident would befall the officer and end their misery. Obviously Boebel could not consent to their plan, but he said he would speak with the man. He did. Boebel first reminded the ranking officer of the American's position as intelligence officer, then said that he had some meaningful information. The American warned the British field officer that he probably would not survive the march out if he did not surrender command to Boebel, who then would listen most closely to advice from the Burmese captain. The British officer did not blink and immediately and without fuss turned over leadership and control to Boebel. Later, after Wingate's staff heard the story, the man was fired and sent home. Apparently something similar had happened during the campaign in Africa, where Field Marshal Bernard Montgomery had fired the offending officer.[10]

A third event was tragic. On the fourth night the small party arrived at the Chindwin. It was wide and fast flowing, the last major obstacle to safety back in Assam. The Chin Hills lay beyond, but the hills meant only numbing physical exhaustion, with opportunities to stop and rest. The river meant death to those swept away in its powerful current.

Of the seventeen men, eight did not know how to swim. Among them was Cpl. Estil I. Nienaber, a small young glider mechanic who wore glasses. He had virtually begged to be taken on the Broadway mission, and the officers had finally agreed. They were unimpressed with his slight physical appearance, but they were taken with his intensity and desire. Heroes seldom look like Hollywood stars.

The men listened quietly as Boebel informed them of the signs of a recent Japanese patrol in the area. Anyone swept along by the current was not to call out, for the noise could alert other Japanese.

The British troops removed their trousers, tied the legs closed, and inflated them to act as makeshift life preservers. The Americans copied their improvisation and, arm in arm, began to wade into the current. It was dark and the water was cold, chilling the men as the river came up to their knees, then their chests, and at last they were floating, paddling, clinging together to their flimsy rafts of government-issued battle dress, swimmers paired with nonswimmers. Somewhere in the darkness, Corporal Nienaber was pulled from the group and swept away.

No one could see him in the gloom. The young man, grimly determined not to put his friends in danger, refused to shout for help. They never saw him again. The British troops were in awe of his self-sacrifice and upon their return talked with newsmen who wrote the story for papers back home. Heraclitus was correct regarding the brave corporal, who would never again step into any river.[11]

Other gliders that went down before reaching Broadway were equally lucky and unlucky. One came down near the Japanese 15th Division HQ. Although most men escaped, the pilot was blinded in the crash landing and captured by the Japanese. One can imagine the tactics used to extract information from the unlucky airman, but he apparently refused to reveal anything. However, the Japanese were able to make some guesses about what was happening by studying the wrecked glider and some of the materials aboard. Another glider came down near a regimental headquarters in the Paungbyin area, and more men were captured. Wingate's previous foray into Burma had the Japanese on high alert; they anticipated that he would once again try something unorthodox in the dry season.

In all, nine gliders went down in Japanese-occupied Burma, at widely dispersed locations. The scattered gliders created a sense among the Japanese that a huge force was hitting them, striking at many targets throughout Burma.

As the enemy focused on defending key rail and communications centers, which had been the chief targets of Wingate's raiders the previous year, Broadway remained undisturbed for more than a week. It was enough.

CHAPTER 19

After Lt. Robert Brackett and his nine men in the engineering unit scraped out a landing field at Broadway, Brigadier General Old, whose long habit was to lead from the cockpit, took off from Lalaghat at 1730 and flew the first C-47 in to the jungle clearing shortly after dark on 6 March. Alison had advised Cochran to send three Dakotas; Cochran, operating on the theory that more is always better, dispatched twelve. They arrived all night long. Cargo and troops were quickly unloaded, and the planes returned to Lalaghat for more.

Aboard Old's C-47 was Sgt. Ed Cunningham, a correspondent for *Yank,* the weekly army magazine. He filed a report that ran in the 5 May 1944 CBI edition. Cunningham was clearly impressed with the mission: the execution of Operation Thursday "made Buck Rogers look like Colonel Blimp."

As Cunningham saw it, construction of even a rough airfield in less than twenty-four hours was a miracle of American ingenuity and determination, and he expressed unbridled admiration for the men who had done it. He noted that after eating only a quick lunch of jam and crackers, the tired GIs had completed the landing field and then collapsed into sleep, their first in thirty-eight hours. When the C-47s arrived just at dark, Alison had set up a control tower in one of the wrecked gliders well off the landing area. The right wing held radios, and two communications men worked the sets. Cunningham observed the activity as

Gooney Birds arrived in a continuous stream all night. Alison told the radio operators to advise the approaching cargo planes to land south to north. While waiting for the first one on final approach to land, Alison asked the enlisted radiomen: "Do you guys realize where we are? We're right in the middle of Jap territory, causing a hell of a racket, and they're not doing anything about it."

"We're too damned busy to think about it, sir," M. Sgt. Otto Grunow replied. "But if we told the folks back home that we were operating an airport 150 miles inside enemy lines, they'd call us liars."

"Yeah, they would," agreed Tech. Sgt. Alex McGregor. "But I'll bet we're doing more business tonight than they are at LaGuardia Field." He might have been right. Cunningham reported that the C-47s arrived in flights of six. He timed the intervals between touchdowns for the first three of one flight: thirty-two seconds between the first and second, thirty-six seconds between second and third. One flight of six landed, unloaded, and departed for India in twenty minutes flat.[1]

A radar unit was flown in and set up to provide early warning of Japanese air attacks. Everyone knew it was only a matter of time before Broadway was found, and a fierce pushback by Japanese forces would result. Antiaircraft guns were delivered and sandbagged gun positions built.

None of the Chindits or Air Commandos was deceived by the lack of an immediate response by Japanese forces. The enemy simply had not discovered their whereabouts yet.

In the meantime it was urgent that the Air Commandos deliver as many troops and as much supplies to Broadway as they could before they were discovered; keeping the air route open might become impossible after that. A virtually continuous stream of American and British cargo planes flew through the darkness to the jungle airstrip: forty-four Dakotas from RAF Transport Squadrons 31, 62, 117, and 194 joined thirty-nine C-47s from the 27th and 315th Troop Carrier Squadrons and the 319th Troop Carrier Squadron of the 1st Air Commandos. In time they airlifted 9,052 troops, along with 1,359 mules, a few horses, and 254.5 tons of supplies and equipment, in to Broadway.[2]

The sight was impressive, even remarkable. British Air Marshal Jack Baldwin, commander of the Third Tactical Air Force who had piloted a Dakota in to Broadway, sent daily reports to Air Chief Marshal Richard Peirse of the RAF and General Stratemeyer of the USAAF. For the most part these are matter-of-fact summaries of the situation, with information on upcoming plans and a précis of men and materiel delivered. By 10 March Baldwin was praising Troop Carrier Command in the highest terms and waxing poetic about the Broadway operation: "Nobody has seen a transport operation until he has stood at Broadway under the light of a Burma full moon and watched Dakotas coming in and taking off in opposite directions on a single strip all night long at the rate of one landing or one take off every three minutes. Wingate and I think you should tell Godfrey that his airborne engineers are superb repeat superb. Within forty eight hours Hurricanes and P-51s will occupy Broadway. That is all."[3]

On the second day following the terrible night smashups on the unimproved clearing, a Burmese chaplain held a memorial service for the men killed. The American dead had been airlifted out, along with the badly wounded, but in the tradition of the British military their dead had been buried near where they had fallen.[4]

After the respectful pause the men put on their headgear and went back to work. Soon the Bofors antiaircraft guns and other defensive arms delivered by the C-47s had been sited and fortified, ready for the inevitable Japanese response.

Reports from Broadway continued to be positive, and the next day, 7 March, Wingate decided to open another field at a clearing code-named Chowringhee, after the congested thoroughfare in Calcutta. Chowringhee was about seventy miles south of Broadway, and because of the bends in the Irrawaddy was situated on the east side of that great river. Brigadier Joe Lentaigne's 111th Indian Brigade would enter the fray from there, the initial pathfinder force to be flown in by glider.

Cochran ordered a dozen Wacos to fly into Chowringhee that night. Leading them would be Flight Officer Jackie Coogan, who had proved to be a good pilot despite his occasional antics and poor judgment on the ground. Coogan's tow pilot was to be Capt. Bill Cherry. All the tows from now on would be single; they had learned their lesson about double tows during the descent to Broadway and would not make the same mistakes again.[5]

The takeoff from Lalaghat went smoothly, and the climb to 4,000 feet over the base was similarly uneventful. The tows and gliders crossed the Chin Hills, with the gliders in the high-tow position out of the prop wash of the tug's engines, but as darkness descended over the region the glider pilots went to low tow, where they could see the exhaust flames from the C-47 engines, as well as the vague outline of the tug against the sky. The tugs were burning so much fuel that the exhaust stacks were bright blue and easily visible. Coogan kept his glider, filled with Chindit troops, in position below Cherry's Gooney Bird, fighting the occasional turbulence and taking up the inevitable towline slack smoothly and without incident. When they arrived over Chowringhee, however, Cherry began his turn to allow room for the usual landing routine of the Waco, and Coogan inexplicably released his glider.

It could have been exciting; it could have been disastrous. It was neither. Recognizing that he had released early, Coogan simply extended his landing pattern and touched down neatly in the moonlit clearing, rolling to a relatively smooth stop. Chowringhee had no logs, no ruts, no hidden watering holes. As soon as the Waco stopped moving, the Chindits bolted from the glider and moved silently and swiftly toward the dark line of jungle, prepared to fight the Japanese they assumed would be there. Once again the silent invasion met no resistance. Coogan set about placing smudge pots in a diamond pattern in the clearing to mark the field for the remaining gliders and positioned a release signal a mile away.

None of the pilots knew what to expect at Chowringhee. No Japanese resistance at Broadway on the 5th was no assurance that they would not meet fierce fire at this clearing. Glider pilots Charles Turner and Harry McKaig had experimented with mounting flexible machine guns in the noses of their CG-4As. When McKaig fired his in a safe area at Lalaghat, the hammering recoil shattered his windscreen. The pair then reinforced Turner's windscreen and replaced McKaig's. As it turned out, neither ever had to fire the jury-rigged guns at enemy troops.[6]

Most gliders landed at Chowringhee without incident, but the one carrying a bulldozer, needed to clear a strip for C-47s to land, sailed over the clearing and crashed into the jungle beyond. Everyone aboard was killed, and the dozer was destroyed.

Flight Officer Turner had landed his glider just ahead of the unfortunate pilot hauling the dozer: "We were doing what we called a blitz approach. Instead of releasing at 1,000 feet and possibly doing a 180 [degree turn], we released at 500 feet and came straight in. We were all overloaded, so our speed was much higher, probably 80 [mph] instead of 60 or 70. When we felt the main wheels touch down, we shoved the yoke forward so the skid would dig in and stop us quickly, and we always had our feet on the instrument panel. There was no protection if we hit something in the dark, and none of us wanted to lose our legs."

When his glider finally stopped, Turner turned to the lance corporal of the Gurkha Rifles, who had been sitting in the copilot's seat. He seemed frozen in place, as did the fifteen or so Gurkha riflemen riding in the rear. Turner, still not certain whether they would take fire from waiting Japanese, shouted at them in his best Hindustani: "Jilte-jow!" (Hurry up and go!) The young lance corporal wasted no more time. He smashed the side window in the cockpit and dove through it. In the rear the Gurkhas hacked their way through the fabric sides of the glider and squeezed out. None used the door.

"So now I was standing outside the cockpit when the glider with the dozer came in," Turner said. "A glider makes a strange kind of whistling noise when it's heavy and fast, and I looked up when he went over. It was dark, of course, but I could see him. He was probably a hundred feet in the air, when he should have been on the ground already. He was high and fast, and then his wing caught the top of a teak tree that was probably a hundred feet high. The glider just went straight in. They were all killed, and the dozer was ruined. They called to Broadway for another dozer, and they brought one in the next day."[7]

Coogan, the former child movie star, would receive the Air Medal for his night's work (he added an oak-leaf cluster for a second hazardous flight into the clearing code-named Aberdeen a couple of weeks later). The *New York Herald Tribune* erroneously reported that Coogan was the first glider pilot in to Burma. It was not a critical issue, but it irritated those who had gone in to the horror at Broadway earlier; it became a festering wound when Coogan, who desperately needed to excel at something since his acting career had stalled, did not correct the report.[8]

The loss of the dozer, and therefore the inability to create a suitable landing strip, threatened to delay the insertion of additional troops at Chowringhee. Cochran immediately dispatched a C-47 to Calcutta to bring another dozer in. Meanwhile Alison loaded the small dozer at Broadway into one of the still-flyable gliders; towed behind a C-47, the glider delivered the heavy machine to Chowringhee at about 2100 (9 p.m.). Plans had called for C-47s to begin landing there the next night, but instead they were diverted to Broadway, which had become a very busy airport indeed. As it turned out Chowringhee was much more exposed than Broadway. After 125 landings of gliders and C-47s, the Air Commandos abandoned the site on the night of 9 March. Shortly after the last two aircraft took off (two C-47s that had been slightly damaged but were repaired), Japanese attacked the strip, but no one was home. The ground troops had also departed, and the results of the Japanese air strike were a lot of damaged trees and many craters in the clearing.

Of the twelve gliders flown in to Chowringhee, only two were in shape to be towed out. Turner, who had just turned twenty, flew one of them. "The worst part was just trying to see. When that C-47 applied full power, it kicked up a duststorm, and I couldn't see a thing," he recalled. "It was scary. But we made it out."[9]

Two days after the initial night landing at Broadway, Wingate himself flew in to look over what he anticipated would become a stronghold, a fortified position in the heart of enemy territory that evoked a sense of biblical history and moral rectitude. Alison, who had worked like a madman since landing his glider in the clearing that first night, met the C-47 as it taxied to a temporary ramp beside the runway. Wingate descended, wearing his sun helmet and a bush jacket complete with ribbons and the red tabs of a general officer. Unlike virtually any other general around, however, Wingate was bearded and he carried a .303 rifle, a weapon he had favored since his days in Palestine with his Special Night Squads. With his beard and deep-set dark eyes he could look as fierce as an Old Testament warrior, but on this day, as he inspected the physical vindication of his long campaign of planning and haranguing, he looked almost beatific. Everywhere were loads of supplies, men hard at work constructing defensive sites, aircraft starting up or taxiing to take off. It seemed hardly possible that all this was the result of just two days' work. But it had come at a high price, and the cost of the effort was clearly visible in the piles of wrecked gliders that still littered the clearing and in the row of simple crosses near the tree line.

Alison, wearing a grubby set of airborne trousers and with a .45 in a shoulder holster, showed Wingate around the bustling clearing-cum-landing strip. It was obvious that the brigadier was impressed, scarcely able to believe what the Air Commandos had been able to achieve in so short a time.

After Wingate's initial inspection of Broadway, Alison ordered an L-5—about a dozen were now parked back in the trees—to be preflighted and topped with fuel. He loaded Wingate into the backseat and flew to Chowringhee to look it over. After a brief inspection there Wingate and Alison flew back to Broadway, where Wingate spent the night. It was a rare treat for him now. As a major general he had about 12,000 men under his command, and he could not lead from the front as was his wont. He was forty years old, the head of seventeen British battalions, as well as five Gurkha and three West African, and the duties of administering such a diverse fighting force did not allow the luxury of fieldwork. He sorely missed it.

The next morning he flew back to Lalaghat, where he was greeted by his aide, Brig. Derek Tulloch (not to be confused with the American medical officer), with news that distressed Wingate. The Japanese had been planning a major attack; Lt. Gen. Renya Mutaguchi was to invade India from Burma, seizing the key towns of Imphal and Kohima in Assam. Aerial reconnaissance seemed to confirm what the Brits had learned from intercepted radio messages: the attack was imminent. The Japanese code had been broken by ULTRA, called MAGIC in the Far East, and Field Marshal Slim was in the loop regarding the Japanese plans.

While Wingate was visiting Broadway and Chowringhee, Slim had notified Tulloch that in the event of a Japanese strike the field marshal might have to use Wingate's two Chindit brigades that were being held in reserve. Slim's plan was to allow the Japanese to cross the Chindwin, then destroy them by using massive airpower and superior numbers of ground troops.

Tactically the plan was sound. Wingate, however, was furious: he had intended to use the reserve brigades to replace those in the field in Burma as they became weakened or depleted. Using all available forces to repel an advance by the enemy sounds like Tactics 101, but this did not deter Wingate from lashing out in rather intemperate terms at what he saw as double dealing or, perhaps from his perspective, incompetence. Besides, Mountbatten himself had assured Wingate that in the event of a long-awaited Japanese attack into India, he would retain command of all his brigades and would be expected to harass and disrupt the Japanese lines of communication and transportation deep inside Burma. He told Tulloch that he intended to fly to Imphal the next morning and confront Slim; if it was not resolved in his favor, he would resign. Wingate had tested Slim before. Dissatisfied with Slim's plan to aid the Chindits, Wingate had told him he could not accept it unless additional aircraft were provided. Slim said that was not possible; Wingate said he could not accept the order. The field marshal told Wingate to study overnight an unsigned copy of the order and to meet the next day in Slim's headquarters to receive a signed copy. "I told him I had never had a subordinate officer refuse an order, but if one did, I knew what to do," Slim recalled. Wingate returned the following morning and, with a wry smile, signed the written order.[10]

Despite that history Wingate's mood was light when he returned to Lalaghat the next day. Tulloch learned that Slim, when confronted by the headstrong Wingate, had insisted that if the two reserve brigades were needed to defend India, Wingate himself would command them, of course. It was a silly showdown perhaps but illustrative of Wingate's fierce determination to maintain the integrity of his special force.[11] That fierce determination, however, did not serve him so well just a short time later, when he stepped in it with Mountbatten himself.

The public relations branch of the South East Asia Command had issued a brief release about operations in Burma that mentioned the invading force as elements of the 14th British Army. Quizzed later, the PR branch claimed the release was designed to excite the interest of correspondents and homefront readers alike; subsequent releases would give more credit and far more details. But the first release—sent out without notifying Wingate—did not mention him, the Chindits, or the Air Commandos. True to form, when Wingate saw the news release at Lalaghat, he exploded.

To be fair, part of his ire probably came from his sense that Cochran especially, but all the rest of the Air Commandos to whom he felt he owed so much, would feel slighted and ill used. Wingate had already had to pacify Cochran—normally laid-back but with a notable Irish temper—after six RAF Spitfires flew in to Broadway before Cochran could send in his Mustangs. Cochran had been furious. Were his men just to be runway laborers for the RAF? Wingate apologized, Cochran was mollified, and Japanese aerial attacks destroyed all the Spitfires (more about this incident in Chapter 21). Now, the first news release about the operation had gone out with not a word about the fine and heroic work of the Air Commandos. Wingate thought it might be the proverbial straw for Cochran. The British commander fired off a communiqué to the head of Mountbatten's public relations arm, castigating him for a poor job and calling the release a "travesty of the truth."[12] That wasn't enough for Wingate; he followed it up with a letter in a similar vein to Mountbatten himself.

Lord Admiral Mountbatten was a likeable and affable man of noble birth and expensive education. But he was not a pushover. He swiftly rebuked Wingate, in firm and certain terms. Wingate apparently wrote a reply to this, but good sense prevailed and he did not send it.[13]

The informality of the forward bases made for team cohesion but not for military appearance or hierarchy. The mess halls at Lalaghat and Hailakandi had been hurriedly constructed, and they housed both officers and enlisted men without regard for class or rank; saluting at any time was nearly nonexistent. One day a visiting U.S. general was invited to dine, and when he stepped into the crowded dining area he stopped, agog at the sight of enlisted men and officers sharing tables, addressing each other by first names. He complained to Cochran, who explained it was the only facility they had, but if the general preferred a private table outside, that was easily arranged. He did, and it was.[14]

He wasn't the only general who was picky about appearances. Patt Meara, who had joined the Air Commandos as a substitute aerial gunner, was driving Brig. Gen. William D. Old, head of the Troop Carrier Command in India, around the airfield in a jeep one day. Meara wore a mechanic's ball cap with the bill snapped up. Before being sent to India, Meara had been in North Africa, where he had obtained some souvenirs, including some rank insignia taken from Italian POWs. A five-pointed star was the insignia of a second lieutenant in the Italian army, and Meara had pinned a souvenir badge to his cap bill.

"I didn't realize we had another brigadier general in the area," Old growled at Meara, who quickly explained where he had obtained the pin. "Take that damned star off right now!" Old insisted. Meara removed it on the spot.[15]

Later that same day Old came across a group of glider pilots who had just unloaded supplies from a train. He was shocked at the slovenly, decidedly unmilitary, appearance of the dirty, bearded, and haphazardly uniformed men who called themselves Air Commandos. Old apparently blistered the ears of the nearest ranking officer, who offered no explanations. Cochran was advised of the incident and on 13 March wrote and posted what surely is one of the most unusual memoranda of the war:

To: All Personnel and Attached Organizations.

Look, Sports, the beards and attempts at beards are not appreciated by visitors.

Since we can't explain to all strangers that the fuzz is a gag or "something I always wanted to do" affair, we must avoid their reporting that we are unshaven (regulations say you must shave) by appearing like Saturday night in Jersey whenever possible.

Work comes before shaving. You will never be criticized for being unkempt if you are so damn busy you can't take time to doll up. But be clean while you can.

Ain't it awful?

> P. G. Cochran
> Colonel, Air Corps
> Commanding[16]

But Brig. Gen. William Old was not just a stickler for military protocol. He was a fearless and accomplished pilot, having flown one of the first planeloads of supplies from India over the Hump to China, in March 1942. He also was at the controls of the first C-47 in to Broadway on the night of 6 March. Within a couple of days of the beard incident, Old had become an Air Commando, at least in appearance. Feeling compelled to pitch in, he too had become dirty and unkempt. He apologized to the officer for tearing off a strip of his hide on the first day. Old now understood what the men at Lalaghat and Hailikandi were going through.[17]

CHAPTER 20

At Hailakandi on 7 March, two days after the first flights in to Broadway, American S.Sgt. Shojiro T. Taketa instinctively leaned closer to his radio set, slowly twisting the tuning dial that brought a steady stream of crackling static through his headset. A whirring hum, rising to a squeal and falling off as the thin needle arced slowly through the frequency spectrum, was a constant assault on his ears. A brief burst of faint garbled staccato syllables caught his attention, but it disappeared. He continued to turn the dial slowly, infinitely slowly. For Taketa the headset and the black crackle-painted radio were magical instruments, the tools of wizards that allowed him to enter a parallel universe, a realm entirely composed of sound, an ethereal galaxy of electrical energy without visual clues, slights, or prejudices.

This solo journey into the radio-band kingdom of kilohertz was soothing. There nothing mattered except the interdiction of sound waves transmitted through the atmosphere.

Taketa was a Nisei, a second-generation Japanese American. He had grown up in California and attended Yuba College in Marysville, where he had been a basketball standout.[1] The executive order that moved him, his family, and thousands of Japanese Americans into relocation centers in Idaho, Wyoming, Montana, and Utah had been like a kick in the stomach, and he had quickly jumped at the chance to enter the army, in part to escape the camp but mostly to publicly declare his allegiance to the only country he had ever known. Taketa had been selected for the Military Intelligence Service and did well at the MIS language schools, where he also learned katakana, a code system based on seventy-one phonetic sounds and thirty-six individual syllables long used by the Japanese to express their words in romanized letters.[2]

Despite the obvious value of using Japanese speakers in the Pacific and the CBI, official policy had forbidden it. Still, many Japanese Americans had been assigned to units—British as well as American—in India and China, including with Stillwell's (but not with his approval). The Air Commandos had picked Taketa. Each day he read the intelligence summaries posted to the unit and spent his time tethered to the radio. For the past several days he had been listening to the Japanese aviation frequencies between 2,500 and 10,000 kHz. These were voice transmissions in the clear between pilots and ground controllers.

Suddenly a faint but authoritative voice, obviously issuing instructions, came through, and Taketa strained to catch every word of the clipped ground-to-pilot conversation. Pilots around the globe, and those whose job it was to communicate with them, had developed precise condensed phrases to convey clear meanings. Sometimes those meanings were camouflaged by using code words, which was the case now. Despite that, the sheer volume of transmissions during the past two days made it obvious that something unusual was happening.

A large number of aircraft were operating in and around an airfield code-named Nagoya. What did it mean? And where was Nagoya? Tom—no one ever called him Sergeant Taketa or even Shojiro—sat back and looked around the dirt-floored basha at Hailakandi that served as the radio shack for the Air Commandos. Taketa normally reported to Major Boebel, but Boebel had left for Broadway; he hadn't made it, and no one knew where his glider had gone down. A conscientious young man, Taketa worked doubly hard to prove—if only to himself—that he was a totally loyal American. He went back through his logs of every intercepted radio transmission and then pored over the daily intelligence briefings forwarded to him. He rose and took four steps to the large-scale map of Burma tacked on the wall and stared at it for several minutes. Colored tacks marked the locations of the intended glider landing sites in northern Burma, as well as known enemy airfields. All maps of Burma provided sketchy details at best; the best known was from a British effort in the early 1920s, but pilots were told not to rely on information regarding mountain heights. Even many villages were unnamed. But it was what they had.

In the two days since the start of Operation Thursday, the Japanese had not retaliated for the glider intrusion. C-47s of the U.S. Troop Carrier Command, together with RAF Dakotas, had made hundreds of deliveries to Broadway and Chowringhee, and the small L-1 and L-5 aircraft daily flew at treetop level to bring in visitors and take out wounded; thus far Japanese warplanes had not harassed or threatened any. Where was the Japanese air force? What were they planning?[3]

Taketa's work was difficult and frustrating. Radio waves are slaves to distance, obstacles, and weather conditions. At his listening post at Hailakandi, Taketa was hundreds of miles from Japanese bases in Burma, and the Chin Hills rose nearly 8,000 feet, a geological wall between him and the enemy that blocked transmissions from lower altitudes. Storms or other atmospheric disturbances also blocked radio signals. Coupled with those problems were the notoriously unreliable Japanese aerial transmitters and their extremely short ranges. But occasionally things went well, and he had been able to pick up numerous signals in recent days. Way too many signals, in fact. The Japanese air force was staging a major buildup somewhere in Burma.

Tom Taketa worked it out in his mind, considering several possibilities and ruling them out. All but the area of Shwebo, that is. A couple of Japanese airfields there fit all the criteria for a large buildup of forces. Yes, it had to be Shwebo, in central Burma.

The twenty-two-year-old Taketa phoned the command basha at Lalaghat, where Colonel Cochran had lived for the last two days. Told who was calling, Cochran was as informal with Taketa as he was with the rest of the Air Commandos. "Hey, Tom. What's up, sport?"

Tom Taketa rapidly detailed what he had deduced. Taketa couldn't see it, but Cochran, taking it all in, grinned. His face had revealed lines of strain from the series of misadventures with the gliders, but he appeared relaxed now. The telephone call was exactly the kind of information that would allow him to start fighter and bomber operations, to be back in his element of action, doing something over which he had some control. He hated paperwork, and now he understood that supervision and administration were not high on his list, either. Cochran called Grant Mahony.

For a few weeks before Operation Thursday began, Mahony and his fighter guys had prowled the skies over Burma. Their Mustangs, painted dull olive drab, were unmistakeable with their five diagonal stripes wrapped around the fuselage; additional horizontal stripes on the tail identified individual Air Commandos. Two stripes denoted Mahony's as well as R. T. Smith's aircraft; a single stripe adorned Maj. Bob Petit's plane; Cochran's Mustang sported three. The visual signs were important when forming up or if silence was imposed or if the radios went down, as happened frequently. Sometimes nose art was the distinctive touch other pilots recognized at a glance. Mahony always looked for "Mrs. Virginia" on the nose of the P-51A flown by his ops exec, Bob Petit; Maj. Walter Radovich flew Mongoose; the nose of Smith's fighter, as well as his B-25, proclaimed it Barbie. Flying in small formations, they sought out wide-ranging targets of opportunity that would keep the Japanese off guard and not call attention to the upcoming invasion site.

Mahony and Cochran talked it over; Taketa's educated guess sounded promising. They decided to arm each of twenty-one Mustangs with a single 500-pound bomb, plus auxiliary fuel tanks and full racks of .50-caliber ammunition. Their excitement was evident in their voices, while each maintained the facade of doing routine work. While the fighters were being armed, Cochran and Mahony quickly briefed the pilots.

It was a turkey shoot. Mahony led the formation first to the Japanese airfield at Anisakan. There, undisguised, were seventeen enemy fighters lined up beside the runway. Mahony had an open and unabated hatred of the Japanese, a trait shared by other CBI pilots who had often been the targets of bombing raids and who knew that captured Allied pilots stood little chance of survival. In matter-of-fact instructions to his Mustang pilots, Mahony pointed out the antiaircraft guns sited around the airfield, and in a line astern they all dropped their bombs and auxiliary tanks on the guns and their crews. With the guns silenced the P-51As began a round-robin series of strafing attacks on the fighters lined up neatly in their sights. Eight or nine passes left all wrecked and smoking.[4]

The strike was not finished. Heading back to Hailakandi, Mahony led his fighters near other Japanese fields at Onbauk and Shwebo, where the exhilarated Allied pilots spotted dozens of enemy aircraft—fighters, bombers, transports, even trainers—either in the landing pattern or already on the ground. Despite having already dropped their bombs on Anisakan and expended much of their ammunition, the eager fighter pilots replicated their earlier attack, hitting first the defensive guns and then strafing the parked and taxiing aircraft. In all the Air Commandos claimed thirty-four Japanese aircraft destroyed, and an intelligence officer labeled the raids "perhaps the most brilliant fighter operation on this front this year."[5]

The attacks were not without cost to the Air Commandos, however. At some point after the attack at Onbauk, Lt. Martin L. O'Berry Jr. disappeared. Following the strafing and bombing at Anisakan, all the fighters met at a predetermined rendezvous, and O'Berry was there. After the raid at Onbauk no one saw him again. The Missing Air Crew Report (MACR) for O'Berry on 9 March states that he was last seen "over enemy territory returning home. No apparent trouble and no radio contact was made after last sighting."[6] An addendum to the MACR by 1st Lt. Younger A. Pitts Jr. stated that he did not see the missing pilot after the attack on Onbauk.[7]

The dive-bombing and strafing P-51s were soon out of ammunition, and the pilots quickly headed home. On the way they spied a lone Oscar fighter trying to evade the victorious group, and a two-ship element comprised of Capt. Erle H. Schneider and 1st Lt. John E. Meyer immediately attacked it from above. The pair had been flying top cover so they still had ammunition.

From 13,000 feet Schneider and Meyer dove to intercept the Oscar, building up tremendous speed as they descended at full throttle. They leveled out at 5,000 feet and closed on the Nakajima. According to Meyer, Schneider opened fire on the Japanese fighter, which burst into flames, and Schneider continued to fire as he closed rapidly.

Meyer described what happened next: "He [Schneider] continued firing and closing until too late to pull away. The P-51's right wing struck the rudder and vertical stabilizer of the enemy aircraft shearing off the tail of the Zero [sic] and about two thirds of the right wing of the P-51. The Zero then crashed. The P-51 did two violent snap rolls to the right and not losing any altitude (due to the extreme speed) and I last saw the ship at 5,000 feet. I then pulled up and lost sight of Captain Schneider due to our extreme speeds. The speed at the time of interception was over 450 mph indicated."[8]

Schneider was killed. The loss of O'Berry and Schneider cast a pall over the giddy fliers, but there was a war on. Mahony had alerted the bomber section as the fighters approached the field, and as soon as the Mustangs landed at Hailakandi, R. T. Smith and Walt Radovich jumped from their cockpits and headed to the bomber pilot briefing. Three-quarters of an hour later they took off to lead a formation of nine Mitchells back to the fields at Onbauk and Shwebo. They bombed the fields from one end to another, once again making several passes, and caught an additional twelve Japanese aircraft in their revetments. They left both fields in flames, with thick black oily smoke rising into the now-darkened sky.

On this single day the Air Commandos had destroyed forty-eight Japanese aircraft, 40 percent of the aircraft destroyed by all units of the Allies for the month. General Stratemeyer was ecstatic. The Air Commandos were beginning to show that the decision not to disperse their assets to other units was a wise one. In this single mission they "obliterated nearly one-fifth of the known Japanese air force in Burma."[9]

Back at Hailakandi, Tom Taketa bent once more over his radio, lost in the world of sound that revealed itself through his headset.

CHAPTER 21

As it turned out, the buildup of Japanese air forces was part of a much bigger military operation. On 8 March, 1944, while Wingate's troops were invading Burma, Japanese forces launched an invasion of India. They intended to surround Imphal and Kohima and block the Kohima-Dimapur Road in an effort to stop the flow of supplies to the American air fields at Chabua and Sookerating that were so vital to keeping supplies flowing into China. Once again, airdrops supplied the besieged Allied troops and after several months the Japanese offensive turned into a major defeat of the emperor's troops. The raging battles in Manipur did not directly involve the Air Commandos.[1] But pilots of the group would soon be involved in a variety of other missions that would test their commitment, courage, and skill.

From 6 March to 24 March, Broadway was transformed from a jungle clearing into an Allied stronghold. Thousands of Chindits and tons of supplies were funneled into Burma through the rough airfield, and the individual stories of Air Commandos and Royal Air Force pilots were a patchwork quilt of confusion, valor, fear, and death.

Air Commando pilots had seen combat now, but they also learned that they could be hurt in many ways other than enemy fire. The original plan for securing fighter pilots for the group was to seek out seasoned combat veterans, but as the war in Europe ground on, it became more difficult. On 11 March, A.R. Van de Weghe and four of his flight school classmates arrived at Hailakani as replacements for pilots who had been killed, wounded, or gone missing in action. The five had graduated as pilots and second lieutenants in October, and none had ever flown a P-51. So on their first day at Hailakandi, Van de Weghe took a Mustang up for an hour to become familiar with his new aerial weapon. Four days later he flew his first combat mission, a two-hour, thirty-minute foray into Burma. When the planes landed, his flight leader asked him how much time he had in a '51.

Van de Weghe looked at his watch. "Counting today's mission . . . three and a half hours, sir!"

The young second lieutenant quickly learned how informal the Air Commandos were. "When I was new in the group, I met Col. Cochran early one morning coming out of the mess basha and gave him a smart salute. He smiled and said, "Hey, sport, you don't have to salute me. I'm just the C.O. around here."

Van de Weghe went on to fly thirty-eight fighter missions before the monsoon floods canceled further operations from Hailakandi. In November 1944 he transferred to the 319th Troop Carrier Squadron of the Air Commandos, flying C-47Bs. Two days after Christmas that year, he was watching the B-25 dubbed Pistol Packing Momma as it was loaded with fuel and ammunition for a mission. The .50-caliber nose gun in the bomber inexplicably fired, wounding Van de Weghe. He was hospitalized for a month.[2]

Another Air Commando P-51 pilot, Lt. William J. Ravey of Fort Worth, Texas, actually shot himself down but lived to tell about it. He was on a training flight far south of Hailakandi, firing at ground targets to simulate close air support of troops. His stream of .50-caliber rounds formed a V that converged about 400 yards in front of his fighter, Texas Kitten, and he could feel the Mustang jerking as the heavy machine guns in the wings spit out hundreds of half-inch bullets. With tracers loaded as every fifth round, he could see the rope of lethal ordnance walking up toward his intended target—and then suddenly it was coming directly back at him. His rounds had struck rocks, ricocheted straight back into the engine of his fighter, and severed control wires. Helpless, Ravey held on as the P-51 smashed into the earth, cartwheeled, and came to rest upside down.

Some Indian workers had seen the accident and rushed to pull the injured pilot from the wreckage. Ravey spent two months in a hospital before being returned to duty. Despite ribbing from his comrades, he declined to paint an American flag victory symbol below his canopy on his replacement fighter.[3]

For S.Sgt. Raymond Ruksas and the other sergeant pilots who had flown their L-5s in to Broadway on 6 March and subsequent days, the coming of darkness each night was a mixed blessing. The black veil that descended at sunset hid their rough airstrip from Japanese aerial patrols, while leaving the Americans to attempt sleep in their crude shelters deep in the jungle—which to them was as alien as another planet, full of strange noises, crawling insects, and the constant fear of Burmese pythons, kraits, and cobras. They slept in hammocks slung in deep foxholes, which the Gurkhas had dug before they departed in columns to harass the Japanese.

The first evening Ruksas was at Broadway, a C-47 landed and taxied to an off-loading area close to the tree line. The ground crew took gasoline, food, and several boxes of hand grenades from the cargo plane and stacked them nearby. They quickly unloaded the plane, so that wounded and injured men could be loaded aboard for the flight back to Lalaghat. Ruksas and several other L-bird pilots were talking in a group nearby when they heard a splintering crash and saw several men peering into a foxhole close to where the materiel had been stacked. Curious, they strolled over and learned that a crate of grenades had fallen into the foxhole.

Ruksas joined the circle of heads peering cautiously over the edge of the hole. No one seemed eager to jump in and retrieve the grenades. Minutes went by, the men embarrassed but still not willing to end the stalemate between hand grenades and warriors. Finally, after perhaps five minutes, a civilian war correspondent sighed theatrically. He bent forward, placing his hands on both sides of the foxhole, and gingerly lowered himself into the pit. He bent down and lifted the wooden box of explosives and then disappeared once more to the bottom of the foxhole. Holding each of the grenades as though they might detonate any second if shown the least disrespect, the newsman handed them to the men lining the hole. He was offered a hand and pulled himself out. Ruksas and the others in uniform were slightly chagrined by this display of commonsense courage. A few weeks later this same newsman boarded an Air Commando B-25 with General Wingate.[4]

Tech. Sgt. Russel E. Prather, another L-5 pilot, recorded some of his impressions of Broadway in a monograph he published more than thirty years later. Prather was assigned to A Squadron of the light plane section, which had been sent to Taro before the invasion at Broadway. When they received the word to move a few days after the initial invasion, their first stop was a small clearing code-named Dixie, close to the Chindwin and about forty-five minutes' flying time from Broadway. They left Taro fully kitted out, unsure when they might return.

Prather wore his airborne jumpsuit with all the pockets, which he filled with K rations, and he wore a web belt with a .45-caliber pistol and extra ammo, a first aid kit, grenades, and a large kukri knife. In his cockpit he stowed a sleeping bag, a folding-stock .30-caliber carbine, and a musette bag with shaving gear, extra clothes, and a second pair of shoes; in an inside pocket he secured the all-important escape kit, which, in addition to the usual silk maps, language booklet, and compass, contained opium and rupees as insurance. A pilot might bribe his way out if forced down.[5]

At Dixie came word that a force of about 300 Japanese troops was within three miles of the natural clearing, so Prather and the others departed for Broadway, where they found that significant progress had been made in a short time to turn the clearing into a stronghold. Barbed wire now rimmed the perimeter of the clearing, a mess tent had been erected, fuel and ordnance dumps established, and sand-bagged machine-gun and antiaircraft positions set up. Deep trenches connected various defensive positions; the airstrip itself was being continuously improved, and the wrecked gliders had been bulldozed into the trees.[6]

Shortly after he arrived at Broadway, Ray Ruksas learned that an L-pilot and his Chindit observer had gone to reconnoiter an area north of Broadway. They never returned, and the loss cast a severe pall over B Squadron. Days later Ruksas and his flying mates were targets of the Japanese, who had found and attacked the growing force at Broadway. Ruksas's hammock was shredded by machine-gun bullets, and that night it rained fiercely, filling his trench with water that soon threatened to drown him if he stayed there. He slept that night in his airplane, and it became his regular sleeping quarters.[7]

Sitting around a small fire the next night drinking whiskey with his friends, Ruksas overheard Sgt. William Barber talking to a friend.

"Take my watch, and my wallet. There's a letter in the wallet to my wife. Please make sure she gets it." Barber was scheduled to fly his first operational mission the next day in his L-5. He was certain he was going to die.

The next morning Barber arose as usual, ate breakfast, and preflighted his L-5. His friend Frank Cowan climbed through the rear door of the small airplane, and shortly after sunrise Barber began to taxi toward Cowan's plane, which was pushed back into the jungle a few hundred feet away.

Barber's plane was in the open when Japanese Oscars appeared low in the east, symbolically and literally out of the rising sun. They targeted Barber's plane, spraying it with machine-gun fire, and the L-5 swerved sharply right and stopped.

When the attack was over, men rushed to the mauled airplane where they found both Barber and Cowan with multiple wounds. Barber was slumped over the stick of the airplane, bleeding heavily; Cowan was also wounded, shot through the body. Both men were carried to Capt. Weldon O. Murphy, who had only recently arrived on foot after his glider went down in the jungle. The medical officer removed a bullet from Cowan's torso, gave him antibiotics and pain medicine, and patched him up. Cowan would live. Murphy could do nothing for Barber.[8]

Soon a small Japanese ground force arrived and began making life miserable for the Air Commandos and Chindits billeted at Broadway. On Technical Sergeant Prather's first night there, he had settled in after a meal of K rations and coffee. The usual desultory talk of home, food, women, sports, and airplanes had taken up the evening, and the L-pilots crawled into their sleeping bags for much-needed rest. Prather lay listening to the night sounds of the Burmese jungle. He homed in on a series of twitterings that mimicked other background noises but seemed off, somehow. Before he could relay his fears to anyone, three explosions shattered the relative calm, followed by small arms fire. Prather and two other L-pilots grabbed their guns and headed for foxholes. What seemed like a fierce battle raged all night, and Prather began to imagine that he and his two friends were the only Allied troops still alive. With morning, however, the firing diminished, then stopped completely, as the Japanese melted back into the thick jungle surrounding Broadway. The kitchen and mess tent were a shambles, and Japanese bodies were strung across the entire clearing but not a single Air Commando or Chindit had been hit.

The Air Commandos tied ropes around the ankles of the dead Japanese, dragged them to a remote corner of the clearing, and buried them with no ceremony. Throughout the day Gurkhas and Chindits patroled the perimeter, occasionally flushing out enemy troops or firing on snipers crouched in trees. At one point a large Allied patrol circled deep into the jungle and drove a strong force of Japanese into the clearing itself, where they were destroyed by machine-gun fire from several fortified positions. Despite their losses, a small but determined force of Japanese kept up a harassing fire most of the following night and the Allies, dug in and now knowing what to expect, once more killed many of the Japanese with no loss of life among the Allies.

The next morning Prather awoke to sporadic mortar fire as the Japanese lobbed shells into the clearing. The Japanese remained a threatening presence at Broadway for weeks.[9]

Incredible as it might seem, the proximity of the Japanese and the attacks from the jungle surrounding Broadway came to be accepted as part of the mission, something to put up with but not to stress about. Cochran, who was not at Broadway, addressed this years later in an interview.

"They would come right in our bases. As an example: One night we had a DC-3 (C-47) run a little too long on the strip, and in trying to turn around, he got stuck. He was down at the end of the strip. I forget what he had a load of, but he and his crew got out. They started to walk back to get help, to get a dozer or something, to help give him a yank and get him out of there. They hadn't walked very far until their whole airplane blew up. So the enemy was that close. When they left it, the enemy sneaked in and planted a few explosives in the airplane and just let her blow. As I say, oddly enough, we got used to that. It didn't seem terribly exceptional."[10]

Alison, of course, was at Broadway from the very first day, and he too recalled the Japanese attacks at the jungle stronghold more as nuisances than serious threats. In a 1979 interview he laughed at the first reaction of the light-plane pilots to combat.

"Our L-5 pilots were living it up. They set up little camps all through the woods, strung their jungle hammocks between trees. This was a great picnic, and then one night the Japanese came. I will tell you, panic hit. Somehow or other, with the British help, they got back inside the British box with the British soldiers who were very experienced at this. I will tell you. As Tex Hill (AVG Ace) said, 'Nothing makes a man shape up quicker than getting shot at.'"[11]

Luck, good and bad, plays a role in war. Ruksas provides another example. At Broadway, to hide planes from enemy aircraft, the Allies pushed them back into the treeline from the clearing that served as landing strip and taxiway. Captain Wilburt H. Edwards approached the sergeant-pilot one morning after breakfast. He looked across the field, narrowing his eyes against the glare.

"Ruksas, you can push your plane three feet farther into the woods if you chop down the tree behind it." The doomed tree was teak, extremely hard, and about a foot in diameter. (Apparently, Edwards had not read his "Pocket Guide to Burma," prepared by the Army Information Branch and issued to all troops in theater. "Soldiers are not expected to go around maltreating large trees, but some of the Burmese venerate these objects and so a special warning is required on the point. Treat every Burmese tree as respectfully as if it were a California Sequoia or Redwood.")[12]

"All I have is a machete, sir." Ruksas did not relish the exhausting business of hacking away at a teakwood tree, which would be only slightly easier than chopping through a metal post.

"You've got all morning to do it, and you aren't scheduled for a mission this morning." The captain turned away, signaling an end to the conversation. For the next four hours the sergeant swung his machete into the iron-hard tree, feeling the shock reverberate through his body with each contact. Other L-pilots wandered by, grinning broadly. Slowly the tree gave up chips and slivers of itself, and shortly after noon the tree toppled, crashing into the thick jungle behind it. Ruksas rested for several minutes, then pushed his plane back into its new position, lifting the tail over the stump and tying down the wings and tail. It was deeper in the woods now, probably not nearly as visible to marauding Japanese pilots. Maybe it had been worth it after all, Ruksas thought. He headed for the chow line.

By late March, the Japanese had settled into a pattern, and one of their routines was to bomb and strafe Broadway at meal times. Dangerous and deadly as the attacks were, they had begun to seem nearly normal: the men would start eating, the Japanese would attack, the men would dive into shelters, and they would resume their meals when the attack was over. So it was this day. But only minutes after Ruksas climbed out of the covered trench in which he had taken shelter, another pilot walked by and informed the group eating with Ruksas that two of the L-birds, parked near where the woods curved, had been destroyed. Fearing the worst, Ruksas started for the site of his recent labors. And, sure enough, his plane and one flown by Sgt. Howard Smith had been burned to little more than twisted blackened metal tubing and melted rubber tires. It seemed a double shame after working half a day to cut down the teak tree.[13]

As the invasion at Broadway progressed, there is no single narrative to account for the many directions it had taken. Air Commando pilots had their stories, the RAF had different experiences and Cochran and the brass back at Lalaghat saw different perspectives.

Broadway was slowly turning from a jungle clearing into a stronghold, more like a primitive air base than a natural open space in a vast woodland. But it remained a perilous place. Wrecked and damaged gliders had been pushed and pulled to one side, C-47s were making regular runs in to the field, light planes were using it as their main base for supplying the Chindits, who had moved out in columns shortly after the successful invasion, and six RAF Spitfires had flown in to provide protection against Japanese raids. One of the RAF pilots, Flight Officer Larry Cronin was less than impressed: "Terribly small runway and very rough. Jungle all round—just drop aircraft in from over the treetops. Wrecked gliders lying everywhere."[14] Another, Alan Peart, sketched the area in a letter to the family of another pilot who was killed at Broadway. His crude drawing shows an east-west runway (the *Yank* correspondent Ed Cunningham reported it as north-south) with a pond at the western end of the rough strip and a marshy area at the east end. Aircraft are arranged in strands of trees within the clearing; the entire clearing is marked as surrounded by jungle and hemmed in by steep hills on both sides.[15]

The arrival of the Spitfires on 12 March had upset Cochran, as well as Mahony, who arrived with four P-51As to take up semipermanent residence at Broadway, only to find the detachment of RAF fighters already there. The flareup was one of the few, and the disagreement did not last long. But it showed Wingate a rougher side of Cochran than he had seen before. Stationing aircraft at Broadway would only invite reprisal raids from the Japanese, Cochran reasoned, and put all his men there in danger. And after doing all the hard work and dangerous flying to open Broadway, if any aircraft were going to protect the airstrip, it would be American—specifically, Air Commando—fighters that would do the job. When Cochran flew to Wingate's headquarters and demanded a meeting, he did not hold back.

"I told him that Johnny Alison and I hadn't been sent over there to support him because we were shrinking violets or because we were babes in the woods. . . . I told him if he wanted to double-deal and wanted to start that, he would find that we were masters at double-dealing. We would come in with the phoniest deck he ever saw in his life." Cochran was aware that Wingate's staff was overhearing the conversation, which was in a converted hangar. He didn't care.

"I said, 'You betrayed us. You did a thing you shouldn't have done, and you double-dealt us. You undercut us.'" Wingate, surprisingly, did not explode. Instead he defused the situation with a quiet admission.

"I did, didn't I?"

With that, Cochran said, Wingate called in one of his staff officers and told him: "Take a screed to the Prime Minister of Great Britain." He listed a series of other luminaries who should receive a copy, including Lord Mountbatten, General Slim, General Marshall, and General Arnold. Wingate then "read off a very concise signal of admission that he had done it, that he had been wrong, and that he wished he hadn't done it, and he apologized." Whether the memorandum was ever sent is doubtful, but it placated Cochran.[16]

The Spitfires were from RAF 221st Group, 81st Squadron. On 10 March Group Capt. G. N. Warrington had flown in to Broadway and determined that it was usable for fighters. He ordered in six Spitfires, along with a small ground crew and a small radar unit.[17]

The radar was installed, but because of the hills and the height of the trees surrounding the clearing—some were one hunded feet tall—it did not provide much advance warning of incoming aircraft. It picked up planes just twenty-five to thirty miles out. The Allies then fired a 105 mm howitzer to warn of an impending raid, but the men had barely enough time to seek shelter and pilots did not have enough time to start their engines, take off, and be in an advantageous position when an enemy formation arrived.

On 13 March, when the Japanese discovered Broadway and attacked, the defenders had about five minutes' notice. Thirty to forty Ki-43s strafed and bombed the jungle strip; five of the six Spits were able to take off and give battle to the attackers. The sixth, however, was shot down immediately after lifting off and Sgt. Pilot Alex Campbell was killed. Several Japanese planes were hit, and one was reportedly shot down by ground gunners.

Three days later Japanese light bombers escorted by fighters came calling once more. The short warning time gave Grant Mahony and the other three P-51 pilots at Broadway barely time to take off before the Japanese force was overhead. They had already decided that Broadway was not a good place to keep their aircraft and were planning to return to Hailakandi later that day. Bombs from the Japanese attackers hit Lt. Hubert L. Krug, the last to take off. His plane began to burn; he struggled to escape as flames entered the cockpit as the Mustang was turning wildly across the clearing. Krug also was worried about ramming some of the fifty-gallon barrels of av gas that were scattered around the landing strip. Eventually he was able to leap from the cockpit but was evacuated to India with serious burns.[18]

The next day, Friday, 17 March, was a disaster for the RAF at Broadway. Once again Japanese fighters and bombers attacked, this time coming in low to avoid the radar. Only two Spitfires managed to take off; one was flown by Squadron Leader W. M. "Babe" Whitamore, a holder of the Distinguished Flying Cross and a veteran fighter pilot, who was able to down one of the attacking Ki-43s. He was then shot down and killed—his loss was termed one of the greatest of the Burma campaign for the RAF—and four Spitfires on the ground were destroyed and a second RAF pilot killed. The sole surviving Spitfire of the original six, piloted by Flight Officer Alan Peart, landed after the attack; his fighter was badly damaged. He withdrew to Kangla, the RAF posted no more fighters to Broadway, and any animosity that the presence of the Spitfires had engendered was quickly forgotten by the Air Commandos, who recognized the high price that the intrepid British fliers had paid.[19]

The Japanese troops around Broadway were by now a weak and largely ineffective force, but they were tenacious and motivated. Despite armed patrols around the dispersal areas where the light planes were parked, Japanese troops still attempted to sabotage the planes by slashing the doped fabric with bayonets and occasionally by holding grenades against the engines of the small aircraft. This always resulted in the death of the soldier but rarely caused extensive damage to the planes.

Russel Prather and his fellow L-5 pilots became inured to the harassing fire of the few Japanese troops that lurked in the jungle surrounding the stronghold. At one point, while they could still hear occasional rifle shots, Prather and two buddies—S.Sgt. James Oliveto and S.Sgt. Alexander "Al" Podlecki—requested permission to inspect their planes after a mortar attack. A squad of Gurkhas was assigned to accompany them as they crept along the edge of the jungle toward the light plane dispersal area. When they arrived with the watchful Gurkhas silently surveying the jungle around them, Prather spotted a Japanese flag draped over the propeller of one of the L-5s. He started for it, eager for a souvenir, but was stopped by Oliveto. Boobytrap, he warned.

Oliveto found a bamboo stick and slowly lifted the flag from the propeller. No explosion. Next the sergeant-pilot tied a rope to the door handle of the airplane, and the fliers and Gurkhas hid behind trees while Oliveto pulled the door open. No boobytrap here, either. The pilots climbed in to their airplanes to taxi to the far end of the field, where they were to ferry out some wounded.

As Prather began to taxi, he heard the light staccato firing of a Japanese machine gun and watched in horror as bullets kicked up a line of dust about ten feet from him. He dove out of the cockpit and headed for the protection of the trees. The shooting stopped, the Gurkhas swiftly sought out the machine gunner, and eventually Prather continued taxiing to the other side of the clearing.

Later Prather flew out with Podlecki to ferry more L-5s in to Broadway to replace several that had been damaged in air raids. Gurkhas set up a covering rifle fire during their takeoff, and Prather sat in the rear cockpit with two grenades to toss out if needed. They flew low over a platoon of Japanese soldiers but were not fired upon, and Prather did not throw his grenades.[20]

One of the C-47s that flew in to Broadway suffered a major malfunction of one of its engines, making it impossible to fly out again. There were no repair facilities, of course, so the decision was made to fly in a complete new engine, with quick attachments for the various lines, and swap engines overnight. Capt. Dick Cole flew the engine in. Asked if he was ever shot at while taking off or landing, he said: "If I was, I never knew it."[21]

In the meantime another rough light plane strip had been fashioned at a site nicknamed White City because of all the parachutes hanging from trees. Each day Air Commandos made airdrops of supplies to Chindits, and, despite fierce fighting there at times, L-5s landed regularly to pick up wounded British troops and fly them back to Broadway for transport in C-47s to hospitals in India.

It was near White City on 22 March that the Air Commando fighters and bombers were first called in for close—very close, about 200 yards—air support, firing machine guns and 75 mm cannon and dropping bombs on Japanese troops near the British position.

Operation Thursday had been an extraordinary operation thus far. The Air Commandos had airlifted an astonishing number of troops in to Japanese-occupied Burma with the only troop casualties caused by accidents. C-47s had towed gliders filled with troops and equipment into a couple of clearings in the vast Burmese forest without opposition; cargo planes continued to land at Broadway, light planes were dispatched from Broadway to the numerous Chindit columns to pick up wounded or ill Chindits without encountering Japanese warplanes; Air Commando fighters and bombers roamed nearly at will across Burma attacking targets of opportunity.

Adding to the unlikelihood of such astounding success was the lack of a clear line of operational authority, the who'd-have-thought-it harmony among the Allies, and the incredibly high morale of the men despite living in ghastly conditions.

On the first night at Broadway the Air Commando gliders delivered 539 men, three mules, and 29,972 pounds of stores and equipment. Beginning the next night, after preparing a rough strip for C-47s to land, the numbers soared: less than a week later they had flown in more than 7,000 Allied troops had been flown into Broadway and more than 2,000 to Chowringhee. Supplies totaling 509,083 pounds were delivered to both sites, together with 1,359 mules and horses. Additional fields in India for loading aircraft, besides Hailakandi and Lalaghat, were established at Imphal and Tulihal. Some aircraft had temporary modifications: bamboo stalls were built in some Dakotas to haul mules; only a handful proved fractious and had to be shot in the air.[22]

British commanders were bountiful in their praise of the American airborne effort. Air Marshal Sir John Baldwin had flown a Dakota in to Broadway on 6 March, and in a cable to Maj. Gen. George Stratemeyer had this to say: "Wingate says also that quote offensive action by CO-CHRAN'S forces powerfully aided by 221 Group have together been responsible for the remarkable fact that up to date the enemy has not been able to interfere with the operation in any way. WINGATE and eye [sic] think you should tell GODFREY [Brig. Gen. S. G. Godfrey] that his airborne engineers are superb repeat superb."[23]

Japanese fighters finally attacked Broadway on 13 March, eight days after the initial assault. Despite their knowledge of the activity at the jungle clearing, they intercepted no Dakotas during the operation (Dakotas flew mainly at night, and Japanese fighters were not equipped for night combat), nor did the Japanese down any L-5s or L-1s, although they flew openly during daylight hours at treetop levels.

After the initial insertion of Chindits at Broadway and Chowringhee, the Air Commandos continued to support the British troops in a variety of ways. The fighters and bombers, operating together, proved to be a potent, effective, and lethal ground-support team. An RAF pilot was assigned to each of the Chindit columns, someone who clearly understood the language of fliers and who also could appreciate exactly what the men in the attacking aircraft needed to clearly identify a target without fear of killing friendly troops. The frequency of 4530 on the RAF radio models 1082 and 1083 was set aside just for air-ground communications after a snafu in which the aerial force held off pressing an attack because of confusion over radio messaging. They worked out a system of marking targets that included marking enemy position with mortar rounds and identifying friendlies with signal flares.[24]

Alison, in an interview in April 1944, described a typical ground-support mission by B-25Hs, which were equipped with six .50-caliber Browning machine guns in the nose as well as a 75 mm cannon that fired a projectile nearly three inches in diameter. The B-25Hs also carried a full load of bombs on every mission.

"The British by radio called their shots for them," Alison said. "First they would put down smoke, then give more directions by radio. 'Will you hit the buildings? There is a machine gun nest over there,' and the bombs would go right in. 'A hundred yards north of that point there are some Japanese—put your bombs in there.' The boys would drop right where they were calling them. The British were terribly impressed." He went on to describe an attack using the 75 mm cannon:

"We had 75 mm cannon in our B-25s, and the action went something like this: 'Bombers from ground. Do you see that white house in the southern part of the town?'

"'Yes, we see it.'"

"'Will you get that for us?' Then they would fly right up to the front door and let go.'

"'Now, do you see the house with the red roof about a block up the street?'

"'Yes,' the bombers would say.

"'Will you get that for us?'

"And the bombers would fly up to the front door of that and let go with their 75 mm. It was very impressive."[25]

A specific instance of ground support by the Air Commandos, directed through radio communication with the Chindit force, is contained in a Joint Intelligence Collecting Agency (JICA) report of 15 April 1944. Three B-25s, covered by six P-51s, hit a target in a wooded position east of Mawlu at the fortified position known as White City. Maj. Walt Radovich, a B-25 operations officer, related the attack:

"Approaching the target, No. 1 B-25 asked 'Tommy,' an R.A.F. officer on the ground, for instructions. The reply was to drop half the bomb load (fragmentation clusters) on the original target, then await results. The target was divided in three parts among the three bombers, smoke was called for and laid on enemy positions, and each bomber then made an individual run.

"'How is the target covered?' Major Radovich asked the ground R.A.F. officer. 'Hold up the rest. That's enough,' was the reply. When the bombers had some difficulty in finding a second target picked by the R.A.F. officer, the commander of the fighter cover, Lt. Col. Grant Mahony, interposed and came down with three P-51s to mark the position for the bombers. The remainder of the bombs were dropped on the area strafed by the Mustangs.

"Two strafing attacks were then made by the B-25s and the P-51s on instructions from 'Tommy.' The fighters circled and strafed warehouses south of Mawlu, while the bombers strafed still another target area close by, weaving back and forth on ground instructions.

"It was, according to 'Tommy,' a 'bloody good show.'"[26]

And while the light planes continued to ferry out wounded and ill Chindits, and to deliver supplies and mail, they also occasionally participated in direct combat, sometimes with Americans and Brits in the same cockpit. Lt. Col. Clinton Gaty, flying an L-5 at an altitude of fifty feet, had discovered a Japanese fuel cache in a cluster of bashas. A few days later Gaty led a raid by P-51s and B-25s to the target; the combat aircraft left from Hailakandi, Gaty from Aberdeen (another landing field in Burma), and they rendezvoused over the target, which was marked by an RAF officer in the backseat of the L-5 who threw smoke bombs out the open window. The target was destroyed.[27]

There were other markers of cooperation and goodwill between the two Allied forces. Capt. Leon S. Dure Jr. of the Joint Intelligence Collecting Agency in the CBI cited the *Calcutta Statesman* of 26 March 1944 in a then-classified report:

Anglo-U.S. co-operation and 100% support for each other has been the basis of the initial success of the forces getting in behind the Japanese in Burma but already there have been instances which have taken such co-operation outside paper plan and operational demand, says the AFI Special correspondent.

The troops themselves are full of praise for the excellence of the work done (by) the U.S. aircraft and personnel but "extras" on the part of the Americans have heightened British enthusiasm for their allies. In one food drop the Americans added cigarettes and U.S. food from their own rations with the message: "We feel the principle of co-operation has gotten too much lip service. There is not much we can do but the boys have gotten a great kick from this."

The British Commander sent a penciled reply: "Your presents were entirely unexpected and you can have no idea how much they are appreciated. At this moment I am sitting on the bank of the Chindwin River watching my men eating American rations, crossing the river in boats brought by American gliders with American out-board motors. I assure you it is no mere figure of speech when I say all my men are indeed grateful and feel we are closely akin to you all."

The postscript said: "No typewriters in jungle."[28]

CHAPTER 22

Nineteen days after the chaotic but successful glider landings at Broadway, disaster struck.

In some ways it was the unofficial beginning of the end of the initial phase of the 1st Air Commando campaign in Burma. In other ways it was a time for reloading, reflection and reassessment. Debate still rages in some quarters about what happened and how; the specific details probably will never be known.

On the morning of 24 March 1944 Maj. Gen. Orde C. Wingate, D.S.O. and two bars, advised the American air commanders at Lalaghat that he wished to visit and inspect Broadway and perhaps other Burma strongholds. This had become a frequent occurrence; the bare-knuckle guerrilla fighter of the Palestine Special Night Squads and the Ethiopian Gideon Force could not resist being close to the action, and he visited his brigade commanders as often as he could. Usually either Col. Johnny Alison or Maj. Walt Radovich flew Wingate in one of the Air Commandos' B-25H bombers. On this day, after a weather briefing at Hailikandi, Radovich flew to pick up Wingate at Lalaghat, where he had transferred his headquarters from Imphal. Accompanying Wingate were his adjutant, Capt. George H. Borrow, and two war correspondents, Stewart Emeny, forty, of the *London News Chronicle* and Stanley Wills, thirty-eight, of the *London Daily Herald*. Emeny was a fearless correspondent who first gained fame during the Ethiopian War in 1935–36; it is believed that it was he who had jumped into the foxhole to retrieve the broken box of grenades at Broadway.

Wingate wore his usual field attire—bush jacket with the red collar tabs and single row of ribbons, and his distinctive old-fashioned coal-shuttle sun helmet—and he carried an infantryman's .303 rifle. He slung a map case over his left shoulder, and a canteen hung from the belt of his jacket. The crew and four passengers boarded the bomber, and Radovich took off for Broadway with a couple of P-51s providing fighter escort. Since the Air Commandos used a single pilot for the Mitchell, Wingate climbed into the copilot's seat, his rank-has-its-privileges position for his inspection flights.

On previous flights Radovich had gotten to know the Chindit commander and did not waste time on conversation or pleasantries. "Wingate was a quiet, moody person, not the kind of person you got to know well. He was always abrupt, no time for small talk," Radovich said in an interview years later.[1]

They landed at Broadway, and Radovich asked when he wanted to be picked up. Wingate replied that he wanted to leave at 1700, so Radovich, unwilling to leave the B-25 exposed to Japanese air strikes, flew back to his home base at Hailakandi. That afternoon he went to operations to check the weather and file his flight plan. Alison was there and pulled him aside.

"Walt, some of the guys are complaining. They say you are taking all the missions, flying too much. I want you to get someone else to pick up Wingate." Radovich was flying bomber and fighter missions at every opportunity.

Radovich shrugged. "Who? Anyone in mind?"

"No. That's up to you."

Alison himself might have picked up the flight but, according to Radovich, the deputy commander "was a hard worker. He always had six things going at once." Radovich sought out R. T. Smith, bomber section commander. Smith suggested 1st Lt. Brian F. Hodges.

Hodges was "a good pilot, steady. He was a typical bomber pilot," according to Radovich.[2] By that, one can conclude, Hodges did not have the hyperaggressive personality fighter pilots demanded of themselves and each other. Competence and unflappability were trademarks of bomber boys, not flamboyance.

Hodges was notified, and he and his crew assembled at ops to review the weather forecast and file a flight plan. They then went out to the flight line to preflight the Mitchell. Hodges's regular aircraft was one that had been christened Sweet Sue, tail number 34329; a painting of an appropriately scantily clad young woman graced the nose. Sweet Sue had been damaged a few days earlier, however, and tonight they would be flying a replacement Mitchell, tail number 34242. Accompanying Hodges were 2nd Lt. Stephen A. Wanderer, navigator, and crew members Tech. Sgt. Frank Sadoski, aerial gunner; S.Sgt. James W. Hickey, radio operator; and S.Sgt. Vernon A. McIninch, flight engineer.

The Mitchell used to transport Wingate and others to and from the strongholds in Burma was one of the operational close-support bombers, with .50-caliber Browning M-2 machine guns in the nose as well as a 75 mm cannon, making it a fearsome ground-attack machine. On this day it was loaded with aviation fuel, bombs, ammunition for the Brownings as well as twenty-one 75 mm shells. All the bombers were kept armed and ready for quick dispatch to a call for help from the Chindits.[3]

After landing at Broadway and conferring with the American and British officers there, Wingate had secured an L-5 and a sergeant-pilot and flown to Aberdeen, and then to White City, where he met with Mad Mike Calvert, informing his brigadier, among other things, that a bar to Calvert's Distinguished Service Order had just been approved. Wingate returned to Broadway, but the B-25 to transport him out of Burma had not arrived. Wingate radioed Cochran, who assured him that the Mitchell had left Hailikandi and would probably be at Broadway within ten minutes.

From Broadway the Mitchell would proceed to Imphal, where Wingate needed to talk with Air Cdre. S. F. Vincent. While waiting to board Wingate and the other four passengers, Lieutenant Hodges had a brief conversation with the commander of the British garrison, Lt. Col. Claud Rome. Rome later detailed the conversation, saying that Hodges was concerned that one of the Mitchell's two engines seemed not to be developing full power. He thought another Mitchell should be dispatched and the balky engine inspected. According to Rome, Hodges did not want to talk with Wingate about it and incur the legendary wrath of the Chindit commander. However, Hodges apparently did, and Wingate pressed him to continue on with the original bomber, because he didn't want to wait for a second Mitchell to arrive.[4]

Rome said he watched as the B-25 rolled down the runway at Broadway, and it seemed to him (a nonpilot) to be using more runway than normal. However, they landed at Imphal without incident, and despite the concerns Hodges had voiced at Broadway, apparently no one serviced the aircraft or inspected the suspect engine. As part of standard procedure close to the front, guards were posted to deter would-be saboteurs. When Wingate completed his conference with Vincent, everyone again boarded the bomber, and Hodges went through the standard pretakeoff checklist, including running up the engines to 2,000 rpm, checking the magnetos on each engine, and monitoring the oil and fuel pressure gauges at 2,400 rpm.[5] Seemingly he found nothing that caused him alarm. The Mitchell took off from Imphal, bound for Hailakandi, at 2005. The weather was clear, but the forecast had warned that local storms were possible, some intense, over the Chin Hills.

Imphal, the state capital of Manipur, sits in a wide valley. Rugged hills rise all around it, some more than 5,000 feet high; the tops are often shrouded in low-hanging clouds, and violent storms build quickly in the moist air. South of the city is a swampy area; runoff from the hills in the rainy season forms a large shallow lake. West of Imphal the hills running north and south are a tangled overgrown wrinkle on the earth's crust; they are inhabited by occasional tiny villages nestled along the slopes.

According to some of Hodges's squadron mates, night flying made him a bit nervous, and his navigator, with the unfortunate name of Wanderer, was fresh to the theater and therefore unfamiliar with the treacherous quick-forming storms in the high hill country.[6]

Hailakandi was about ninety miles due west of Imphal. The flight should have taken no more than half an hour. However, the Wingate party's arrival time came and went, and mild concern soon turned to alarm. Field Marshal Slim, at Comilla when the signal came in that Wingate was missing, wrote that "gloom descended upon us."[7]

Frantic calls went out from Hailakandi to Lalaghat, Imphal, and numerous makeshift airfields across the region. No word. No one had heard a distress call, but the Air Commando pilots and the British staff officers who stood around in small groups discussed the forecasted localized storms as they drank coffee or tea, checked their watches, and called out for news to anyone wandering by. There was none.

Cochran had been scheduled to meet with Wingate that night; time wore on, and he began to think he had mixed up the meeting date or time. He called Imphal and was told that Wingate had taken off from there. To verify, they included the pilot's name and the aircraft number. Then Cochran received a message from Capt. Richard L. Benjamin, one of the C-47 pilots going in to Broadway, that he had just seen an explosion in the hills west of Imphal: "Doggone if I don't think that was an airplane." Cochran advised him to mark the location on a map as best he could.[8]

The next morning at first light, aircraft filled the skies as a search began. S.Sgt Lloyd I. Samp, piloting an L-5, was the first to spot wreckage on the side of a ridge barely twenty miles west of Imphal. The crash site was on the opposite side of the direction in which Hodges's Mitchell should have been flying, and the wreckage itself was confined to a small area, but one wing was clearly identifiable as a B-25 airfoil. Samp stayed over the area, directing a British search-and-recovery party, until his engine carburator iced up and he was forced down. His plane was damaged, but he was unhurt.[9]

When the ground team arrived and surveyed the site of the Mitchell crash, it was obvious that no one could have survived. The bomber appeared to have gone straight into the hillside, and it was difficult to find any human remains, let alone identify anyone. A poignant—and conclusive—discovery was made nearby. The Wolseley sun helmet, so often seen on Wingate's head, a mark of his eccentricity and adherence to personal tradition, was found virtually intact on the hillside about thirty yards from the tangled wreckage.

Cochran notified Mountbatten's headquarters and was advised to keep Wingate's death quiet while they determined the best course to take and whom to appoint to head the Chindits.[10] The recovery crew gathered what few human remains it could find, and they were buried in a common grave near the village of Bishnupur—"land of the dancing deer"—in what today is the state of Manipur, India. A few years later the remains were transferred to a British war cemetery near Imphal, and in 1950 a minor squabble erupted when the remains were once again disinterred. This time they were reburied at Arlington National Cemetery beneath a single white marble marker that listed the names of all aboard the Mitchell that day. This offended British sensibilities, but the U.S. position was hard to deny: How to separate the few bone fragments and teeth to determine which were the mortal remains of the British general? This was long before the use of DNA to identify human remains.

Wingate's death sent shock waves throughout the region as well as London and Washington.

Encomiums and panegyrics flowed in from around the world. Churchill said of his Chindit leader: "With him a bright flame was extinguished." Vinegar Joe Stilwell, who could never be accused of flattery, told reporters at his Burma headquarters that Wingate's death "is a distinct loss to us all out here. He was a real fighter whose combative spirit was inspiring." The GI editors of *CBI Roundup* ran news of his death as the top story, avowing that his passing was "a tragedy to American as well as British arms. By his daring, his desire to come to grips with the enemy and his unorthodox methods he had captured the imagination of most of the people in the English-speaking world."[11]

Field Marshall Slim, in his account of the campaign in Burma, said that "the immediate sense of loss that struck, like a blow . . . was a measure of the impact [Wingate] had made."[12] But Slim was not willing to canonize the general. His intensity and single-minded purpose had infuriated many, Slim acknowledged, and despite Wingate's legion of devoted disciples, the field marshal thought Wingate's greatest fault was his own belief that he was a prophet. None of that was stated at the time, of course; it just isn't done.

Wingate was controversial, to state the obvious. He was eccentric, often rude, convinced of his own superiority, and could be maddeningly pig-headed and narrowly focused. He had at times been his own greatest publicist and his own worst enemy; he had offended ordinary rank-and-file soldiers and the Supreme Commander, South East Asia Command, equally. Yet there was no denying that his imagination, drive, and bloody single-mindedness about irregular warfare had been the soul of the long-range penetration groups. His passion for the Chindits and the idea of operating behind enemy lines in Burma had been the sustaining energy behind Project 9 and the Air Commandos. His loss was a body blow to Cochran, Alison, and the other American officers and men who had made possible the first aerial invasion of a country in the history of warfare.

Walt Radovich, who had been slated to fly Wingate out of Broadway that evening, said of Wingate's death: "It just kind of took the starch out the 1st Air Commandos."[13]

To be sure, plenty remained to be accomplished: still more combat, more aerial supply and medical evacuations. But it had a different feel now that the short slight man with the beard and the topi would not be seen again, offering advice on the siting of a machine gun or proselytizing about the benefits of eating raw onions.

The cause of the crash remains a bit of a mystery. No black boxes recording radio traffic and flight details existed; there were no witnesses. The AAF concluded that perhaps an engine had failed, perhaps while the plane was being buffeted by a violent storm, and that the Mitchell had entered a spin and crashed nearly vertically into one of the higher hills in the Chins.

What is indisputable is that no one survived to tell the story of the horrible last seconds of the ill-fated flight, and nine men died violently on the side of a mountain far from their homes and loved ones.

CHAPTER 23

Four days after Wingate's death in late March 1944, Gen. Hap Arnold sent a wire calling John Alison back to the Pentagon. Alison, still ensconced at Broadway, got word from Cochran over the radio. Virtually all radio traffic was sent in the clear now, to ensure against loss of time decoding as well as to prevent any misunderstandings in either sending or receiving a cipher.

"John, you've got a message, and I think you'd better come back tonight and read it."

Alison looked around for a likely airplane to fly out. The L-5s and L-1s were too valuable to take out of service, and the fighters had all pulled out following the destruction of the RAF Spitfires and P-51s based at the remote jungle strip. The cargo ships and B-25s always unloaded quickly and departed without delay to avoid being caught on the ground by the occasional roving Japanese fighters. But at one end of the dirt strip sat an RAF Dakota with some damage to a wing caused by striking another Dakota while taxiing on the uneven narrow strip. It had been there a couple of days, partially hidden under a pile of brush. To Alison its presence was an invitation for the Japanese to bomb the airstrip again.

He walked to the Dakota and carefully inspected the damage. About three feet of the leading edge of the right wing was bent and gashed near the wingtip, and the aileron on the trailing edge was also inexplicably bent and crushed, although it appeared firmly attached to its hinges. Despite the external damage the main spar—a beam that runs the length of the wing and is the core of the wing's structural integrity—appeared to be undamaged. It would fly, he reasoned. He ordered the brush removed and told the British flight sergeant, who had been awaiting parts to repair it, that he was going to fly it out. The sergeant objected. Alison reminded him that he was the commanding officer of the airstrip and mollified the worried enlisted man by stating that he would assume all responsibility for the aircraft. Capt. Charles Russhon, the ubiquitous photographer for the group, climbed aboard, and Alison told him that he had never flown a C-47 before. "It doesn't make any difference. Let's go." Alison took off without incident, despite having only one aileron, and set a course to Hailakandi. He read a placard on the instrument panel detailing the procedure for raising the gear. Over Hailakandi he called the tower and asked for an experienced C-47 pilot. He then verified the procedure for lowering the gear. "You're safe, come on in," the cargo pilot assured him.[1]

Alison reported to Cochran, who handed him the wire from General Arnold ordering Alison stateside. As he was making preparations to leave, however, he received yet another cable, this time from the headquarters of the Supreme Allied Commander in Europe. Gen. Dwight Eisenhower wanted Alison to report to him personally, without delay.

Alison cabled Arnold requesting permission to report to Eisenhower before returning to Washington and received authorization for a two-day stopover in England. He left India on 1 April 1944 and reported to Eisenhower's headquarters, where he was ushered into the Supreme Allied Commander's office.

The famous grin greeted him. Eisenhower stood and offered his hand. "Alison, I am glad you are here. The reason we wanted you, we are planning to cross the Channel, and we are going to use gliders. You have had a brand-new experience, and we would like to understand the problems that you encountered." The five-star insisted on personally taking him to the office of Gen. Carl Spaatz and chatted amiably with the diminutive colonel while they strolled about a quarter-mile to Spaatz's office. After talking with Spaatz, whom Alison had known while stationed at Langley Field, Virginia, before the war, Alison talked with Gen. Hoyt Vandenberg, the man who had been instrumental in recommending Cochran and Alison to lead the Air Commandos. Vandenberg was now in charge of tactical air support for the coming invasion. Among Alison's recommendations was the use of single tows for glider operations.[2]

After Alison arrived in Washington, he met with a very pleased General Arnold. News of the Air Commando operation had been quite positive, and soon major articles and photos would appear in a variety of high-profile magazines and newspapers. More important, the worth of the concept had been proved to Arnold's satisfaction, and now he wanted Alison to begin setting up as many as four additional Air Commando groups. Alison asked where the new units would be sent, and Arnold replied that they would join the 1st Air Commando Group in Burma. Alison shook his head. In his view, he told Arnold, the British did not intend to retake Burma from India, so more air commando groups would not be welcome there, at least not to be used in support of British invasion troops. Arnold sent for Cochran to confirm Alison's impressions; in a few days the overworked head of the Air Commandos appeared at Arnold's office in the Pentagon. He agreed with Alison: the British Army brass had no compelling interest in wresting Burma from the Japanese. Arnold bundled both Alison and Cochran into his car and drove to see his friend Sir John Dill, the most senior British military officer in Washington. Dill confirmed the impressions of the two American colonels.

Mountbatten, a staunch supporter of the air task force concept from the beginning, also began to flag in his zeal for the long-range penetration incursions envisioned by Wingate. Further, the monsoon season was nearly upon the forces in Burma, and the coming of the torrential rains would mean the end of effective operation there until much later in the year. General Stratemeyer cabled Arnold from India that the entire campaign in Burma was now an air commando–style operation, and that the British staff had little enthusiasm for long-range penetration groups in the image of the Chindits. The staff much preferred an amphibious assault from the south.[3]

The original goal of Project 9 had been realized, and the viability of Wingate's vision of guerrilla-style operations supported entirely from the air had been proved, so the first chapter in the book of the Air Commandos was now largely complete. Wingate was dead; Alison was out of theater; the monsoons were soon to drench the flying fields and turn jungle trails into treacle.

This is not to suggest that the situations of individual air commandos changed overnight. The war ground on, and they continued to try new weapons and new tactics. On 4 April, P-51s took off from Hailakandi by 0800 and headed to Aungban, Burma, prepared to use for the first time the rockets that Cochran and Alison had worked so hard to procure. The tubes that had been fabricated specifically for the Air Commando Mustangs were attached to hard points under the wings, and when P-51s arrived over the Japanese airfield they found enemy fighters arrayed around revetments. Mahony ordered the attack. When the

Mustangs headed for home, they left behind a ruined airfield spouting plumes of dark oily smoke; they claimed twenty-four bombers and fighters destroyed on the ground, while the plucky Capt. Paul Forcey accounted for one more in the air. There were no losses among Air Commando aircraft.

One of the P-51 pilots that day was A. R. "Van" Van de Weghe, who discovered the physical discomfort of long combat flights on this mission. It was a two-hour flight each way. About thirty minutes from Aungban, Van de Weghe became acutely aware of a need to urinate. A relief tube below his seat provided an opportunity, but in the process of setting up for that procedure, the young pilot failed in marksmanship. The result was a soaked flight suit. That left him "ready to face the enemy, with wet pants."[4]

The small contingent of YR-4 helicopters and their crews proved their value in this period. The small underpowered machines were difficult to fly, and the forward bases in India offered poor facilities and weather conditions. Two of the four helicopters had been lost in crashes. One was aboard a C-46 that was lost in a storm; another crashed after hitting a telephone wire while hovering, killing the passenger, a fighter pilot who had been curious about the "eggbeaters" and wanted a ride. The hot and humid air in Assam proved nearly fatal to the success of the choppers; during the heat of the day taking them any higher than the surrounding trees was difficult.[5]

But on 21 April the word came in: an L-1 flown by S.Sgt. Edward F. "Murphy" Hladovcak and carrying three wounded British troops had gone down in Japanese-controlled terrain. No good open areas existed for L-planes to land to pick up the men, all of whom survived, so 1st Lt. Carter Harman volunteered to retrieve them. The closest stronghold was Aberdeen; it took several legs with stopovers to get there, but finally on 23 April he arrived in the flimsy craft. Taking off from Aberdeen, he found the men in the hills near the L-1, but the tiny prototype helicopter could carry only one passenger at a time. After four trips over two days all the men were safe and eventually transported to hospitals in India. The helicopter unit itself was ordered back to India in early May. The rotary-winged craft had proved their concept was feasible, but it would be several years before helicopters replaced light planes as flying ambulances. Before helicopters could become an icon of American military might, they would need a bigger, more reliable, engine, one not so prone to overheating.[6]

And several L-pilots, including Ray Ruksas, gained acclaim and saved lives when they went to the aid of Merrill's Marauders. Japanese had encircled the Marauders at Nhpum Ga in northern Burma, and their own

Piper L-4s could not evacuate sick and wounded troops. Joe Stilwell ordered the L-1s of the nearby Air Commandos to try medical evacuations from a 700-foot strip carved out of the jungle. Ruksas, and staff sergeants John J. Hyland, Joseph H. Sparrow, and Thomas E. Purcell Jr. evacuated more than 350 sick and wounded men; Purcell was killed when his Vigilant failed to clear trees at the end of the tiny runway. The flying ambulances presaged the ubiquitous med-evac helicopters that were to prove so valuable in Korea and Vietnam.

In June, when the rains made the fields at Lalaghat and Hailakandi unusable, Cochran moved the Air Commando operation to an abandoned RAF base at Asonol. It was drier, and the facilities were permanent and much nicer. Lt. Steve Uminski, a glider pilot, painted the interior of the Officers' Club with oversized characters from *Terry and the Pirates*. The droll humor of American GIs was evident in the names of some of the facilities: Terry's Tavern was the Noncommissioned Officers' Club; the dining hall displayed a sign proclaiming it the Old Greasy Spoon.

Tim Bailey, the glider pilot who had bailed out while an instructor in New Mexico, joined the 1st Air Commandos at Asanol. He was too late for the invasion at Broadway, but he did take part in flying CG-4As to deliver drums of gasoline behind Japanese lines and then a jeep with five troops. Like most of the glider pilots, Bailey often flew as copilot on C-47s.[7]

The typewriters that Cochran had tried to banish from shipment to India eventually earned their keep. Cochran and Alison held fast to Arnold's directive ("The hell with paperwork!"), but some record-keeping was vital. For example, no one had filed Missing Air Crew Reports—MACRs—for the first casualties, and finally a statistical control officer was sent to Air Commando headquarters at Hailakandi to try to sort out the mess and bring a sense of order to the chaos. A Joint Intelligence Collecting Agency report described him as "on the verge of despair" at what he found.[8]

Even awards and decorations were given informally. Medals usually are presented in formal circumstances, with men neatly aligned in ranks and rows, while a general or colonel pins the medals on the chests of recipients. (Napoleon is reported to have said, at an awards ceremony: "With such baubles, men are led.") Walt Radovich reported that Cochran and Alison awarded Air Medals, Purple Hearts, and Distinguished Flying Crosses with the same casualness that they approached everything except combat. They would pin a note to the main bulletin board: "If you have any medals coming, pick them up from the basket in Operations."[9]

In May Cochran himself was ordered home. He had not been in good health throughout the war, frequently working himself to exhaustion.

An officer from the investigative branch of the air force had been in India and had had several meetings with Cochran. The officer notified Arnold that Cochran clearly was physically ill and needed to be recalled. Years later Cochran revealed that before the war he had been advised by a clinic in Boston that he was hypoglycemic, that is, low blood sugar. This could lead, in extreme situations, to a person's passing out. Cochran knew if he revealed it to the army, he would be permanently grounded and likely be medically discharged. He learned to control the condition to an extent, but when full-blown fatigue set in, it could take him as long as six weeks to be fit again.[10]

With Cochran's return to the States, Project 9 (though not the entire Air Commando campaign) could be considered officially ended. What was its record? How do we assess it?

The use of light planes to evacuate hospital cases, coupled with the close air support of the Air Commando P-51s and B-25s working with British forward air controllers, characterized the more conventional use of the 1st Air Commando Group for the rest of the campaign in Burma. The group had an enviable list of firsts, including the first use of air-to-ground rockets, the first use of a helicopter in combat, the first air unit designed with complete autonomy, the first use of light planes in a combat role. A booklet published as part of the Air Force History Museums programs spells out these and other notable achievements.[11] The first combat use of light planes might be debatable, since Operation Torch used liaison planes in November 1942. Other firsts listed in the booklet include the first night glider recovery and the first use of gliders to haul animals. As difficult and dangerous as those feats were, it's hard to give complete credit to those however, since military forces never used gliders after World War II. Being first does not always translate to progress or advancement.

Noteworthy at the time of Operation Thursday were the morale and esprit de corps of the 1st Air Commandos. It is common, perhaps, for servicemen to recall fondly—or not so fondly—certain incidents or personnel who stand out over the decades. Time has a way of making even the most difficult tasks seem easy and of making laughter possible even when recalling the most terrifying events. Self-effacement is the standard mien for gatherings of old warriors, and it was much in evidence at the Final Reunion of the 1st Air Commandos Group in Fort Walton Beach, Florida, in October 2012. The talk flowed freely as they retold old stories, and laughter was the order of the day. But what cannot be disregarded as mere bonhomie is an intelligence report written in late March 1944 by Capt. Leon S. Dure Jr., of the Joint Intelligence Collecting Agency. Dure spent several days with the Air

Commandos shortly after the flights in to Broadway, and he was clearly impressed:

> The status of discipline in the air commando force is said to have confounded more than one high-ranking visitor, confused by the fact that enlisted men and officers of all ranks share and share alike, and the further fact that no point was ever raised about personal appearance. About morale, however, there can be no doubt. "If Phil (or John) says do it, then by God we do it," is a common expression that ends all question. The existence of a commander and deputy commander in such perfect accord that the decision of one is automatically the decision of the other is not the least remarkable aspect of the air force.[12]

Perhaps the most important contribution of Project 9 was the coordinated use of air power and ground action in unconventional ways to effect limited goals as part of a larger strategy. The 1st Air Commando Group could be called the father of modern special forces warfare, the progenitor of special operations commands that use a variety of weapons and tactics in most unconventional ways.

Eventually, the 2nd Air Commando Group would deploy to the region, and the third would be active in the Philippines, but the highly unorthodox methods of the original group led by Philip Cochran and John Alison would not be used again during World War II. The cross-Channel invasion of France in Overlord, as well as in Holland during Market Garden, included gliders. But the risky night tow of gliders into jungle clearings would never be duplicated, and the world would never again see such an autonomous unit of highly individualistic men equipped with fighters, bombers, light planes, gliders, and helicopters. Never again would a commander declare, "To hell with paperwork! Get out there and fight!" Planning, logistics, research and development, all neatly detailed by paperwork in triplicate have become a hallmark of modern industrialized warfare. The days of horsehide flying jackets, Natal boots, and crusher caps are gone forever. A new breed of irregular war fighter—fliers, soldiers, mariners—has replaced the devil-may-care charm of the early Air Commandos; this new breed is no less dedicated or fearless but far more anonymous and more highly trained in unconventional and asymmetrical warfare. Sophisticated weapons and eyes-in-the-skies intelligence have removed much of the need for boots in the cockpit or on the ground, and weaponized drones now go anywhere without putting a pilot in harm's way. No doubt this will prove both more lethal to our enemies, and more protective of the warriors we send in our name to far-off places.

But for sheer daring, audacity, and perseverance in the face of adversity, it is hard to beat the true story of the Air Commandos and the invasion of Burma. By glider. At night.

NOTES

CHAPTER 1

1. Sewell, "Campaign in Burma," 496.

2. A list of films about Burma during World War 2 may be found at Wikipedia. The author makes no claim to being expert in war films; readers should use their best judgment

3. Ibid., 504.

4. *Combined Chiefs of Staff: Conference Proceedings.*

5. *Compton's Pictured Encyclopedia,* vol. B (1936), 279.

6. Thant Myint-U, *River of Lost Footsteps.*. The author, who holds a PhD in history, is the grandson of the former secretary-general of the United Nations, U Thant, and has written extensively about Burma.

7. Thant Myint-U, "Fall of the Kingdom," chap. 1, in *River of Lost Footsteps.*

8. Ibid., 12–30.

9. Ibid., 198–219.

10. Stokesbury, *A Short History of World War II.* 44.

11. For a detailed account of the horrors of that battle, see Chang, *Rape of Nanking.*

12. "How to Tell Japs from the Chinese," 81–82; see also Harvey, *Meanwhile,* 376–77.

13. Ford, *Flying Tigers,* 68.

CHAPTER 2

1. Bierman and Smith, *Fire in the Night,* 69.

2. McNeely and Plake, "U.S. Navy Air Combat Information."

3. Scores of books have been written about Wingate. I found Rooney, *Wingate and the Chindits,* and Bierman and Smith, *Fire in the Night,* to be balanced and informative.

4. Rooney, *Wingate and the Chindits,* 15.

5. Ibid., 17.

6. Bierman and Smith, *Fire in the Night,* 22–23.

7. Ibid., 41–43.

8. Ibid., 66.

9. For a more complete discussion of Wingate's detailed plans, see Rooney, *Wingate and the Chindits,* 32–34.

10. Ibid., 39–40.

11. Ibid., 40.

12. Bierman and Smith, *Fire in the Night,* 124.

13. Ibid., 155–216.

CHAPTER 3

1. Shelford Bidwell makes a case that Wingate suffered some form of mental illness, which manifested itself in his inability to control his outbursts. Bidwell asserts that Wingate was a manic depressive, or cyclothyme, but was focused, purposeful, and goal directed. Bidwell, *Chindit War,* 39.

2. U.S. War and Navy Departments, *Pocket Guide to Burma,* Department 1.

3. Bierman and Smith, *Fire in the Night,* 243–44.

4. Rooney, *Wingate and the Chindits,* 77–78.

5. Bierman and Smith, *Fire in the Night,* 262.

6. Rooney, *Wingate and the Chindits,* 79.

7. Ibid., 81.

8. Bierman and Smith, *Fire in the Night,* 263.

9. Ibid., 281.

10. Ibid., 279–81.

11. Ibid., 284–85.

12. Aung San was the father of Aung San Suu Kyi, who was awarded the Nobel Peace Prize in 1991 for her nonviolent opposition to the brutal rule of U Ne Win. Field Marshall William Slim referred to the Burmese National Army as the "Burmese Traitors Army." Near the end of the war, after the BNA turned on the Japanese, Slim agreed that the BNA should receive Allied support. Slim, *Defeat into Victory,* 484–85.

13. Op. Cit., 301.

14. Rooney, *Wingate and the Chindits,* 100.

15. Churchill, *Closing the Ring,* 67.

CHAPTER 4

1. Churchill, *Closing the Ring,* 80.

2. Ibid., 81.

3. The phrase "dogs of war" first appears in William Shakespeare's *Julius Caesar,* 3.1.273. The prologue to *Henry V* names the dogs: Famine, Sword, and Fire.

4. My wife's great-grandfather, Robert Johnston, was a member of the Canadian militia, a reserve force that turned away the Fenians in 1870. We have his Canada General Service Medal, with the rim engraved to him.

5. Churchill to FDR, telegram, in Churchill, *Closing the Ring,* 81.

6. Coffey, *Hap,* 21.

7. Wright and Wright, *Papers of Wilbur and Orville Wright,* Vol. 2, (New York: McGraw-Hill, 1953), 2:1203. On 22 March 1913 Orville Wright wrote to then-Lt. Henry H. Arnold describing the 1912 Model D, built to meet the army's requirement for a speed scout: "The light-scout machines are not at all difficult to handle; in fact I think it is [*sic*] the easiest machine that we build. Its high speed in landing is its only drawback. It is a very strong machine and has a larger factor of safety than any of the other models."

8. Miller, *Masters of the Air,* 143.

9. Bierman and Smith, *Fire in the Night,* 319.

10. *Combined Chiefs of Staff: Conference Proceedings,* hereafter *CCS,* 449.

11. Ibid., 450.

12. Bierman and Smith, *Fire in the Night,* 319.

13. Operation Sledgehammer was an early Allied plan for a cross-Channel invasion of Europe in 1942, part of a second front to relieve pressure on Russia. The United States and Russia enthusiastically supported the idea; Churchill said it was premature since the Allies at that stage had neither the equipment nor personnel for a successful campaign. Operation Roundup was a similar plan for invading northern France in 1943. It likewise did not receive the support of the British.

14. *CCS,* 401.

15. Ibid.

16. Ibid., 289.

17. Operation Torch was the successful invasion by U.S. and British troops of Morocco and North Africa in November 1942.

18. *CCS,* 403.

19. Ibid..

20. Ibid., 469.

21. Ibid., 410.

22. Ibid., 411.

23. Ibid., 493–94.

24. Bierman and Smith, *Fire in the Night,* 320.

25. Churchill, *Closing the Ring,* 75–77.

26. Ibid., 90–91.

CHAPTER 5

1. A good source for the history of the Pentagon is the website of the Department of Defense, Historical Office of the Office of the Secretary of Defense: http://history.defense.gov.

2. Arnold, "Aerial Invasion of Burma."

3. Harvey, *Meanwhile,* 448.

4. Philip G. Cochran, interview by Dr. James C. Hasdorff, 20–21 October and 11 November 1975, U.S. Air Force Historical Research Agency file K239.0512-876, 5, Maxwell Air Force Base, Montgomery, AL

5. Ibid., 14–16.

6. Ibid., 28–30.

7. Boltz, "Phil Cochran and John Alison," 28. See Bainbridge,

8. Harvey, *Meanwhile,* 382–87; Cochran, interview by Hasdorff, 20–21.

9. Cochran, interview by Hasdorff, 42.

10. The raid on Tokyo led by Lt. Col. Jimmy Doolittle involved sixteen B-25Bs launched from the USS *Hornet* on 18 April 1942. Doolittle's bomber was the first one to take off.

11. Op. Cit., 47.

12. Ibid., 49–51.

13. Ibid., 55.

14. Ibid., 94–95.

15. Ibid., 101–02.

16. Ibid., 118–27.

17. Ibid., 132–33.

CHAPTER 6

1. John R. Alison, interview by Maj. Scottie S. Thompson, 22–28 April 1979, Air Force Historical Research Agency file K239.0512–1121, 7, Maxwell Air Force Base, Montgomery, AL. The pages of the transcribed interview are numbered.

2. Ibid., 10–12.

3. Ibid., 13–14.

4. Ibid., 21–24.

5. Ibid., 45.

6. Ibid., 43–44.

7. Ibid., 58.

8. Ibid., 59.

9. Hubert "Hub" Zemke went on to become the leader of the famed 56th Fighter Group and was credited with sixteen aerial victories before his P-51 fighter was torn apart in a thunderstorm over Europe. He bailed out, was captured, and finished out the war as a prisoner of war in Stalag Luft 1 near Barth, Germany.

10. Alison, interview by Thompson, 68–72.

11. Ibid., 122.

12. Ibid., 128.

13. Boltz, "Phil Cochran and John Alison," 54. A field at Supreme Headquarters, Allied Expeditionary Forces, in London would be named for Griffiss during the war, and later, an air force base would bear his name in Rome, New York.

14. Alison, interview by Thompson, 154.

15. Ibid., 186–94.

16. Bond and Anderson, *A Flying Tiger's Diary*, 202–204.

17. Otha Spencer, *Flying the Hump: Memories of an Air War* (College Station: Texas A&M, 1992), 28.

18. Alison, interview by Thompson, 55.

19. Hill and Schaupp, *"Tex" Hill*, 187.

CHAPTER 7

1. The globe, in its oak floor stand, now rests in a glass enclosure in the main lobby of the Air Force Historical Research Agency, Maxwell Air Force Base, Montgomery, AL.

2. Arnold's khaki summer uniform—with the three ribbons topped by silver Command Pilot wings and with the original gold Signal Corps Military Aviator wings below—now is displayed at the National Air and Space Museum in Chantilly, Virginia.

3. Barney McKinney Giles had an identical twin brother, Benjamin Franklin Giles, also a general officer in the Army Air Forces.

4. Philip G. Cochran, interview by Dr. James C. Hasdorff, 20–21 October 1975 and 11 November 1975, U.S. Air Force Historical Research Agency file K239.0512-876, 145, Maxwell Air Force Base, Montgomery, AL..

5. Ibid., 145–47.

6. Ibid., 148.

7. Ibid., 144–49.

8. John R. Alison, interview by Maj. Scottie S. Thompson, 22–28 April 1979, Air Force Historical Research Agency file K239.0512–1121, 346, Maxwell Air Force Base. The pages of the transcribed interview are numbered.

9. Mason, Bergeron, and James A. Renfrow, *Operation Thursday*, 10. What Arnold told them has been repeated hundreds of times but does not appear in any official reports of the meeting.

10. Cochran, interview by Hasdorff, 150.

11. Ibid., 152.

12. Ibid.

13. Ibid., 150.

14. Ibid., 154–56. Arnold's published diaries record that he met Cochran in Iceland, but he does not detail the conversation. Arnold, *American Airpower Comes of Age*, 2:43.

CHAPTER 8

1. Philip G. Cochran, interview by Dr. James C. Hasdorff, 20–21 October 1975 and 11 November 1975, U.S. Air Force Historical Research Agency file K239.0512-876, 162, Maxwell Air Force Base, Montgomery, AL.

2. Ibid., 162–63.

3. Ibid.,157.

4. Ibid., 157–58.

5. Ibid., 158–59.

6. Ibid., 159.

7. Ibid., 160.

8. Richard E. Cole, interview by author, 8–11 March 2013, Boerne, TX.

9. Ibid.

10. Lewis went on to represent the Senators in the 1947 All-Star Game; the outfield that year was Joe DiMaggio, Ted Williams, and Lewis. *Gaston (N.C.) Gazette,* 19 February 2011.

CHAPTER 9

1. Holley, "Evolution of the Liaison-type Aircraft."

2. John R. Alison, interview by Maj. Scottie S. Thompson, 22–28 April 1979, Air Force Historical Research Agency file K239.0512–1121, 24, Maxwell AFB. The pages of the transcribed interview are numbered.

3. Duohet, *Command of the Air.*

4. McFarland, *Papers of Wilbur and Orville Wright,* 2:1203.

5. Holley, "Evolution of the Liaison-type Aircraft," 94.

6. Ibid., 94.

7. Ibid., 101.

8. Ibid., 90.

9. Love, *L-Birds,* 7.

10. The Civilian Pilot Training Program was initiated before the United States was officially involved in the war. Seeing an urgent need

to train more pilots (the Army Air Forces had only 4,502 pilots in 1939, according to the National Museum of the Air Force), the CPTP trained 435,165 pilots in civilian flying schools around the country from 1938 until the program was disbanded in the summer of 1944. "Civilian Pilot Training Program," 8 February 2011, fact sheet, National Museum of the Air Force, www.nationalmuseum.af.mil/factsheets/factsheet.asp?id=8475 accessed 9 April 2013.

11. Bill Cartwright, interview by author, October 2012, Fort Walton Beach, FL, at the Final Reunion of the First Air Commandos. Cartwright later flew L-5s for the First Air Commandos. The L-5 "was bigger, faster, and had an electric starter!" he told me.

12. Devlin, *Silent Wings*, 10–11.

13. Ibid., 27–28, 74.

14. Ibid., 32–35.

15. Ibid., 66–67.

16. Air Force Statistical Digest.

17. Devlin, *Silent Wings*, 112–13.

18. McNarney, "Glider Pilot Training Program."

19. MacWilliam and Callendar, "Third Lieutenants."

20. Ed Cook to Col. Jim Mrazek, 12 May 1978. Courtesy Silent Wings Museum, Lubbock, TX.

21. Tim Bailey, "Memories from Silent Wings Drive," 12–13, unpublished memoir, revised 2012.

22. Richard E. Cole, interview by author, 8–11 March 2013, Boerne, TX.

23. Alison interview by Thompson, 349.

24. Thomas, *Back to Mandalay*, 91–92; Cochran, 173–74.

25. The designation *Y* in prewar and wartime military aviation meant that an aircraft model was experimental or was still undergoing acceptance testing. The *X* designation was first used in 1946; the Bell X-1 became the first airplane to break the speed of sound, piloted by Capt. Chuck Yeager, in 1947.

26. Philip G. Cochran, interview by Dr. James C. Hasdorff, 20–21 October 1975 and 11 November 1975, U.S. Air Force Historical Research Agency file K239.0512-876, 164, Maxwell Air Force Base, Montgomery, AL.

27. Ibid., 168.

28. Alison, interview by Thompson, 362.

29. *TM9–1276 War Department Technical Manual, Carbines, Cal. .30, M1, M1A1, M2 and M3* (Washington, DC: War Department, 1947).

30. Mason, Bergeron, and Renfrow, *Operation Thursday*, 16; Thomas, *Back to Mandalay*, 93–94.

31. John R. Alison, interview by Interrogation Branch of Assistant Chief of Air Staff, Intelligence, 25 April 1944, Air Force Historical Research Agency file 142.052, 3, Maxwell Air Force Base, Montgomery, AL. The pages of the transcribed interview are numbered.

32. Arnold, *American Airpower Comes of Age*, 1:487.

33. Thomas, *Back to Mandalay*, 95.

CHAPTER 10

1. "Factsheets: Seymour Johnson Air Force Base History," 2 August 2006, www.seymourjohnson.af.mil/library/factsheets/factsheet.asp?id=4331, accessed 9 April 2013.

2. Thomas, *Back to Mandalay*, 100.

3. Ibid.

4. U.S. Army Air Forces (USAAF), *Pilot Training for the CG-4A Glider*, 44. On a ship the hawse pipe holds the anchor cable.

5. JICA, "Report of Glider Operations," 10. In addition to Taylor and Rose, the officers included nineteen second lieutenants and fifty-four flight officers; one technical sergeant, three staff sergeants, six sergeants, five corporals, nine privates first class, and one private comprised the ranks of enlisted men.

6. Albert E. Piester, interview by author, October 2012, Fort Walton Beach, FL.

7. Charles B. Turner, telephone interview by author, March 2013.

8. John Forcey, son of Paul Forcey, e-mail to author.

9. Special Orders, no. 278, 5 October 1943, Army Air Forces School of Applied Tactics, Orlando, FL, in the personal files of Jim Miller, son of Capt. Donald V. "Red" Miller.

10. Morgan, *Famous Aircraft*, no page numbers.

11. USAAF, First Motion Picture Unit, *Troop Carrier Airplanes*, Training Film T-33,

12. USAAF, *Pilot Training for the CG-4A Glider*, 10.

13. Ibid., 21.

14. Ibid., 44.

15. USAAF, *Pilot Training Manual for the C-47*, 94–95.

16. JICA, "Report of Glider Operations," 20.

17. Harry McLean, interview by author, October 2012, Fort Walton Beach, FL.

18. Richard E. Cole, interview by author, 8–11 March 2013, Boerne, TX.

19. JICA, "Report of Glider Operations," 12–13.

20. Ibid., 12.

21. Turner, interview by author.

22. Van Wagner, *Any Place, Any Time*, 29.

CHAPTER 11

1. Philip G. Cochran, interview by Dr. James C. Hasdorff, 20–21 October 1975 and 11 November 1975, U.S. Air Force Historical Research Agency file K239.0512-876, 377, Maxwell Air Force Base, Montgomery, AL..

2. Bierman and Smith, *Fire in the Night,* 329.

3. Cochran, interview by Hasdorff, 206.

4. Ibid., 211.

5. Ibid., 379.

6. Dickson, "Our Troop Carriers in Burma," 4.

7. JICA, "Report of Glider Operations," 20.

8. Ibid., 13–14.

9. Ibid., 12.

10. Albert E. Piester, interview by author, October 2012, Fort Walton Beach, FL.

11. Ibid.

12. Richard E. Cole, interview by author, 8–11 March 2013, Boerne, TX.

13. Charles B. Turner, telephone interview by author, March 2013.

14. Van Wagner, *Any Place, Any Time,* 33.

15. Baisden, *Flying Tiger to Air Commando*, 86.

16. James Eckert, personal interview.

17. Cole, interview by author.

18. "Basha Blues," published in *Hump Express,* 15 February 1945. Published by India China Division, Air Transport Command.

19. Thomas, *Back to Mandalay,* 150.

20. Harry McLean, interview by author, October 2012, Fort Walton Beach, FL.

21. Van Wagner, *Any Place, Any Time,* 36.

22. Walter V. Radovich, interview by Dave Thompson, n.d., Walter V. Radovich Collection, AFC/2001/001/4173, Veterans History Project, American Folklife Center, Library of Congress.

23. Patt Meara, interview by author, October 2012, Fort Walton Beach, Florida.

24. Smith, *Tale of a Tiger,* 8.

25. The North American B-25 was one of the most recognizable, and one of the most effective, medium bombers of World War II. First flown in 1940, it was used in every theater of the war, and was also flown by RAF and Russian pilots. Lt. Col. James H. Doolittle led sixteen B-25Bs on the daring raid on Tokyo in April 1942.

26. "The Flying '75," *Air Force,* February 1944, 55.

27. Baisden, *Flying Tiger to Air Commando,* 88.

28. Turner, interview by author.

29. John R. Alison, interview by Maj. Scottie S. Thompson, 22–28 April 1979, Air Force Historical Research Agency file K239.0512–1121, 369, Maxwell Air Force Base, Montgomery, AL. The pages of the transcribed interview are numbered.

30. Cochran, interview by Hasdorff, 186–87.

31. Sir Charles Blake Cochran (1872–1951) was renowned for his musical revues featuring young women performing at his Trocadero Caberet in London. The troupe was known as Cochran's Young Ladies.

32. Cochran, interview by Hasdorff, 193.

33. Ibid., 193–94.

34. Ibid., 190.

35. Ibid., 192–97.

CHAPTER 12

1. Bowman, *USAAF Handbook, 1939–1945,* 148.

2. JICA, "Report of Glider Operations," 18.

3. John R. Alison, interview by Interrogation Branch of Assistant Chief of Air Staff, Intelligence, 25 April 1944, Air Force Historical Research Agency file 142.052, 10, Maxwell Air Force Base, Montgomery, AL. The pages of the transcribed interview are numbered.

4. Harry McLean, interview by author, October 2012, Fort Walton Beach, FL.

5. Thomas, *Back to Mandalay,* 129.

6. Ibid., 131.

7. Ibid., 134–35.

8. Ibid., 136.

9. Brad Smith, interview by author, Brad Smith is the son of R. T. Smith.

10. *Air Force,* June 1942, 1.

11. Thomas, *Back to Mandalay,* 138.

12. Ibid., 142.

CHAPTER 13

1. Harry McLean, interview by author, October 2012, Fort Walton Beach, FL. World War II field rations were designed specifically to introduce high-calorie portable meals on a short-term basis to troops who would otherwise not have access to field kitchens. The K-ration, considered a survival ration, delivered 2,830 calories in three meals. C-rations were to be used for no more than three days and also were considered only part of a survival kit. D-rations were chocolate bars, usually to be included with C-rations. None of the rations received high marks from troops on issues of palatability or diversity.A thorough discussion of World War II field rations can be found at the website of the U.S. Army

Quartermaster Foundation, Fort Lee, VA, www.qmfound.com, which has reprinted chap. 1 of *Franz A. Koehler, Special Rations for the Armed Forces, 1946–53, QMC Historical Studies, series 2, no. 6 (Washington, DC: Office of the Quartermaster General, Historical Branch, 1958).*

2. McLean, interview by author.

3. Henry M. "Hap" Arnold, *American Airpower Comes of Age: World War II Diaries,* John H. Huston, ed. (Maxwell AFB, AL: Air University Press, 2002), 1:485–86.

4. Maguire and Conway, *American Flight Jackets,* 80.

5. This description of a city in India is an amalgam of stories. My father-in-law was a B-29 crewman stationed in Chakulia and often told stories of what he had seen; his photos are in my collection. Bill Ravey, an Air Commando P-51 pilot, also provided me with many photos of the sights in Indian cities. Oliver Townsend, "India," *AF Newsletter,* May 1942, also describes typical scenes.

6. The glider section unit patch is visible on flight jackets in the photo section.

7. Fighter section and cargo section unit patches are visible in the photo section of this book.

8. Patt Meara, interview by author, October 2012, Fort Walton Beach, FL, and Charles B. Turner, telephone interview by author, March 2013. Both former Air Commandos independently told similar tales of Coogan's often crude stories about Hollywood women.

9. Cary, *Jackie Coogan: The World's Boy King,* 189–90.

10. Devlin, *Silent Wings,* 142–43.

11. Turner, interview by author.

12. Richard E. Cole, interview by author, 8–11 March 2013, Boerne, TX.

13. Page, "Medical History of Project 9."

14. Ibid., 109.

15. Bidwell, *Chindit War,* fn. 79. Herring's Chindit column was to organize guerrilla bands of Kachin tribesmen to fight Japanese troops; Dah Force was named for the Burmese knife with a long curved blade. It was indigenous to Burma much as the kukri was to Nepal.

16. Van Wagner, *Any Place, Any Time,* 37.

CHAPTER 14

1. Olin B. Carter, interview by Don Arends, n.d., Olin B. Carter Collection(AFC/2001/001/16725), Veterans History Project, American Folklife Center, Library of Congress.

2. James Eckert, interview.

3. Carter, interview by Arends.

4. Van Wagner, *Any Place, Any Time,* 39.

5. Fergusson, *Wild Green Earth*, 15.

6. Ibid., 19–20.

7. Ibid., 56.

8. JICA, "Burma—Invasion of First Air Commando Force," 7–8.

9. Op. cit., 56.

10. For further reading see Slim, *Defeat into Victory.*

11. Slim, *Defeat into Victory*, 233.

12. Ibid., 240–41; Sewell, "Campaign in Burma," 500.

13. JICA, "Burma—Invasion of First Air Commando Force," 7.

14. Dickson, "Our Troop Carriers in Burma," 4–5.

15. Slim, *Defeat into Victory,*246.

16. Albert E. Piester, interview by author, October 2012, Fort Walton Beach, FL. Olin Carter died in January 2012. Piester visited him weekly while Carter was hospitalized.

17. Piester, interview by author.

CHAPTER 15

1. Mahony's DSC citation is reprinted in full in *Air Force,* May 1942, 10. His name is misspelled as Mahoney.

2. Philip G. Cochran, interview by Dr. James C. Hasdorff, 20–21 October 1975 and 11 November 1975, U.S. Air Force Historical Research Agency file K239.0512-876, 291, Maxwell Air Force Base, Montgomery, AL.

3. Sakaida, *Japanese Army Air Force Aces*, 33–36.

4. Copy of telegram from the files of Jim Miller, son of Capt. Donald V. Miller.

5. Grant Mahony to F. E. Miller, in the files of Jim Miller. The secret contents of thesurvival gear included opium, which was used as money in some regions of Burma, according to Cochran (interview by Hasdorff, 394–98) and Alison (324–26). Pilots also carried money, but American money was virtually useless in the jungle and dangerous to friendly villagers if they were found with it, so Cochran and the Air Commandos carried a two-inch cube of opium. This of course was in addition to silk maps, blood chits written in a variety of languages, and survival gear such as a compass, knife, matches, first-aid kit, and a small supply of food. For arms carried by aircrew see discussed above.

6. Mahony to F. E. Miller.Copy of Mahony letter courtesy of Jim Miller.

7. Miller survived internment in Rangoon, but the experience scarred him for life. His son said that Donald Miller never talked about the war, and his mother warned their children to never, under any circumstances, ask their father about the war. Jim Miller, interview by author.

8. Cochran, interview by Hasdorff, 293.

9. Ibid., 294–95.

10. Chant, *Aircraft of World War II*, 254.

11. Ibid., 261.

12. Cochran, interview by Hasdorff, 293.

13. Ibid., 298.

14. Ibid., 296–97.

15. Ibid., 297.

16. Ibid., 299–301.

17. Flight log in the files of Brad Smith, son of R. T. Smith.

18. Cochran, interview by Hasdorff, 302.

19. Ibid., 301.

CHAPTER 16

1. JICA, "Burma—Invasion of First Air Commando Force," 9.

2. Ibid., 9.

3. Richard E. Cole, interview by author, 8–11 March 2013, Boerne, TX.

4. For further reading on the Doolittle raid, see Glines, *Doolittle Raid*, and Doolittle and Glines, *I Could Never Be So Lucky*.

5. Thomas, *Back to Mandalay*, 196.

6. Print sources have reported several versions of this meeting.; it was also recorded on film by Lt. Charles Russhon. The scene is included in the 2007 documentary film *Silent Wings: The American Glider Pilots of World War II*, directed by Robert Child. Thomas reports in *Back to Mandalay* that Cochran concluded this way: "Nothing you've ever done, nothing you're ever going to do counts now. Only the next few hours. Tonight you are going to find your souls" (197). I have quoted Cochran as depicted Although the film and recording of Cochran are contemporary with the invasion, it seems to me to have been rehearsed and lacks spontaneity; it might have been shot immediately following the original briefing, but there is no way to determine that.

7. Albert E. Piester, interview by author, October 2012, Fort Walton Beach.

8. Philip G. Cochran, interview by Dr. James C. Hasdorff, 20–21 October 1975 and 11 November 1975, U.S. Air Force Historical Research Agency file K239.0512-876, 242, Maxwell Air Force Base, Montgomery, AL.

9. Thomas, *Back to Mandalay*, 204.

10. It is generally agreed today that Burmese teak cutters placed the logs across Piccadilly to dry, and that they were unaware of the plans to land gliders there and were not working for the Japanese. See Slim, *Defeat into Victory*, 265.

11. Cochran insists that he did not make the final decision, that it was made by Wingate alone (244–46). Slim says he pulled Wingate aside for a

private conversation after the Chindit commander became agitated upon hearing the news about Piccadilly. Wingate was convinced Operation Thursday had been betrayed and the mission should be canceled. Slim writes in *Defeat into Victory* (261–62) that he said the operation should proceed; Wingate looked relieved at not having to make the decision.

12. Y'Blood, *Air Commandos Against Japan*, 92.

13. Cole donated the knife, along with some letters and a circular flight computer, to Ohio University, Athens, which he attended before leaving for the military in 1940.

14. Richard E. Cole, interview by author, 8–11 March 2013, Boerne, TX.

15. Ibid.

16. Ibid.

17. Cochran, interview by Hasdorff, 261.

CHAPTER 17

1. John R. Alison, interview by Maj. Scottie S. Thompson, 22–28 April 1979, Air Force Historical Research Agency file K239.0512–1121, 409, Maxwell Air Force Base, Montgomery, AL. The pages of the transcribed interview are numbered.

2. Earl C. Waller, letter, courtesy Silent Wings Museum, Lubbock, TX.

3. Ibid.

4. Bellah, "Password Was Mandalay."

5. John R. Alison, interview by Interrogation Branch of Assistant Chief of Air Staff, Intelligence, 25 April 1944, Air Force Historical Research Agency file 142.052, 5, Maxwell Air Force Base, Montgomery, AL. The pages of the transcribed interview are numbered.

6. Op. c., 34.

7. Alison, interview by Thompson, 372.

8. Bellah, "Password Was Mandalay,"34.

9. Alison, interview by Interrogation Branch, 6.

10. Bierman and Smith, *Fire in the Night*, 354–55.

11. Waller to .

12. Alison, interview by Interrogation Branch, 6.

13. Alison, interview by Thompson,, 403.

14. JICA, "Burma—Invasion of First Air Commando Force," 11.

15. Alison, interview by Interrogation Branch, 7.

16. Olin B. Carter, interview by Don Arends, n.d., Olin B. Carter Collection (AFC/2001/001/16725), Veterans History Project, American Folklife Center, Library of Congress.

CHAPTER 18

1. Van Wagner, *Any Place, Any Time*, 53; JICA, "Report of Troop Carrier Command Participation," 2.

2. Page, "Medical History of Project 9," 80.

3. Ibid., 80.

4. Ibid., 81.

5. JICA, "Report of Glider Operations," 19.

6. Op.cit., 81.

7. Thomas, *Back to Mandalay,* 233.

8. Ibid., 235.

9. Ibid., 236.

10. Ibid., 238.

11. JICA, "Burma—Invasion of First Air Commando Force," 18.

CHAPTER 19

1. Cunningham, "Burma Air Invasion,".

2. JICA, "Report of Troop Carrier Command Participation," 4.

3. Baldwin to Peirse and Stratemeyer, secret cipher message, 10 March 1944, document 9 in file of John R. Alison, "Operation Thursday: Allied Landings in Northeast Burma," in Other Materials file, Veterans History Project, Library of Congess, http://lcweb2.loc.gov/diglib/vhp/story/loc.natlib.afc2001001.07422/pageturner?ID=pm0006001&page=9, sccessed 13 April 2013.

4. My great uncle Leonard Raymond Nicholls of the 2nd Battalion, King's Own Royal Regiment, was killed 21 November 1941 in Libya. He is buried in Knightsbridge War Cemetery there. My great uncle Dennis Nicholls of the Royal Army Ordnance Corps was killed in Korea and is buried there.

5. Cochran was asked to report on the loss of gliders on double tow. On 28 March 1944 he submitted a single-page report to Commanding General USAAF, China Burma India Theater, India Burma Sector. Cochran's conclusions: about 30 percent of the gliders on double tow did not reach their destinations because of the difficult flight conditions, overloaded gliders, and inexperienced crews. His recommendation: "As a rule of thumb we advise the following: For day operations or operations with the moon for medium distances and over level terrain, double tow should always be used to get maximum lift. For peak performance conditions such as crossing high mountains at night or where heavy loads have to be carried for extreme ranges, single tow is recommended." He also recommended more training for glider pilots.

6. Charles B. Turner, telephone interview by author, March 2013.

7. Ibid.

8. *New York Herald Tribune,* 19 March 1944.

9. Turner, interview by author.

10. Slim, *Defeat into Victory,* 220.

11. Bierman and Smith, *Fire in the Night,* 362–63.

12. Ibid., 364.

13. Ibid., 364.

14. Albert E. Piester, interview by author, October 2012, Fort Walton Beach, FL.

15. Patt Meara, interview by author, October 2012, Fort Walton Beach, FL.

16. Van Wagner, *Any Place, Any Time,* 58.

17. Thomas, *Back to Mandalay,* 149.

CHAPTER 20

1. Taketa was inducted into the Yuba College Athletic Hall of Fame in 2000 for his prowess on the basketball cort in 1941–43.

2. McNaughton, *Nisei Linguists,* 287.

3. Brig. Gen. William D. Old, head of Troop Carrier Command in India and Burma, filed a report on 16 March. He noted that "it is inconceivable that the Japanese Air Force in Burma permitted this operation to proceed night after night without any attempt to interfere" (JICA, "Report of Troop Carrier Command Participation," 5).

4. JICA, "Burma—Invasion of First Air Commando Force," 14.

5. Ibid.

6. Missing Air Crew Report, 8 March 1944, in the files of Jim Miller. O'Berry's P-51A, tail number 43–6119, carried four .50 caliber machine guns, and the MACR notes the serial numbers for each.

7. Pitts's statement in the addendum, dated 9 March 1944, reads: "After the attack on Anisakan the planes met at a predetermined rendezvous. I saw Lt. O'Berry at this point. The flight left this point and saw a number of airplanes at Onbauk. An attack was made on grounded aircraft and the flight returned home. I did not see Lt. O'Berry after the rendezvous."

8. Missing Air Crew Report, 9 March 1944, in the files of Jim Miller.

9. Van Wagner, *Any Place, Any Time,* 57.

CHAPTER 21

1. Taylor, *Air Supply in the Burma Campaign* 75.

2. A. R. Van de Weghe, personal communication with author, April 2013.

3. Bill Ravey, interview by author, October 2012, Fort Walton Beach, FL.

4. Ray Ruksas, "No. 1 Air Commando on Broadway," *Ex-CBI Roundup,* March 1992, www.cbi-history.com/part_vi_1st_air_commando_gp2.html.

5. Prather, *Easy into Burma*, 38.

6. Ibid., 39.

7. Ruksas, "No. 1 Air Commando on Broadway."

8. Ibid.

9. Prather, *Easy into Burma*, 39–40.

10. Philip G. Cochran, interview by Dr. James C. Hasdorff, 20–21 October 1975 and 11 November 1975, U.S. Air Force Historical Research Agency file K239.0512-876, 234, Maxwell Air Force Base, Montgomery, AL.

11. John R. Alison, interview by Maj. Scottie S. Thompson, 22–28 April 1979, U.S. Air Force Historical Research Agency file K239.0512–1121, 379–80, Maxwell Air Force Base, Montgomery, AL. The pages of the transcribed interview are numbered.

12. U.S. War and Navy Departments, *Pocket Guide to Burma*, 38.

13. Ruksas, "No. 1 Air Commando on Broadway."

14. Shores, *Air War for Burma*, 177.

15. Ibid., 186; Cunningham, "Burma Air Invasion."

16. Cochran, interview by Hasdorff, 277–79.

17. Op.cit., 176.

18. Ibid., 182–83.

19. Ibid., 183.

20. Prather, *Easy into Burma*, 40–41.

21. Richard E. Cole, interview by author, 8–11 March 2013, Boerne, TX.

22. JICA, "Burma—Invasion of First Air Commando Force," 14.

23. Ibid., 13–14.

24. Ibid., 17.

25. John R. Alison, interview by Interrogation Branch of Assistant Chief of Air Staff, Intelligence, 25 April 1944, Air Force Historical Research Agency file 142.052, 9, Maxwell Air Force Base, Montgomery, AL. The pages of the transcribed interview are numbered.

26. JICA, "Burma—Supplemental Report," 5.

27. Ibid., 5–6.

28. JICA, "Burma—Invasion of First Air Commando Force," 18.

CHAPTER 22

1. Walter V. Radovich, interview by Dave Thompson, n.d., Walter V. Radovich Collection, AFC/2001/001/4173, Veterans History Project, American Folklife Center, Library of Congress.

2. Ibid.

3. Ibid.

4. Bierman and Smith, *Fire in the Night*, 372.

5. *B-25 Pilot Manual,* 31.

6. Op. cit., 373–74.

7. Slim, *Defeat into Victory,* 269.

8. Philip G. Cochran, interview by Dr. James C. Hasdorff, 20–21 October 1975 and 11 November 1975, U.S. Air Force Historical Research Agency file K239.0512-876, 283–84, Maxwell Air Force Base, Montgomery, AL.

9. Van Wagner, *Any Place, Any Time,* 66.

10. Cochran, interview by Hasdorff, 285.

11. Churchill, *Closing the Ring,* 566; *CBI Roundup,* 6 April 1944.

12. Slim, *Defeat into Victory,* 269.

13. Radovich, interview by Thompson.

CHAPTER 23

1. John R. Alison, interview by Maj. Scottie S. Thompson, 22–28 April 1979, U.S. Air Force Historical Research Agency file K239.0512–1121, 413, Maxwell Air Force Base, Montgomery, AL. The pages of the transcribed interview are numbered.

2. Ibid., 414.

3. Van Wagner, *Any Place, Any Time,* 83.

4. A. R. Van de Weghe, personal communication with author, April 2013.

5. Alison, interview by Thompson, 362–64.

6. Van Wagner, *Any Place, Any Time,* 70.

7. Tim Bailey, "Memories from Silent Wings Drive," 19–20, unpublished memoir, revised 2012.

8. JICA, "Burma—Invasion of First Air Commando Force," 16.

9. Walter V. Radovich, interview by Dave Thompson, n.d., Walter V. Radovich Collection, AFC/2001/001/4173, Veterans History Project, American Folklife Center, Library of Congress.

10. Philip G. Cochran, interview by Dr. James C. Hasdorff, 20–21 October 1975 and 11 November 1975, U.S. Air Force Historical Research Agency file K239.0512-876, 232–34, Maxwell Air Force Base, Montgomery, AL.

11. Mason, Bergeron, and Renfrow, *Operation Thursday,* 44–45.

12. JICA, "Burma—Invasion of First Air Commando Force," 5.

REFERENCES

Arnold, Henry H. "Hap." "The Aerial Invasion of Burma." *National Geographic,* August 1944, 129–48.

———. *American Airpower Comes of Age: World War II Diaries.* Edited by John H. Huston. 2 vols. Maxwell Field, AL: Air University Press, 2002.

Bailey, Tim. "Memories from Silent Wings Drive." Unpublished memoir. Revised 2012.

Baisden, Chuck. *Flying Tiger to Air Commando.* Atglen, PA: Schiffer, 1999.

Bellah, James Warner. "The Password Was Mandalay." *Reader's Digest,* September 1944, 33–34.

Bidwell, Shelford. *The Chindit War: Stilwell, Wingate, and the Campaign in Burma, 1944.* New York: Macmillan, 1979.

Bierman, John, and Colin Smith. *Fire in the Night: Wingate of Burma, Ethiopia, and Zion.* New York: Random House, 1999.

Boltz, Richard W. "Phil Cochran and John Alison: Images of Apollo's Warriors." Master's thesis, School of Advanced Airpower Studies, Air University, Maxwell Air Force Base, Birmingham, AL. June 2001.

Bond, Charles R. Jr., and Terry Anderson. *A Flying Tiger's Diary.* College Station: Texas A&M University Press, 1984.

Bowman, Martin W. *USAAF Handbook, 1939–1945.* Thrupp, Gloucestershire, UK: Sutton, 2003.

Cary, Diana Serra. *Jackie Coogan: The World's Boy King. A Biography of Hollywood's Legendary Child Star.* Lanham, MD: Scarecrow Press, 2007.

Chang, Iris. *The Rape of Nanking: The Forgotten Holocaust of World War II* (1997.

Chant, Chris. *Aircraft of World War II.* New York: Barnes and Noble, 1999.

Child, Robert, dir. *Silent Wings: The American Glider Pilots of World War II.* Blawnox, PA: Inecom Entertainment, 2007.

Christian, John L. "Burma." *Annals of the American Academy of Political and Social Science* 226 (March 1943): 120–28.

Churchill, Winston S. *Closing the Ring.* Vol. 5 of *The Second World War.* Boston: Houghton Mifflin, 1951. Coffey, Thomas M. *Hap: The Story of the U.S. Air Force and the Man Who Built It, General Henry H. "Hap" Arnold.* New York: Viking, 1982.

Combined Chiefs of Staff: Conference Proceedings, 1941–1945. Vol. 2, *Quadrant Conference, August 1943.* Papers and Minutes of Meetings. Washington, DC: Office of the Combined Chiefs of Staff, 1943. Dwight D. Eisenhower Presidential Library, Abilene, KS.

Compton's Pictured Encyclopedia. Vol. B: "Burma." Chicago: Compton, 1936.

Cunningham, Ed. "Burma Air Invasion." *Yank,* 5 May 1944. Available online at Comcast.net/~cbi-theater-2/yankcbi. Accessed 25 April 2013.

Devlin, Gerard M. *Silent Wings: The Story of the Glider Pilots of World War II.* New York: St. Martin's, 1985.

Dickson, H. B. "Our Troop Carriers in Burma." *Air Force,* June 1944, 4–5. Air Force Historical Studies Office, Joint Base Anacostia, Washington, DC.

Doolittle, James H., with Carroll V. Glines. *I Could Never Be So Lucky Again.* New York: Bantam, 1991.

Fergusson, Bernard. *The Wild Green Earth.* London: Fontana, 1956.

Ford, Daniel. *Flying Tigers: Claire Chennault and the American Volunteer Group.* Washington, DC: Smithsonian Institution Press, 1991.

Glines, Carroll V. *The Doolittle Raid: America's Daring First Strike Against Japan.* Atglen, PA: Schiffer, 1991.

Harvey, Robert C. *Meanwhile . . . : A Biography of Milton Caniff, Creator of Terry and the Pirates and Steve Canyon.* Seattle: Fantagraphis Books, 2007.

Hill, David Lee. "Tex," with Reagan Schaupp. *"Tex" Hill: Flying Tiger.* San Antonio, TX: 2003.

Holley, Capt. Irving B. Jr. "Evolution of the Liaison-Type Airplane,

1917–1944." *Army Air Forces Historical Studies* no. 44 (April 1946). AFHRA.

"How to Tell Japs from the Chinese." *Life,* 22 December 1941, 81–82.

JICA (U.S. Joint Intelligence Collecting Agency). "Burma—Invasion of First Air Commando Force." *China-Burma-India Report* no. 1448 (29 March 1944). Air Force Historical Research Agency, Maxwell Air Force Base, AL, hereafter AFHRA.

———. "Report of Glider Operations." *China-Burma-India Report* no. 1449 (1 April 1944). AFHRA.

———. "Report of Troop Carrier Command Participation in 'Thursday Operation' [*sic*]." *China-Burma-India Report* no. 1579 (16 March 1944; 1 April 1944). AFHRA.

———. "Burma—Supplemental Report on First Air Commando." *China-Burma-India Report* no. 1834 (15 April 1944). AFHRA

Love, Terry. *L-Birds: American Combat Liaison Aircraft of World War II.* New Brighton, MN: Flying Books International, 2001.

Lowden, John L. *Silent Wings at War: Combat Gliders in World War II.* Washington, DC: Smithsonian Institution Press, 1992.

MacWilliam, J. H., and Bruce D. Callander. "The Third Lieutenants." *Air Force Magazine: Online Journal of the Air Force Association* 73, no. 3 (March 1990). www.airforce-magazine.com. Accessed 28 December 2012.

Maguire, Jon, and John P. Conway. *American Flight Jackets: A History of U.S. Flyers' Jackets from World War II to Desert Storm.* 2d ed. Atglen, PA: Schiffer, 2000.

Mason, Herbert A. Jr., Randy G. Bergeron, and James A. Renfrow Jr. *Operation Thursday: Birth of the Air Commandos.*" Air Force History and Museum Program. 1994. Reprint, Washington, DC: Air Force Historical Studies Office, 2007. www.afhso.af.mil/shared/media/document/AFD-100928-052.pdf.

Mauer, Mauer, ed. *Air Force Combat Units of World War II.* Washington, DC: Office of Air Force History, 1983.

Wright, Orville, and Wilbur Wright. *The Papers of Wilbur and Orville Wright.* Edited by Marvin W. McFarland. Vol. 2: 1906–48. New York: McGraw-Hill, 1953.

McNarney, Betty J. "The Glider Pilot Training Program, 1941 to 1943." *Army Air Forces Historical Studies,* no. 1.

McNaughton, James C. *Nisei Linguists: Japanese Americans in the Military Intelligence Service During World War II.* Washington, DC: U.S. Army, 2006.

McNeely, Lt. D. G., and Lt. F. N. Plake. "U.S. Navy Air Combat Information, Observations of Operational Forces in India-Burma. Direct

Air Support to Long Range Penetration Groups of the Third Indian Division in North Burma." First Air Commando Group, US-AAF Report no. 1, 8 May 1944. AFHRA file GP-A-CMDO-1-HI, 11.

Miller, Donald L. *Masters of the Air: America's Bomber Boys Who Fought the Air War Against Nazi Germany.* New York: Simon and Schuster, 2006.

Molesworth, Carl, and Steve Moseley. *Wing to Wing: Air Combat in China, 1943–45.* New York: Orion, 1990.

Morgan, Len. *Famous Aircraft: The Douglas DC-3.* Fallbrook, CA: Aero, 1980.

Nicholas, William H. "Gliders: Silent Weapons of the Sky." *National Geographic,* August 1944, 149–60.

Ogburn, Charlton Jr. *The Marauders.* New York: Crest, 1964.

Owen, Frank. *The Campaign in Burma.* Tiptree,UK: Arrow, 1957.

Page, Robert C. Major. "Medical History of Project 9." April 1944. AFHRA.

Prather, Russel E. *Easy into Burma.* Privately printed memoir. Kettering, OH. 1977.

Rooney, David. *Wingate and the Chindits: Redressing the Balance.* London: Cassell, 1994.

Ruksus, Ray. "No. 1 Air Commando on Broadway." *EX-CBI Roundup,* March 1992. www.cbi-history.com. Accessed 1 September 2012.

Sakaida, Henry. *Japanese Army Air Force Aces, 1937–45.* London: Osprey, 1997.

Sewell, Horace S. "The Campaign in Burma." *Foreign Affairs* 23, no. 3 (April 1945): 496–504.

Shores, Christopher. *Air War for Burma: The Allied Air Forces Fight Back in South-East Asia, 1942–1945.* London: Grub Street, 2005.

Slim, William Viscount. *Defeat into Victory: Battling Japan in Burma and India, 1942–1945.* New York: Cooper Square Press, 2000.

Smith, R. T. *Tale of a Tiger.* Van Nuys, CA: Tiger Originals, 1986.

Stokesbury, James L. *A Short History of World War II.* New York: William Morrow, 1980.

Taylor, Joe G. *Air Supply in the Burma Campaign: Historical Analysis of the 1st Air Commando Group Operations in the CBI Theater, August 1943 to May 1944.* Maxwell Air Force Base, Montgomery, AL: Air Command and Staff College. March 1997. www.afhra.af.mil/shared/media/document/AFD-090601-072.pdf.

Thant Myint-U. *The River of Lost Footsteps: A Personal History of Burma.* New York: Farrar, Straus and Giroux, 2006.

Thomas, Lowell. *Back to Mandalay.* New York: Greystone, 1951.

U.S. Army Air Forces. *Pilot Training Manual for the C-47*. Foreword by H. H. Arnold. n.d. Reprinted in Len Morgan, *The Douglas DC-3*. Fallbrook, CA: Aero, 1980.

————. Office of Flying Safety. *Pilot Training for the CG-4A Glider*. AAF Manual 5-17. March 1945. Reprinted by George A. Petersen.

U.S. Secretary of the Air Force. *Handbook: Flight Operating Instructions, B-25J, TB-25J, PBJ-1J*. AN 01–60GE-1. 7 September 1949.

U.S. War and Navy Departments. *Pocket Guide to Burma*. Rev. ed. Washington, DC: GPO, April 1944.

U.S. War Department. *Jungle Warfare*. Basic Field Manual FM 31–20. Washington, DC: GPO, 15 December 1941.

Van Wagner, R. D. *Any Place, Any Time, Any Where: The 1st Air Commandos in World War II*. Atglen, PA: Schiffer, 1998.

Wakefield, Ken. *Lightplanes at War: U.S. Liaison Aircraft in Europe, 1942–1945*. Charleston, SC: Tempus, 1999.

Y'Blood, William T. *Air Commandos Against Japan: Allied Special Operations in World War II Burma*. Annapolis, MD: Naval Institute Press, 2008.

INDEX

Wright Field, Dayton, Ohio, 78, 83, 90, 95–96, 122
YR-4 helicopter. *See* Sikorsky YR-4 helicopter

Zemke, Hubert (Hub), 64–66